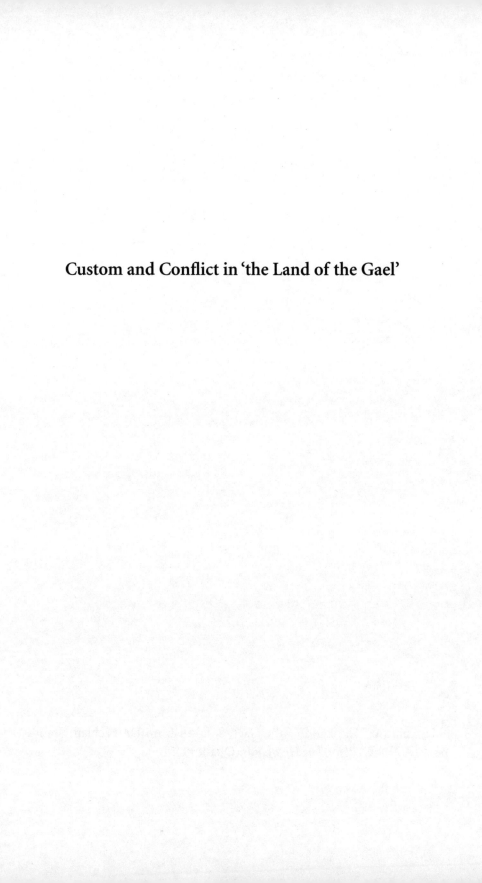

Custom and Conflict in 'the Land of the Gael'

* The phrase, 'The Land of the Gael', is taken from Dr. Lachlan Grant's book, *A New Deal for The Highlands* (Oban, 1935).

CUSTOM AND CONFLICT IN 'THE LAND OF THE GAEL': BALLACHULISH 1900-1910*

NEVILLE KIRK

MERLIN PRESS

© Neville Kirk, 2007

First published 2007 by The Merlin Press Ltd.
96 Monnow Street
Monmouth
NP25 3EQ
Wales

www.merlinpress.co.uk

ISBN. 9780850365702

British Library Cataloguing in Publication Data
is available from the British Library

Printed in Great Britain by
Cromwell Press, Trowbridge, Wiltshire

Dedication

To Anne and Will Thomson of Glenachulish

Contents

Illustrations, Maps and Documents

Acknowledgements

The research for this book was made possible by funding received from the Arts and Humanities Research Board under the Research Leave Scheme. Manchester Metropolitan University provided matching financial support. I am very grateful for their help. Without it the book would not have seen the light of day.

I am also very grateful for the assistance of staff at the following institutions: Argyll and Bute Council Archives, Lochgilphead; the British Newspaper Library, Colindale; Fort William Library; the General Register Office for Scotland; the Glencoe and North Lorn Folk Museum; Manchester Central Library; Manchester Metropolitan University Library; the National Archives of Scotland; the National Library of Scotland; the National Museums of Scotland; University of St Andrews Library, Special Collections Department.

Several individuals have been extremely generous in their support and encouragement. In Scotland relatives of Dr. Grant and the quarrymen, professional and non-professional scholars, librarians and archivists extended a warm hand of friendship and provided invaluable help and guidance to an 'outside' historian largely untutored in Scottish history. In this context I am heavily indebted to the following individuals: Alan Bell, Heather Brunton, Ewen Cameron, Duncan Clark, Pam Cranston, Rob Duncan, William Kenefick, Dorothy Kidd, Murdo MacDonald, Allan Macinnes, Christine MacKay, Michelle MacKay, Roddy Macleod, Ian McCormack, Arthur McIvor, Rita Potts, Sheena Roddan, Tessa Spencer and Maggie Wilson. In England Janet Beer, Mike Winstanley, Chris Wrigley and Tony Zurbrugg were equally supportive and helpful. Valuable comments were made by participants in seminars at the Humanities Research Centre, the Australian National University, Work and Organisational Studies, University of Sydney and by the Friends of the Manchester Centre for Regional History, Manchester, England.

Professor Mike Savage, University of Manchester, kindly read an earlier version of the entire manuscript and offered valuable comments. Finally I am grateful to Tony Zurbrugg for publishing an original research monograph in these 'post-modern' days of instant and often sketchy knowledge and understanding.

Introduction

Between 1902 and 1905 the remote Scottish Highland community of Ballachulish, standing 'at the foot of the wild Pass of Glencoe, famous in history for the massacre of the Macdonalds',[1] was shaken to its foundations by two major, protracted and bitter conflicts of a non-military kind. These involved, on the one hand, the dominant local employer, the Ballachulish Slate Quarries Company Limited, and on the other, the quarrymen and the local community. The purposes of this book are to describe and explain these conflicts, situate them in the context of the local community in which they arose and evaluate their wider regional, national and historical significance. In so doing I aim to rescue them from near historical invisibility.

Before proceeding to an overview of the conflicts, it is important briefly to acquaint the reader with the key conceptual and methodological issues and assumptions which inform this study. Above all, I offer a continuous engagement and critique of the theory of rational economic choice, both in general terms and with reference to the particular case of social movements. According to this theory, and notwithstanding variations and qualifications to its core elements, individuals throughout history have acted *exclusively* to 'maximize their personal benefits and reduce their costs'.[2] Two related propositions of direct relevance to this study are that the mobilization of resources has been the key task and feature of social movements,[3] and that it has often been in the 'rational' interest of individuals to forego involvement in social movements, to 'free ride' on the backs of participants. The rationale for the latter is that non-involvement 'would provide the same share of collective goods at less cost' to themselves as involvement.[4]

In direct opposition to this theory and the related claims stated above, I demonstrate that members of the working class and local community involved in the social movements and conflicts at Ballachulish were influenced by far more than economic self-interest and the mobilization of resources, and did not perceive non-involvement to be a rational alternative choice. They were *socially-embedded* human beings with the capacity, as social agents, to influence and change, albeit in sometimes unintended ways, their largely unwilled conditions of existence, rather than being blindly driven by an abstract, metaphysical notion of 'rational self-interest' operating above and beyond the course of human history. As complex historical actors rather than one-dimensional, a-historical abstractions, they were influenced in their values, norms and actions by a combination of sometimes inconsistent and conflicting factors. These included altruism, self-sacrifice, solidarity and the public good as well as the maximisation of narrow self-interest, of considerations of social as well as individual choices and interests.[5] Furthermore, they willingly entered the fray against their quarrying masters, encouraged those in the outside community to provide material and ideological support, and strongly disapproved of actual and potential 'free-riding' non-participants among their ranks. Far from acting 'rationally', the latter were portrayed as being irrational, weak, immoral and selfish. The participants on both sides appreciated not only the importance of leadership, organisation and the mobilization of support, but also the battle for hearts and minds, to the outcome of the disputes.

Just as with the participants, the conflicts themselves were rooted in a wide range of socio-economic, cultural and political factors rather than economic self-interest alone. Above all, I maintain that the conflicts were crucially informed by a conflict between, on the one hand, the 'customary' or 'moral-economic'[6] actions, norms, values and expectations of the quarrymen and many in the local community and among their supporters (including some employers), and, on the other hand, the 'rational' or 'contractual' values and behaviour of the company. The former centrally comprised established codes and practices of 'fairness', 'reciprocity' and 'justice' in social relations, including economic relations, while the latter was rooted in the 'business-minded', competitive and individualistic imperatives of 'the market'. According to the majority of those running the company, 'moral' questions and issues were largely irrelevant to the unsentimental goals of profit maximisation, cost minimisation, the full assertion of managerial prerogatives and the elimination of opposition. The pursuit of self-interest and absolute control and power was seen by the leading figures in the company both as the 'natural' or 'commonsensical' way for human beings to behave (or at least those with the necessary 'entrepreneurial' drive about them), and the key not only to the survival and success of the company, but also the material well-being of its workforce.

In sum, I maintain that it is important to set the specific conflicts within the wider context of a fundamental clash of values and practices concerning 'human nature', the 'proper' way to behave both individually and towards others, and the 'legitimate' pursuit and exercise of power, control, authority, rights and responsibilities. To argue in this way is to lay claim to the historical existence of *different, contested* and *contextualised* interpretations, as opposed to a *single, consensual* and *unchanging* definition, of 'rational' motivations and behaviour, especially of an economic kind. As a corollary, a serious question arises concerning the extent to which the notion of economic rationality employed by rational choice theorists is essentially an ideological construct, reflecting the interests and outlook of specific individuals and groups of people at specific points in time, rather than being the fixed and universal defining characteristic of humankind.[7]

In moving to a brief description and analysis of the conflicts, we should observe that the first conflict began in July 1902, involved a twelve months lock-out, and lasted eighteen months. It revolved less around expressed worker grievances concerning unsatisfactory labour contracts, inadequate wages and excessive charges for the powder, coals and other materials supplied by the company, than the latter's summary dismissal of the medical officer, Dr. Lachlan Grant, from both his work in the quarries and his post as Medical Officer for the Parish Council District of Ballachulish. Grant's dismissal was widely perceived to transgress established and largely shared employer and employee notions of fairness and trust, and the customary right of the workers' elected representatives on the Medical Committee to have the majority voice in the appointment of the medical officer for the quarries. Indeed, the Ballachulish Slate Quarries Company Limited, which had begun to work the quarries in 1894, had fully agreed to the appointment of Grant in 1900 and, at least in the opinion of the men's representatives, appeared to be satisfied with the doctor's work up to the very point of his removal. An initial and widespread sense of shock and anger at his dismissal was followed by a remarkable and sustained display of worker and community solidarity. Reinforced by impressive external moral and financial support, the dispute was eventually resolved in favour of the locals. Grant was reinstated to his former posts in the quarries and the community, and the workers both made wage gains and, in a place of work and locality previously noted for a lack of interest in trade unionism and industrial militancy, established and received the company's recognition for a union of the 'new' type which, unlike 'craft' or 'old' trade unionism, embraced all grades of quarrymen.

The second dispute, which had simmered throughout the previous winter and spring months, came to the boil in the summer of 1905. It saw a crowd 'numbering between two and three hundred persons' proceed to the house and break down the door of the unpopular quarry manager, Archibald Maccoll, and successfully achieve, by means of 'threatened violence', his written resignation and 'an undertaking to leave Ballachulish on the following … morning'. Members of the crowd had charged Maccoll with 'autocratic', 'dictatorial' and 'unfair' behaviour towards both Dr. Grant and members of the quarrying labour force and the community. Twelve members of the crowd were subsequently charged with 'mobbing and rioting', but received either modest fines, were found not guilty or, in one case, had the charge withdrawn.[8]

In addition to the traditional crowd actions of these 'mobbers and rioters', the company was also faced with increasingly depressed market conditions and a massive surplus of unsold slates. During the second half of 1905 there was short-time working, unemployment and the closure of the quarries for five months. The dispute ended in a compromise. Following the appointment of a more conciliatory chair, the company agreed to recognise trade unionism and collective bargaining, and a conciliation board, formed at the end of the first dispute, was resurrected. The depressed state of both the company and its product markets induced the workers to accept, in return, what they hoped would be temporary reductions in their numbers, the length of the working week and their wages. However, despite recurring optimistic forecasts between early 1906 and mid 1907, neither market conditions nor workplace relations showed substantial and sustained improvement. Matters deteriorated sharply from July 1907 on-wards when, in the face of poor trade and the refusal of the quarriers any longer to tolerate 'considerable reductions on contracts and standard wages in order to keep matters going', the quarries were closed once again, and remained so until the New Year. The company's continuing inability to meet its liabilities left an Extraordinary General Meeting no option but to wind up the business and to call in the liquidator in August 1907. Fortunately, a new company, the Ballachulish Slate Quarries Limited, was formed in December 1907 and work was resumed early in 1908.[9] Grant continued his medical practice until his death in 1945, and quarrying continued to take place at Ballachulish until 1955.[10]

Of immediate and major significance to the participants and of obvious historical importance, nevertheless, the Ballachulish disputes have barely figured in the published oral, visual and written historical records. Unlike the equally important, long running and acrimonious disputes which were taking place at the quarries of the autocratic Lord Penrhyn in north Wales between the 1880s and early 1900s – in which Penryhn doggedly and successfully defended the principles of 'managerial prerogatives' and non-unionism – the even more re-mote and, doubtless in many metropolitan eyes, 'peripheral' and 'parochial' Ballachulish disputes, failed almost entirely to capture the attention of the national mainstream press and the national government at Westminster. For example, searches through issues of *The Times* and the *Manchester Guardian* at key moments during both disputes, revealed only silence. Furthermore, none of the witnesses or cases cited in the *Report of the Royal Commission on Trade Disputes and Trade Combinations*, of 1906, had any connection with slate quar-rying at Ballachulish. The Board of Trade's *Report on Strikes and Lockouts in the United Kingdom and on Conciliation and Arbitration Boards*, for 1903, did contain a relevant, but partial, brief account of the first dispute. This read:

On 5th January a stoppage of work took place at the Ballachulish slate quarries, in which 370 workpeople were involved. The matter in the dispute related to the appointment of the medical officer at the quarries, and the general conditions of employment. An attempt to arrange a reference of the dispute to arbitration by the Board of Trade was unsuccessful. The dispute was, however, eventually settled between the parties themselves after a duration of over 11 months.[11]

There was no reference in the account either to the fact that the 'stoppage of work' was effectively a lock-out, or that it was part of a conflict dating back to July 1902. The Board of Trade's annual *Reports on Strikes and Lockouts*, between 1904 and 1906, contain no further mention of Ballachulish.

Students of trade unionism and industrial relations in late Victorian and Edwardian Britain have been equally neglectful. With the exception of references to developments at the Penrhyn quarries, workplace relations in slate quarrying have either been completely ignored or very briefly mentioned in the relevant published academic literature. R. Merfyn Jones's seminal study of quarrymen, their communities and workplace relations not only at Penryhn, but also throughout north Wales, *The North Wales Quarrymen 1874-1922*, is the exception to this general rule. Moreover, Jones's book contains a short reference to 'one long and bitter dispute', a 'strike' of the 'Scots quarrymen of Ballachulish in 1903'. [12] However, to the best of my knowledge, none of the other regionally- or nationally-based published histories of 'old' and 'new' trade unionism and industrial relations during this period contains any reference to the Ballachulish disputes.[13]

This is perhaps somewhat surprising in the Scottish case where, given the predominantly rural, albeit heavily urbanised, nature of the country,[14] and the slow development of national, as opposed to local, trade unions in comparison with England,[15] one might have expected labour historians to have unearthed more examples of industrial worker protest and organisation in the Highlands and other rural areas beyond the coalfields and the major urban centres. However, the Ballachulish disputes simply do not figure in the published Scottish labour history literature. In truth, the dominant and in many ways understandable concern of Scottish labour historians has continued to rest with urban workers, especially in 'red Clydeside', and coalminers[16] – workers often assumed to be more 'advanced', less 'backward', and more in the mainstream than their 'docile' Highland cousins standing on the periphery of national and Scottish labour movement development. This was also a common assumption among early twentieth-century commentators. For example, in October 1903 'Gavroche', writing in the socialist weekly, the *Labour Leader*, argued that the dispute at Ballachulish was 'unique'. For,

Here was a body of men living in a remote part of the country, living under conditions and traditions such as usually foster an instinctive deference to the powers
that be, uninfluenced, even up to the present moment, by agitation from the outside, with no previous experience of trade unionism...[17]

There has, of course, been considerable academic interest in the transformation of modern Highland society. This transformation resided in the decline
of the rule of the clans and the traditional social relationships, values and customs of Gaeldom (the 'landlord-protector', popular loyalty and deference and
'the guarantee of land possession'), and the strong growth of the unsentimental
commercial exploitation of the land by (increasingly large numbers of Lowland
and English) individualistic capitalist landlords rather than by 'patrons and
protectors of their clansmen'. [18] A large part of this interest has focused upon
the strains and stresses of the process of transformation– the 'bitter, if sporadic,
protest and deep hostility' resulting from the advancement of capitalist agriculture, and the persistent demand for 'access to the land', and security of tenure
and fairness of rents repeatedly expressed by crofters and others among the
many economically threatened and dispossessed smallholders and tenants in
the Highlands. However, among historians of Scottish Highland protest there
has not been a corresponding interest in industrial wage earners in these remote
rural settings.[19]

Lastly, in terms of the published secondary sources, there is useful, but limited, coverage of the first Ballachulish conflict in two articles by Kris Misselbrook in the *Lochaber Free Press*, 18 and 25 February 1977, and brief references
to the same conflict in the work of local historian, Barbara Fairweather, and in
the Slate Display Room at the Glencoe and North Lorn Folk Museum in Glencoe village. Professor Allan Macinnes also brought the 'lockout of 1902-03' to
public attention in his informative short piece on the Scottish slate industry,
published in the *Sunday Mail Magazine* in 1989.[20] Professor Macinnes, who was
brought up in Ballachulish, remembers friends and relatives with recollections
and memories of both disputes. However, and notwithstanding the fact that
'much' of Fairweather's information on quarrying in Ballachulish was collected
from 'the men who worked in the quarry', there are no surviving oral history
tapes, transcriptions and deposits.[21]

This absence has been corroborated by Dr. Grant's sole surviving daughter,
Mrs Sheena Roddan and her cousin, Mr. Duncan Clark, a retired solicitor and
son of Angus Clark, a Ballachulish quarrymen. Twenty-one years old in 1902,
Angus Clark was Secretary of the Medical Committee (see the photograph on
page 7). He became the future brother-in-law and a close and lasting political ally of Grant. Duncan Clark, who has extensively researched the disputes,

Ballachulish Slate Quarriers' Medical Committee (National Library of Scotland)
Dr. Grant is in the centre of the front row.

generously shared his knowledge with me. I am extremely grateful for his help and that of Sheena Roddan. I also owe a great debt to Dr. Roddy Macleod of Ballachulish, owner of *Craigleven,* the house purchased by Grant in 1928, who has a keen interest in Grant's life and career and who first put me in touch with Mrs. Roddan.[22] Finally, Mrs. Maggie Wilson of Ballachulish kindly showed me around Laroch House in Ballachulish, Maccoll's place of residence and the object of the 'mobbing' attack in 1905, and alerted me to Dr. Macleod's interest in Grant.

In sum, the secondary literature contains no substantial published account of the conflicts. Moreover, my extensive conversations and contacts with labour and social historians both north and south of the border have revealed little or, more commonly, no academic knowledge of the 'Scottish Bethesda'.

There is some compensation for the meagreness of the secondary literature in the far more voluminous, if frequently limited and uneven, evidence to be found in a variety of primary sources. As noted above, there is virtually nothing of relevance to be found in parliamentary papers and reports and the main-stream national press. The 1903 Minutes of the Parliamentary Committee of the Scottish Trades Union Congress, the Minutes of the Lismore and Appin Parish Council for 1903 and 1904, and the 1905 Report of the Chief Constable of Argyllshire, however, all provide very useful and significant, if often tantalising, insights into, respectively, the nature of the correspondence and support among labour activists in the wider Scottish movement and those in Ballachulish, the termination and re-appointment of Grant to his post of Medical Officer for Ballachulish, and the 'mobbing and rioting' incident of 1905.[23] Furthermore, and more substantially, the widespread, but uneven, coverage of the conflicts in the organs of the local and wider Scottish press partly offsets the deafening silence of their mainstream national counterparts. In terms of the former, the traditionally radical *Oban Times*, followed by the progressive *Highland News*, provide the most detailed and informative press treatment of both the conflicts and the socio-economic, political and cultural characteristics of the Ballachulish district. Useful, but often discontinuous, accounts can also be gained from the pages of the *Glasgow Herald*, the *Glasgow Evening News*, the *Oban Weekly News* and the *Oban Telegraph and Express*. I found no references to the events at Ballachulish in the main newspaper for Inverness and its region, the Whig-Liberal *Inverness Courier*, complete with its very conservative and stuffy coverage of the political, personal and leisurely doings of mainly 'the great and the good', both at home and across the Empire.[24]

I expected to find considerable coverage and interest in the Ballachulish conflicts in the pages of the socialist press, but, with the major exception of the Independent Labour Party's weekly organ, the *Labour Leader*, in 1902 and 1903, my search proved to be very disappointing. This was by no means initially the case. In 2000 and 2001, while trawling the pages of the *Labour Leader* for British socialist attitudes to class, race and empire during the late nineteenth- and early twentieth-centuries, I inadvertently came across 'Gavroche's'[25] reports of the 'extraordinary' and 'dramatic' events taking place in Ballachulish upon Grant's dismissal. Sensing their very unusual and, in all probability, historically neglected but significant character, I decided to revisit these events, courtesy of 'Gavroche', at the earliest possible opportunity. Before so doing, a literature search of the published academic literature and the many kind responses to my queries from colleagues in Scotland and elsewhere convinced me that my initial curiosity and growing sense of excitement were fully justified: Ballachulish, unlike Penrhyn, was, at least for the vast majority of the present generation of scholars with relevant knowledge and expertise, 'hidden from history'. After completing my research on class, race and empire, I duly and eagerly revisited the *Labour Leader*, gratefully to become aware that 'Gavroche' provided the reader with regular and quite detailed reports of the entire first dispute, between July 1902 and January 1904. The second chapter of this book, charting the nature and chronology of the conflicts, relies heavily on 'Gavroche's' reports. It was indeed the latter which not only aroused my curiosity in the first place, but persuaded me to pursue my mounting interest in more depth and breadth.

Unfortunately, the socialist press offered precious little else in the way of further enlightenment. 'Gavroche' continued to provide the readers of the *Labour*

Leader with regular and informative accounts of the fluctuating fortunes of the socialist movement in Scotland. However, neither these accounts nor the *Labour Leader* as a whole made any reference to the second dispute at Ballachulish in 1905.[26] Detailed searches of the pages of the two other national socialist weeklies, the *Clarion* and *Justice*, the respective journalistic organs of the Clarion movement and the Social Democratic Federation, also proved to be largely fruitless. Between 1902 and 1905 the Ballachulish conflicts entirely escaped the attention of *Justice*, while the *Clarion* contained only two brief items. The one was a letter in 1903 seeking to enlighten readers about the 'Scottish Bethesda'; the other, in September 1905, provided a short account of the disputes, including reference to the attack on Maccoll's house, and offered the conclusion that 'For the last three years there has been nothing else but trouble in the valley of Glencoe'.[27] *Forward*, the Scottish socialist weekly newspaper which began publication only in 1906, made no mention of the continuing conflicts in the Ballachulish quarries during 1906 and 1907.[28]

In company with the *Labour Leader*, rather than the socialist press as a whole, the medical press, and especially the *Lancet*, with its national base and appeal, provided a good source of information and enlightenment concerning the first dispute. For the 'Grant case' raised very important issues for medical practitioners and other professionals *nationally*, according to the *Lancet*. These revolved around their contractual rights and responsibilities, their relations with their employers, including the latter's 'appropriate' and 'customary' respect for their expertise, professional judgement and control over vital aspects of their work, and their freedom properly to carry out their duties towards their patients and clients. In sum, much in the manner of workplace relations between the quarrymen and the Ballachulish Slate Quarries Company Limited, established or 'customary' issues of mutual rights and responsibilities, control, independence and respect, were perceived to lie at heart of the escalating conflict between Dr. Grant and the company. According to the *Lancet*, neither the professional man, Grant, nor the 'skilled', able and respectable quarrymen were being afforded the respect and fairness of treatment 'reasonably' due to them. Rather they were being treated as dependant, unthinking and helpless 'slaves' by a company 'immorally' intent upon maximising its power at the expense of 'fair' and 'just' relations with its employees, whether of professional or manual status.[29] Significantly the *Lancet's* sentiments were widely shared in the medical press nationally, including the *British Medical Journal* and the *Edinburgh Medical Journal*. As we will see in the chapters below, they make for fascinating reading. However, once again in the manner of the *Labour Leader*, the medical press did not provide coverage of the 1905 dispute.

Many of the insightful reports in the medical press are to be found in the first three of Dr. Grant's fourteen volumes of press cuttings. Deposited in the National Library of Scotland, Edinburgh, by Sheena Roddan and Duncan Clark in 2003, these cuttings proved to be invaluable. Indeed, along with the contemporary press they constituted the most important primary source for reconstructing the narrative of events between1902 and the summer of 1905.[30] Beyond the latter date references in Grant's cuttings to developments at the quarries become very thin. (The doctor probably spent much of his time in the period immediately following his re-instatement in attending to his patients and building up his geographically extensive medical practice which stretched from Ballachulish in the north to Bridge of Orchy in the south east and to Appin in the south west, according to Sheena Roddan. He was also a key figure in the establishment, in 1906, of the Highland Crofters' and Cottars' Association.[31]) A clipping from the *Glasgow Herald*, for 5 October 1907, records that the Ballachulish Slate Quarries were now 'For Sale by Private Tender' and, ironically and sadly in view of the prevailing depression, the liquidation of the company and the short-time working and unemployment among the quarrymen, that 'The slate in these quarries is of exceptional quality and always commands a high price'.[32] But neither the formation of the new company, nor its fortunes and those of its workers up to the eve of the First World War figure in Grant's volumes. However, by way of compensation, they do contain, especially when read in conjunction with the relevant issues of the *Oban Times* and *Highland News*, much fascinating and valuable material about the cultural and socio-economic aspects of local Ballachulish and wider Highland life. Moreover, especially from Volume Three (1903-1908) onwards, they chart Grant's impressive range of activities as a champion of 'the land of the Gael' and 'the preservation of everything Celtic and national', a very committed and hardworking radical doctor and pamphleteer, social and land reformer, educationalist, temperance advocate, JP, sports enthusiast (shinty and golf), active Liberal with socialist connections and leanings, and by the 1930s, founder of the New-Deal inspired Highland Development League.[33] Of limited relevance to the present study, these middle and later volumes will prove to be of paramount importance to students of Grant's life and work beyond the disputes. Given the remarkable range and depth of his activities and his indefatigable pursuit of radical and progressive causes, Grant urgently merits a detailed biography.

The census returns and the valuation rolls also cast important light upon the nature of the local community in which the conflicts took place.[34] These sources contribute greatly to our knowledge and understanding of key socio-structural characteristics of Ballachulish – of its household, property and occupational structures, its gender roles, and the birthplaces and patterns of geographical and social mobility of its inhabitants. I offer the thesis in the chapters that follow that when read in conjunction with those cultural sources reflecting people's perceptions and representations of themselves, their community and the wider world, the census and the valuation roll sources provide evidence testifying, above all else, to the 'closeness' and relative homogeneity of the community under scrutiny. Furthermore, it was this very 'closeness' which to a large extent underpinned the remarkable level of and sustained support for Grant and the quarrymen between 1902 and the autumn of 1905. I also suggest that by the latter date the escalating economic difficulties of the company and growing labour market divisions and fragmentation among the quarrymen around the issue of selective employment in the quarries, placed severe strains upon that very community solidarity which had been their mainstay in the face of considerable adversity.

Finally, in addition to the vehicles of the press and Grant's *Papers*, insights into the views and actions of the Ballachulish Slate Quarries Company Limited have been gained from the slim extant records of the company, 1893-1907, held at the National Archives of Scotland, in Edinburgh. These records provide the reader with useful information concerning the company's finances and the occupational profile of its directors and shareholders. However, they do not contain any references to the disputes, Dr. Grant and labour-capital relations in the quarries.[35] Somewhat surprisingly, the *Slate Trade Gazette*, published monthly in Hull and reflecting the views of the National Association of Slate Merchants and Slaters and Kindred Trades, contained little of substance concerning the Ballachulish Slate Quarries Company.[36]

The theoretical concerns, and the absences, limitations and unevenness in both the sources and the historiography, as outlined above, have logically set the five point agenda of this book. First, in Chapter One I reconstitute those features of the community and the workplace relevant to the disputes. Second, I then piece together, in Chapter Two, the nature and chronology of the two disputes, including the effects of the second dispute on the doomed company and the quarrymen down to the latter part of 1907. It will be evident that the first two chapters are primarily concerned to bring to light predominantly 'lost' and 'hidden' characteristics of the community, the workplace and the disputes.

Third, I then adopt a more analytical approach, both to explain the successes, failures and compromises achieved by the main players in the two disputes and to explore the wider historical and historiographical significance of my Ballachulish case study. These two tasks are undertaken in Chapter Three. It may be useful at this stage briefly to outline to the reader my main conclusions in relation to the first task, and the issues and areas addressed with reference to the second.

I suggest that a combination of factors explains the successful outcome of the first dispute in favour of the doctor and the quarrymen and defeat for the company. These may be outlined in the following way. The cohesive, stable and united character of the local community and the very close correspondence between, on the one hand, family and community and, on the other, the workplace, were conducive to strong organization and the impressive and sustained mobilization of resources both at work and in the village of Ballachulish itself.[37] The widespread and sustained support offered locally, regionally and beyond to the 'morally just' cause of the 'upstanding' and 'respectable' quarrymen and 'their' doctor also made an important contribution to the their success. In contrast, the 'outside' company made itself extremely unpopular by riding roughshod over 'customary' and locally cherished norms, ideas, values and practices and by its generally 'insensitive', 'highhanded' and 'tyrannical' attitudes and behaviour. The company also failed to maintain a united front in the face of continuing opposition. Finally, the availability of suitable alternative means of employment crucially enabled the locked-out workers to retain their independence, to maintain themselves and their families and the material means to continue their struggle.

Deteriorating conditions in the product market, a less favourable labour market situation and the emergence of cracks in the hitherto impressive workers' unity strongly underpinned the compromise settlement reached by the company and the workers at the end of the 1905 dispute. The softened attitude of the company, the crowd's successful action against Maccoll and the growth of institutionalised collective bargaining and conciliation also made an important contribution to this outcome. However, between 1905 and the end of 1907 the company was dealt a deathblow by its sharply deteriorating market and financial situation and the determination of the quarrymen to resist making further concessions on pay and working conditions.

In terms of the disputes' wider significance, I first discuss the nature of, and relationship between, 'customary' culture and social protest – for example, their 'backward' and 'forward-looking' or 'modern' characteristics and their location in material life as well as in ideas. My discussion is conducted with reference to the relevant scholarly literature, and especially the work of E.P. Thompson.[38] This is followed by an investigation of the complex and shifting attachments, entanglements and identities of custom, community, locality, class, gender, region and nation which manifested themselves during the disputes. In the course of this investigation I both engage with the appropriate literature on place, space and identity[39] and pay particular attention to what I see as emergent labour-consciousness and leadership, including elements of class attachment and belief, within the 'customary' community and workplace of Ballachulish. I consider the implications of this local form of 'labour consciousness' for conventional beliefs in labour-movement and wider working-class weakness and division both in the Highlands, as compared with many other, and especially urban, areas of Scotland, and in the latter as a whole as compared with other parts of Britain, especially England.[40]

I then move to an examination of the role and attitudes of both the company and other employers and propertied members of society directly and indirectly involved in the disputes and the local community. In the course of this I consider the light cast by the Ballachulish experience upon the 'regional peculiarities' of Scottish capitalism – the latter allegedly characterised by more united, autocratic and anti-union employers than in much of Britain.[41]

Finally, I highlight the key leadership role played by Grant and his small group of middle-class professionals both in the first dispute and in the community as a whole. Special attention is paid to their close identification, and in many instances shared culture – rooted in Gaelic, religion, respectability, education, temperance and progressive causes – with their working-class neighbours and quarrymen leaders. I suggest that these revealed local patterns of leadership and social networks cast further light upon debates concerning both national and international patterns of class, community and social movement, including labour movement, organization, mobilization and consciousness,[42] and the importance of ties between middle- and working-class radical-liberal 'respectables' and 'improvers' to the development of modern Scottish and English progressive politics.[43]

The fourth item on my agenda is further to extend our analytical and substantive terms of reference by means of a consideration of the extent and ways in which the actions and beliefs of the protesting members of the community and quarrying workforce at Ballachulish carry implications for the wider study of modern social protest movements. This forms the subject matter of Chapter Four. Concern rests with issues of rationality, spontaneity, organisation and leadership, the role of industrial workers, and especially 'skilled' and independent-minded workmen, in rural protest movements and the question of methodology. In terms of the latter, I make a case for a holistic approach to the study of social movements. In contrast to the limited perspective offered by a resource mobilisation, rational choice approach, I examine not only structural but also cultural factors – questions of agency, motivation and consciousness as well as resources and their organisation. In addition, I pay close attention to historical context, chronology and patterns of continuity and change. In adopting this approach, I draw upon aspects of 'social choice' theory – of the study of the ways in which different individuals within society 'arrive at cogent aggregative judgments' about 'the public good', 'the public interest'.[44]

Fifth, in the Afterword I return to a more descriptive mode in order to tie up the loose ends of my story. I outline developments in quarrying in Ballachulish from the formation of the new company in 1907 up to the end of the decade. Significantly, this new company, the Ballachulish Slate Quarries Limited, adopted both a new spirit and a new approach. It set out to restore customary bonds of trust and mutuality with, and to improve the living standards of, the local community by taking serious cognisance of the views of the quarrymen and by modernising production methods in slate quarrying by means of capital investment and technological change. In addition to reviewing these developments, I briefly consider the legacy of the disputes for trade union development in the Highlands up to the latter part of 1910, and indicate some potentially fruitful avenues for future research.

In conclusion, my study reconstructs and explores the significance of those social conflicts, structures and relations which dominated the west Highland community of Ballachulish between the appointment of Dr. Grant in 1900 and the promise of reconciliation and modernisation displayed by the new company up to and including 1910. In so doing, I am seeking both to rescue the disputes and their workplace and community contexts from near historical invisibility and, in establishing their significance to wider historical and theoretical issues and debates, to demonstrate that they hold more than peripheral or parochial interest to the study of modern social movements and social structures. My book will hopefully appeal to readers with a particular interest in Scottish history, and to students and professional academics across the humanities and social sciences.

Chapter One
The Community and the Workplace

In its 'Appeal for Funds', published in March 1903, the Medical Committee of the locked-out quarrymen described Ballachulish as 'a peaceful village', 'romantically situated' and 'embosomed by mountains'.[1] Ballachulish and its neighbour, Glencoe, had a combined population of around 1500 in the 1890s and 1800 by the mid 1900s.[2]

Ballachulish lay on the shore of Loch Leven, twenty-six miles north-north-east of the nearest coastal centre, Oban, to which it was in the process of being connected by the construction of a railway line, and fourteen miles south of Fort William, the latter situated in the north-east corner of Loch Linnhe. Ballachulish's closest neighbouring village was that of Glencoe, just over a mile away, east north-east, while almost six and a half miles beyond Glencoe, in the same direction, lay Kinlochleven, the latter situated at the head of Loch Leven (see map on page 16). Between 1904 and 1909 Kinlochleven, 'made up of two shooting lodges and their cottages and one small farm', would be 'altered completely' by the unremitting toil of three thousand largely itinerant and Gaelic-speaking workers, many from the Isles. For it was these workers who impressively made the Blackwater dam (at that time the largest in Europe), blasted the rock and laid the water pipes in Kinlochleven's steep and rugged mountain backdrop to supply the power houses at Kinlochleven itself. The 'waterworks' generated electricity which, in turn, was used for the smelting of aluminium by the British Aluminium Company in its Kinlochleven factory. A temporary smelter, opened in 1907, closed two years later when 'the main smelter began working'.[3]

References to 'romantic' Highland locations and straight-line distances, of course, are most deceptive. They convey nothing of the many perils and hardships and roughness of work, life and travel often involved in this remote and extremely mountainous area, complete with its very harsh winters and high level of rainfall. For example, in his 1908 Annual Report, Dr. Roger McNeill, the Medical Officer for Argyll, both commended the Lochleven Water and Electric Power Company upon its efforts to provide decent accommodation and other material comforts for its electricity and aluminium workers in the 'new village' by the loch, and criticised the accommodation and sanitary conditions

The geographical context
(courtesy of Ella Kirk)

of those who toiled away on the mountainside in the 'preliminary operations'. Among those enjoying the relative material comforts provided by 'the generation of electricity and the manufacture of aluminium', between July and December 1907, were many quarriers from Ballachulish. These men had literally and successfully 'walked away' from the Ballachulish Slate Quarries Company's demand that, in order to ensure its continued viability in the face of severe market difficulties, they agree to further 'concessions' in terms of pay and working conditions.[4] Those involved in construction, drilling and blasting and other 'preliminary' tasks numbered between 1040 and 2750 workers during the period covered by McNeill's report. Included in their ranks were many 'tramping navvies'. They 'lived', according to McNeill,

> in wooden or corrugated iron huts, scattered over a distance of over 5 miles from the pier to the water reservoir, which is being constructed at a height of about 1,000 feet. The conditions of life can scarcely be described as satisfactory.

Among these unsatisfactory 'conditions of life' were 'primitive arrangements' for the disposal of refuse which had led to ill-health and infectious disease. McNeill recommended the appointment of a local sanitary inspector, but stopped short of 'insisting on what might be considered by some ... as necessary improvements'.[5]

Far more vivid and detailed insights into the truly awful working and living conditions prevailing among the workers engaged in the 'preliminary operations', were provided by tramp, navvy and socialist Patrick MacGill in his remarkable autobiography, *Children of the Dead End*, first published in 1914. Having heard on the tramping grapevine that 'pay was good and the work easy' in the 'Mecca' of Kinlochleven, MacGill and his tramping, fighting, gambling and drinking partner, 'Moleskin Joe', made the long 'pilgrimage', by foot, from Glasgow. 'Eager to get on to Kinlochleven and make money to send to my own people in Glenmornan', in Donegal, MacGill was soon to be severely disillusioned with his new life. On approaching the 'bald cliffs' of Kinlochleven, MacGill and 'Moleskin Joe' 'sat on a rock, lit our pipes and gazed on the Mecca of our hopes'. The prospect was far from romantic or paradisiacal:

> A sleepy hollow lay below; and within it a muddle of shacks, roofed with tarred canvas, and built of driven piles, were huddled together in bewildering confusion. These were surrounded by puddles, heaps of disused wood, tins, bottles and all manner of discarded rubbish. Some of the shacks had windows, most of them had none ...

> Although it was high mid-summer the slush around the dwelling rose over our boots ... the building, which was a large roomy single compartment that served the purpose of bedroom, eating-room, dressing-room, and gambling saloon ... The room, forty feet square, and ten feet high, contained fifty bed-places, which were ranged around the walls, and which rose one over the other in three tiers reaching from the ground to the ceiling. A spring oozed through the earthen floor, which was nothing but a puddle of sticky clay and water.[6]

In the rainy season the flooring in MacGill's shack was 'always under the water'. During the evenings of the bitterly cold and snowy winter months MacGill and his army of 'despised outcasts', the men 'with no fixed address', the 'scarecrows of civilisation', either 'crouched around the hot-plate' or 'scrambled into bed and sought warmth under the meagre blankets'. During the day-time, 'unkempt, ragged and dispirited', they 'slunk' to their toil, the 'snow falling on their shoulders and forcing its way insistently through our worn and battered bluchers', while their tools 'froze until the hands that gripped them were scarred as if by red-hot spits'.[7]

MacGill and 'Moleskin Joe' were part of a team employed on the 'very dangerous' jobs of hammering five-foot steel drills into and blasting the rock. Those holding the drills often suffered injury and sometimes death at the hands of the other members of the team wielding their hammers. The latter task, observed MacGill, 'requires nerve and skill': it was, nevertheless, 'classed as unskilled labour'. Confident expectations of having 'money enough and to spare' ('Sixpence an hour meant thirty shillings a week, and a man was allowed to work overtime until he fell at his shift') were soon 'dispelled before the hard wind of reality'. For most of those employed in construction at Kinlochleven seemingly spent their money on heavy drinking and gambling sessions. Apart from these pastimes and fighting matches, both spontaneous and organised in character, there was virtually nothing else to do, according to the very bleak and depressing picture drawn by MacGill.[8]

It would certainly have been extremely difficult for MacGill and his mates to 'have a night out' and pursue more approved forms of leisure. Up to the First World War there was no road to Kinlochleven. The 'local' men from Glencoe and Ballachulish employed there, either walked over the hills or arrived by boat. Down in the village, however, there were signs that the 'respectable' and 'improving' activities of education, the co-op. and mutual improvement society were making some, albeit limited, headway in Kinlochleven in the years before the First World War.[9]

At the time of the first dispute, in 1902, Ballachulish was also geographically remote, but far less so than Kinlochleven. The railway link between Oban and

Ballachulish would be completed in the following year. And even though the soaring 'Munros' of Sgorr Dhearg and Agorr Dhonuill, situated on the fine, curving ridge of Beinn a' Bheithir (Hill of the Thunderbolt), guarded Ballachulish's south-western flank, and the long and precipitous wall of the Aonach Eagach Ridge to the east and the massive presence of the Three Sisters (Aonach Dubh, Gearr Aonach and Beinn Fhada) towered above the Pass of Glencoe,[10] there was road access from Ballachulish to the east, west and south. To the south south-east, a railway ran from Tyndrum, situated some distance below the wide expanse of Rannoch Moor, to Glasgow. Furthermore, the pier at Ballachulish was the point at which the roofing slates from the local quarries were traditionally loaded onto boats on Loch Leven to meet, via the sea loch of Loch Linnhe, the housing demands of Britain's mushrooming urban dwellers. Loch Linnhe also provided water access to Fort William and the North, and to Oban and points further south. As in the case of the quarrying communities of north Wales, Ballachulish's relative geographical remoteness did not signify economic 'backwardness'. For, in both north Wales and the Scottish Highlands and Islands, the slate industry tied people with a very strong sense of local place and pride, whether willingly or not, into the wider world of industrial capitalism, characterised by its fluctuations of demand for slate and the consequently unsettling effect on the quarriers' and their families' regularity and security of employment and earnings.[11]

Unlike the 'frontier' and, for many of its transient workers, temporary settlement of Kinlochleven, with its heterogeneous collection of 'rough' and casual construction workers and the increasingly more 'regular', 'steady' and 'respectable' element in the powerhouses and the aluminium plant,[12] Ballachulish was an altogether more settled, homogeneous and tightly-knit village by the late nineteenth century. The latter's communal 'closeness' is clearly demonstrated in both the visual and quantitative sources pertaining to the physical layout and social structure of the village and its immediate area, and in the qualitative sources concerning the inhabitants' patterns of thought, behaviour and values and attitudes.

Evidence contained in maps, the census for 1891 and 1901 and the valuation rolls for 1901-2, 1902-3 and 1905-6, shows that the village of Ballachulish and its vicinity were dominated by the quarries, their predominantly male labour force and their families. Furthermore, these families both struggled to 'make ends meet', on the basis of the wages paid mainly to the male head and his sons and other resident male relatives of working age (the latter almost invariably pursuing the same occupation as the former) and the predominantly unpaid activities of their female members. They also displayed massive residential stability and continuity.

The 1898 map of Ballachulish, reproduced on page 21, shows that the core quarters of the village, East and West Laroch, were situated between the two quarrying areas. Most of the villagers lived in West Laroch, within a few minutes walking distance of the main quarry in East Laroch. Information extracted from the valuation rolls – the latter usefully listing the number, proprietor, tenant, (principal) occupier/inhabitant and annual value and yearly rent or value of the property concerned– indicates that between 1901and 1906 the streets of East and West Laroch were inhabited mainly by male quarrier heads of households and their families. For example, out of a sample of sixty-five principal inhabitants/occupiers drawn from the valuation roll for East Laroch in 1901-1902, forty-five were male quarriers. Of the remaining twenty, there were six labourers, six of no stated occupation (comprising five women and one man), two enginemen, two foremen and one nurse, widow, smith and piermaster (see Appendix One, Valuation Rolls, 1901-1906, pp. 418-19 – from Dugald Henderson, quarrier, to Alexander Wilson, quarrier). In West Laroch there was the same preponderance of male quarrier heads. A sample of ninety-one principal inhabitants/occupiers taken from the valuation roll for West Laroch in 1905-6, reveals that fifty-eight were quarriers, nine paupers (eight women and one man), four labourers and three were widows. Of the remaining seventeen, seven (four women and three men) had no listed occupation, two were enginemen, two were minors and there were single listings for the occupations of grieve, roadman, foreman, joiner, blacksmith and postman (see Appendix One, Valuation Roll 1905-1906, pp. 446-448 – from Catherine Cameron, pauper, to Allan McLachlan, quarrier).

The valuation rolls also alert us to a lower- and middle-class presence in East and West Laroch. For example, Hugh McColl and subsequently Miss Nancy McColl, bakers, Barr and Co., storekeepers, Archibald McAlpine, joiner, Hugh Macinnes, butcher, Donald Campbell, farmer, Hugh McColl, tailor and the Argyll Highland Rifle Volunteers and its drill instructor, Peter Campbell, rented their properties in East Laroch from the proprietor, 'F.C. Beresford Drummond and another'. In West Laroch Lachlan Grant, M.D., rented a house possessing an annual value of £30 per annum from Dugald Cameron, a tailor, while his immediate adversary in the first dispute, Archibald Maccoll, the quarry manager, let a shop and bakehouse, also valued at £30 per year, to Andrew Cochran. They were joined, as neighbours, either in West Laroch or elsewhere in Ballachulish, by a teacher, Archibald McCallum, M.A., Grant's close friend Rev. Duncan McMurchy, minister at the South Ballachulish United Free Church, Robert McInnes, a grocer, and James Skinner, station master and employee of the Callander and Oban Railway Company (see Appendix One, pp. 418, 422, 425, 444, 448). In truth, the local middle class had a very limited numerical presence

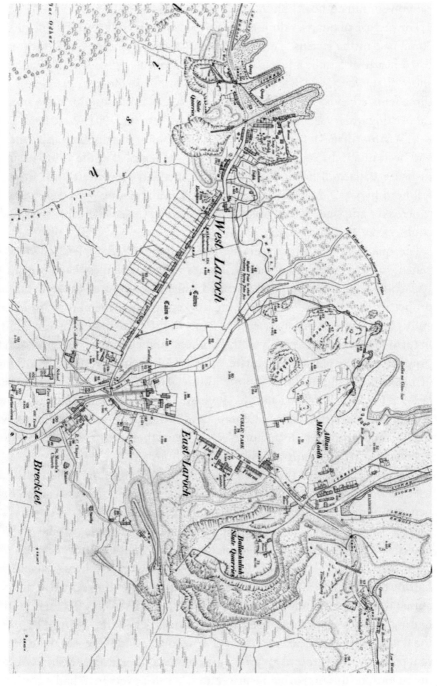

Ballachulish - OS County Series (1/2500) 2nd Edition 1898 (National Library of Scotland)

in Ballachulish. However, we will see that some of its members, such as Grant and McMurchy, possessed impressive organisational, leadership and ideological powers and authority among the local population.

The picture of quarrier dominance in the village is confirmed by information contained in the census. Thus a sample of forty-one houses and thirty-seven listed heads of families, taken from the 1901 census returns for West Laroch, shows that twenty-five of these heads were working in the slate quarries. A mere three female heads, widowed and keeping house, came second in the numerical pecking order (see Appendix Two, Census Returns, 1901, West Laroch, pp. 6-14 – from Allan McLachlan to Duncan Matheson). Ten years earlier matters had been much the same. Of forty-three heads sampled in the 1891 census returns for Ballachulish Rd., West Laroch, fully thirty-three were slate quarriers, followed by six widow-housekeepers, one laundress, one retired servant, one shoemaker and one crofter (see Appendix Three, Census Returns, 1891, Ballachulish Rd., West Laroch, pp. 3-11).

The quarriers and other working-class inhabitants/occupiers listed in the valuation rolls rented their modest homes in East and West Laroch from the Ballachulish Quarries Company Limited which had acquired the lease on these properties in 1894. Before that date the workers had held their homes independently of the lessee of the quarries. The Ballachulish Quarries Company Limited, in turn, took out its lease both on the workers' homes and the quarries from the proprietor of the Ballachulish estate, Francis Colebrook Beresford Drummond, of Ballachulish House, 'and another', both 'trustees of the late Sir George de la Poer Beresford of Ballachulish'. Resident at Ballachulish House and owners of the Ballachulish estate, 'Captain' and 'Mrs.' Beresford Drummond were wealthy and prominent local notables who gave their active support to a range of educational and leisure activities in Ballachulish.[13]

The annual values of the workers' rented properties in the Ballachulish district lay between £1 and £4, with the majority in East and West Laroch being between £1 and £2. Furthermore, only a small minority of these properties carried 'grazing rights' by the 1900s. These facts suggest both the inability of Ballachulish's worker families to afford high rents and their dependence upon their own labour power, both paid and unpaid, as their main source of livelihood. During the middle years of the nineteenth century properties rented at under £4 annually and not on long leases had merited 'little detail' in the valuation rolls. During the same period of time most of the quarriers' three-roomed houses on the Ballachulish estate had an attached 'cowhouse'; and there was the option to rent pasturage and ground for growing potatoes and vegetables nearby. According to local historian, Barbara Fairweather, 'almost every man had a cow'.[14] By the turn of the century some quarrying families doubtless continued to grow vegetables, but the vast majority no longer possessed 'pasturage' or 'grazing' rights. As observed by Jones for north Wales, 'for the majority of quarrymen … agriculture was no part of their livelihood; that was gained in the rocks of the quarry … and their lives were lived in the … streets of their industrial villages'.[15]

The wages of their male members constituted the sole source of paid income for almost all Ballachulish's quarrying families. While the male head of the family was the main paid 'breadwinner', it was commonly expected among quarrying families that, once they reached working age, sons and other resident male relatives would also seek paid employment. As clearly demonstrated in the census for both 1891 and 1901, this meant in practice that the overwhelming majority of the latter would join the former in the quarry. This was to be expected in a locality in which quarrying constituted by far the main means of paid work. Many sons and other male relatives would initially work as helpers, but would hope eventually to move into the specialised and more 'skilled' jobs performed by many of the male heads of families. The failure of the census enumerators more finely to break down the various job classifications in quarrying in Ballachulish – most workers are listed simply as 'quarriers' or 'slate quarriers' and a few as 'slate dressers' and 'slatemakers' – means that it is impossible to calculate the extent to which this precise hope was fulfilled. However, we can safely conclude, on the basis of the census information, that occupational self-recruitment and continuity were extremely high among Ballachulish's male quarrymen, both absolutely and in relation to the wider occupational picture for working-class fathers and sons.[16]

For example, of the 25 male quarrier heads in my sample of the 1901 census for West Laroch, twelve were listed as having sons or 'extended' male relatives living with them (brother, brother-in-law and nephew being the most common in terms of the latter category) in paid work. In all these cases slate quarrying was the listed 'profession or occupation'. For example, Hugh McKechnie, slate quarrier, and Catherine, his wife, had four sons, all of whom were slate quarriers, while Donald McInnes, slate quarrier, headed a family comprising his mother, Dorothy, a housekeeper, his brothers Dugald, Alex, John and Robert, all of whom were slate quarriers, and Bella McDonald, his 'Neice' (sic), who was listed as a servant. Hugh McDonald's family household even included a nephew and grandnephew, living alongside Hugh himself, his sister Christina, and his brother Charles. All the male members of this household were listed as being employed in the slate quarries, while Christina was simply afforded the description of 'Sister' (for these examples see Appendix Two, pp. 7, 9, 12).

My sample from the 1891 census for Ballachulish Rd. reveals a very similar picture. Of 32 slate quarrying heads listed (including two retired quarriers),

seventeen had a total of 33 sons or other resident male relatives in gainful employment. Only three of the 33 were not employed in slate quarrying. One,
a son, was a joiner, while of the other two, brothers, one was a tailor and the
other a postman. The families of Allan Robertson and Archibald Clark typified
the experiences of this sample. Robertson, the married head of the family and a
slate quarrier, lived with his wife, Mary, and their two sons, Ronald and Donald,
both slate quarriers. Archibald Clark's family home included Clark himself, the
unmarried head, and his married sister, Isabella, a housekeeper, and her hus-
band, Gael McPhee and their two children, John and Margaret. All of the three
men in the house were slate quarriers (see Appendix Three, pp. 8, 9).

The endeavours of its male members – of both the 'normal' nuclear unit and
its extended parts[17] – thus supplied the family with its paid income. In this context it is also worth noting the presence of very few lodgers and boarders and
the general lack of paid work for female members of the family. Only two lodgers appeared in my sample of 43 heads and one hundred and 96 inhabitants
for 1891. They were both unmarried joiners, Robert Wallace and Alex McKay,
lodging with the Cameron family (see Appendix Three, p. 9). My 1901 sample,
based upon 41 houses, with a total of 179 inhabitants, included a higher figure
of lodgers and boarders, thirteen in all. However, it is highly significant that
all of the latter were temporary workers employed in navvying and the construction of the railway line (six navvies, five railway labourers and two railway
gangers), and all had been born outside of Ballachulish. One was from Ireland
and ten from Scotland, with six hailing from Ross-shire and three each from
Inverness-shire and Lanarkshire (see Appendix Two, pp. 8, 9, 10, 11, 12, 13).
As such, they were not part of the extremely close, strong and enduring family
network of the local quarrying labour force. In Ballachulish employment in the
quarries and local family background, traditions and connections, in terms of
both nuclear and extended families, went hand-in-hand. As such, Ballachulish
had, once again, much in common with the quarrying communities of north
Wales.[18]

Women and girls, while key members of the family, were very much on the
margins of the paid workforce, both in quarrying and beyond. Most of the local population depended upon the quarries for paid employment. Apart from
labouring, there was little else. Both these areas of employment were dominated
by males. The *Oban Times* estimated in February 1903 that around 50 'women
and children', out of a total workforce of just under 400, were usually employed
in the Ballachulish quarries.[19] However, it is highly likely that most, and perhaps
all, of these were male 'children', including the boys and young men employed as
helpers and on other ancillary tasks in quarrying. Certainly, no female presence
in quarrying appears from my, albeit limited, samples of the census returns and

the valuation rolls. (Jones reaches the same conclusion for the slate quarrying communities of north Wales.)[20] Furthermore, the small size of the local middle and upper class meant that, in contrast to Glasgow, Edinburgh and many other urban and rural parts of Britain, there was little demand for domestic servants. The latter, of course, were the largest group of paid female workers in nineteenth- and early twentieth-century Britain.[21] The Beresford Drummonds did employ servants, but they were the exception to the general rule. All this has led Fairweather to conclude that many of the young women and girls of Ballachulish 'had to leave home owing to lack of employment'.[22] Finally, and taking into account its under-representation of the true extent of women's work (in 1901 the vast majority of wives and many daughters in Ballachulish were afforded no 'profession or occupation'),[23] the census confirms the extremely limited nature of paid employment opportunities for women in Ballachulish. Thus both my samples, for 1891 and 1901, show that 'housekeeper' was the most commonly listed occupation for adult women and 'scholar' for daughters. In the 1891 sample housemaid, general servant or general domestic, lady's nurse, dressmaker and laundress, and shirtmaker and laundress followed in order of descending numerical importance (see Appendix Three) In my 1901 sample three general/domestic servants, two housemaids and one ladies nurse, dressmaker and laundry maid were listed along with twelve housekeepers and scholars (see Appendix Two). In sum, in keeping with the national picture, including the quarrying communities of north Wales, women in Ballachulish played a key role in the home and the wider community in 'providing' and 'caring', mainly on an unpaid basis, for the needs of their menfolk, their families and local 'notables'.[24]

The highly gendered, limited and sectional nature of paid employment opportunities in Ballachulish should not allow us to lose sight of my conclusion that it was almost invariably the case that sons and other male family members followed in the occupational footsteps of the male quarrying heads of families. We will also see in due course that this very high level of occupational self recruitment strongly underpinned the impressive degree of cohesion and solidarity displayed by the male quarrying workforce during the disputes.

Notwithstanding the fact that there was no formal system of apprenticeship in quarrying, the key male jobs of drilling and blasting the rock and splitting and dressing the slate (cutting it to the required size) necessitated much skill and accuracy, attention to detail and safety, and intimate knowledge and experience of local quarrying conditions. In common with their brothers in north Wales, the Ballachulish quarrymen had great pride in their practical skill and 'local' knowledge. This was often seen as superior to the 'mere book learning' of increasing numbers of quarry managers.[25] The 'quarrymen proper' of rockmen, splitters and dressers, who constituted about half of the quarrying workforce, were often in great demand and were by no means easily replaceable. As the *Glasgow Evening News* declared in 1903, 'no labourer, or ordinary quarryman can do the work', and 'if trained men are not available the quarries are useless'.[26] In buoyant market conditions they could expect to receive relatively high wages, of around 28 or 30 shillings per week, with a minimum set at no less than 25 shillings 'whether the contract turns out well or ill'.[27] The small number of skilled carpenters and smiths were paid approximately the same as the 'quarrymen proper'. The overwhelming employment of the generic terms 'quarrier', 'slate quarrier' and 'labourer' in the valuation rolls and the census means that it is very difficult to trace the number and identities of labourers who worked specifically in the slate quarries (very few of the latter being so listed) . On the basis of my discussion of employment patterns and family structure, it is, however, logical to assume that many of them were the sons, brothers and male in-laws of the 'quarrymen proper' who often stood at the head of the family. In any event, the historical sources tell us that the wages of adult male quarry labourers were listed as being between eighteen- and twenty shillings per week. In addition the wages of the mainly younger male helpers and other ancillary workers constituted generally small, but useful, supplements to the family income.[28]

The predominantly favourable light cast by this data concerning nominal wages on the living standards of the quarrying families, however, must be seriously questioned. For such data constitutes only one part of the much larger body of evidence to be considered. And the latter lends itself, on balance, to a far more unfavourable or pessimistic conclusion in relation to overall living standards. For example, as we will observe in more detail below and in the following chapter, the generally and more frequently depressed markets for slate during the period in question exerted strong downward pressure upon the earning capacities of the quarrying labour force. Furthermore, in common with many other quarrying enterprises, the Ballachulish Slate Quarries Company Limited set the cost of powder, coals and other essential workplace and household materials against the quarrymen's wages. The result was that their actual earnings sometimes fell below the 25 shillings 'minimum', being, at least according to 'Gavroche', 'probably under twenty shillings per week'.[29] As such, they did not compare well with earnings for skilled men in many other industries in Scotland, especially in the industrial counties.[30] 'Gavroche' went so far as to claim that 'taking all the year round', the quarrymens' earnings were 'less than unskilled labourers' wages for work that requires skill and knowledge and is at all times arduous and dangerous'.[31] This was probably an exaggerated claim. However, there is no doubt that both the estimate of 28 to 30 shillings and the 25 shillings 'minimum' should be viewed as a very rough and ready figures and, as such, treated with great caution.

We will also see that during both disputes and beyond, the migrating Balla-chulish quarrymen repeatedly complained that they could earn significantly higher wages and take home pay in both quarrying and other industries in Scotland than in their home quarries. Donald McMillan, a leading figure in the quarrymens' cause, even maintained in 1903 that those labourers from Ball-achulish who were temporarily employed in one of the quarries in the west, 'were earning better wages than skilled quarrymen were when at work in the quarries under the Ballachulish Slate Quarries Company'.[32] Moreover, working hours and earnings, especially for many of those of the quarrying workforce employed outside the Bank Sheds – where the sawing, dressing and splitting into slates took place – were seriously affected by the vagaries of the weather and the amount of daylight offered by the changing seasons. And the quar-rymen took repeated issue with the Ballachulish Quarries Company Limited over its policy of six weekly, as opposed to monthly (four weekly) payments to its quarrying crews. The men's argument was that it was very difficult to make their money stretch over the longer period in order adequately and regularly to support themselves and their families.[33]

There were also the issues of health and welfare to consider alongside those of wages, earnings and hours. Once again, a predominantly gloomy picture emerges. For example, Dr. Grant, Dr. Farquharson, who was Grant's predeces-sor both in the quarries and as Medical Officer for Ballachulish , Dr. Roger Mc-Neill, the Medical Officer for Argyll referred to earlier, and 'Gavroche', were all of the strong opinion that the health and welfare not only of much of the wider Scottish, but also the local, working class were being adversely and 'acutely' affected by poor housing, overcrowding and very inadequate sanitary arrange-ments.[34] Not all three doctors may have fully endorsed 'Gavroche's' unsubstan-tiated claim that the 'hovels' and 'the housing problem' in Ballachulish, under the tenancy of the Ballachulish Slate Quarries Company Limited, were as bad and 'as acute as … in Whitechapel', but they probably would have argued that they were on a par with congested conditions afflicting the working classes in many urban areas.[35] In addition, Grant and the quarrymen's leaders also con-demned, during the first dispute, the 'excessive' assessments, for both parish and county purposes, being imposed upon their tenants in Ballachulish by the company.[36] As a portent of things to come, the latter did not hesitate to register its determination firmly and unambiguously to brook no criticism and opposi-tion, whether from professional or manual worker sources. For example, Dr. Farquharson's criticisms of the company's workplace and housing policies met with a decidedly cold reception. In 1900 Farquharson resigned from his posi-tions in the workplace and the community and left Ballachulish for Manchester because, in a view widely shared within the local community and published in the *Labour Leader*, 'matters were made so uncomfortable for him by the quarry management'.[37]

Their living standards lower than reference to wage levels alone would suggest, and compelled during the disputes to seek work elsewhere in Scotland,[38] the Ballachulish quarrymen nevertheless exhibited, much in the same way as their counterparts in north Wales, an exceedingly strong combined sense of occupational 'calling' and local 'place' or 'home'.[39] By the early 1900s many Ballachulish quarrymen saw their jobs, their homes, their neighbours, their friends and their local community as being 'for life'. As in north Wales, this outlook was a reflection far more of a positive and proud, rather than a demoralised and fatalistic, approach to life. The reader's attention has already been drawn to the facts of strong occupational pride and self-recruitment among Ballachulish's quarrymen. It is now time to turn to consider the equally strong commitment to 'place' – to Ballachulish as 'home'.

As reflected in both the valuation rolls and in the census, there was an extremely high incidence of residential stability among Ballachulish's quarrying (and non-quarrying) working-class families. Thus, the valuation rolls for East and West Laroch between 1901 and 1906 show that, apart from isolated changes in the name of the inhabitant/occupier (and these uniformly *within* the same family and often the result of the death of the male inhabitant/occupier previously listed), there was virtually *no* residential movement in the core quarrying areas of Ballachulish, even of the very short-distance, 'street-hopping' kind so characteristic of the behaviour of the nineteenth-century urban working class in Britain.[40]

To make my point more precisely, the information in Table I below, extracted from the valuation rolls, shows that the houses numbered 15-31 of the Quarry Cottages in East Laroch, were occupied by *exactly the same families*, albeit with a few changes in the name of the occupier, between 1901-2 and 1905-6.

Table I, Occupancy of Quarry Cottages, East Laroch, Ballachulish, 1901-6

House	Occupier	Year 1901-2	1902-3	1905-6
15	Dugald Henderson, quarrier	✓	✓	✓
16	Angus McInnes, quarrier	✓	✓	✓
17	Donald McColl, quarrier	✓	✓	Alexander McColl, quarrier
18	John Stewart, quarrier	✓	✓	✓
19A	Ronald McInnes, labourer	✓	✓	✓
19B	Archibald McKenzie, quarrier	✓	✓	✓
19C	Archibald Rankin, quarrier	✓	✓	Jessie Rankin, pauper
20	Duncan Clark, quarrier	✓	✓	✓
22	Catherine McKenzie	✓	✓	✓
23	Allan Robertson, quarrier	✓	✓	✓
24	John Kennedy, quarrier	✓	✓	✓

House	Occupier	Year 1901-2	1902-3	1905-6
25	Alexander McDonald	✓	✓	✓
25A	Mrs. William Cameron	✓	Mrs. Margaret Cameron, widow	
	Alexander Cameron, quarrier	✓	✓	✓
	Alexander MacDonald, quarrier	✓	✓	✓
27	Thomas MacDonald, quarrier	✓	✓	✓
	Archibald Carmichael, quarrier	✓	✓	✓
	Mrs. Duncan Clark, widow	✓	✓	John Clark, quarrier
30	Donald Turner, quarrier	✓	✓	✓
31	John McDonald, labourer	✓	✓	✓

Source: *Valuation Rolls for the County of Argyll* (National Library of Scotland), 1901-1902 (pp. 418-419), 1902-3 (pp. 425-426), 1905-6 (pp. 444-445).

The same pattern of almost uniform residential stability manifested itself among the occupants of those houses numbered between 32 and 90 in Quarry Cottages, East Laroch (there being only one change in the period covered, in 1905-6),[41] and among the predominantly quarrying families in the homes numbered 1-84, West Laroch, between 1901 and 1906. In terms of the latter there was only one extra-familial change in occupancy between 1901-2 and 1902-3, and four between the latter date and 1906.[42] Furthermore, those quarriers working in Ballachulish but living just outside the village itself, were also very settled in their homes. For example, the Quarry Cottages at Tayfuirst, near the pier at Glencoe, were occupied overwhelmingly by the same quarrier families, once again with minor changes in personnel, between 1901 and 1906.[43]

It will be evident to the reader that my conclusions so far concerning residential stability are based upon a single source, the valuation rolls, and upon the short time span of five years. However, they are supported by evidence taken from other sources. For example, the relevant census information for Ballachulish in 1891 and 1901 overwhelmingly lends itself to the conclusion that by the late nineteenth- and early twentieth centuries we are dealing with a very stable and settled community.

Difficulties, sometimes of considerable magnitude, do arise in an attempt to draw precise and accurate conclusions on the basis of a comparative study of the 1891 and 1901 census enumerators' returns for Ballachulish. These difficulties reside mainly in the absence of numbers for houses, different streets and/or areas sometimes being given for many of the same houses and their inhabitants (for example, Ballachulish Rd. in 1891 and West Laroch in 1901), and, in some cases, the different and confusing sequence in which the houses and their families are listed in 1891 and 1901.[44] However, detailed scrutiny of these sources, combined with the cross-checking of census information against the valuation rolls,[45] enabled me to arrive at two direct comparisons. First, in both 1891 and

1901 the majority of families in my samples were resident in the same street and in all probability the same house. Second, the movement that did occur was typically of the very limited, short-range type (within the same street or part of West and East Laroch). It was frequently occasioned by death or marriage within the family unit. For example, there is a perfect match for the first five families listed in my census samples for 1891 and 1901. Thereafter the sequence becomes less uniform. While there is no match for the following three families, a pattern of correspondence, albeit broken by some absences and some movement, does reassert itself for the remaining thirty directly comparable families. For example, the sequential listing of the Fraser, McGregor, McInnes, Cameron and Rankin families in the 1891 census is replicated ten years later, with the qualification that the listing for Rankin now comes between McInnes and Cameron (see Appendix Two, pp. 9-10, Appendix Three, pp. 6-7). Between 1891 and 1901 Alex McColl, slate quarrier, and the brother of John McColl, listed as the head of family in both census years, gets married and, with his wife and son, moves into a house next door to John (see Appendix Two, p. 12, Appendix Three, p. 9). During the same decade Catherine Clark, listed as a widowed head and housekeeper in 1891, dies and her son Donald, a slate quarrier, becomes the head of the family. However, as a result of a different sequential listing in the 1901 census, as compared with that for 1891, it is not clear whether Donald and his sister Mary, the housekeeper, George, his nephew, and two navvying boarders, stay in the same house or move slightly along the street. However, I suspect, the former to have been the case, with the census enumerators for 1891 and 1901 being somewhat inconsistent in making entries for houses in accordance with their street order (see Appendix Two, p. 13, Appendix Three, p. 9).

Another important conclusion, derived from the census material alone, is that the vast majority of the local population had been born and bred in Ballachulish and other parts of Argyllshire. Thus, out of my sample of 196 people in 1891, 153 had been born in Ballachulish and a further twenty elsewhere in Argyllshire. Of the remaining 23, only one person, an English pauper and father-in-law to the head of the family, had been born outside Scotland. Ten years later the picture was much the same. Out of my total sample of 179, only two had been born outside of Scotland, one in England and one in Ireland. 177 had been born in Scotland, with 141 in Ballachulish itself. In sum, we are dealing overwhelmingly with a population of Scots in which a massive 78 per cent, in both 1891 and 1901, were local to Ballachulish.

This conclusion highlights the importance of both 'the regional' and, more especially, 'the local' and matters familiar and immediate (the family, the street, the neighbourhood, the village and the workplace) to the people of Ballachulish. This was in keeping, albeit in a particularly pronounced way, with the experience of the British working class as a whole.[46] The conclusion also adds considerable weight to my claim that there existed in Ballachulish an extremely stable, closely-knit and homogeneous community, complete with very limited experience of geographical and occupational mobility and a restricted view of the world. For most of this community even the kind of relatively short-distance and regular migration (from adjacent counties and within counties) most common among the British working class, was something beyond their experience.[47] This is not to deny the fact and importance of examples and patterns of long-distance and sometimes forced migration and emigration from the Highlands, the Scottish quarrying communities themselves, and other parts of Britain during the nineteenth century.[48] However, it is to insist upon the crucial importance of matters local and customary to my subjects in Ballachulish by the period in question.

Furthermore, it would appear to be the case that this was by no means a new state of affairs. For example, Fairweather informs us that as early as the mid-nineteenth century the men working the Ballachulish quarries 'were local and descended from local people'.[49] By my period Ballachulish largely mirrored the experience of north Wales. 'By the last quarter of the nineteenth century', observes Jones, 'immigration into the quarrying towns had slowed down and the slate craft had become the possession of those already resident in them'.[50]

The community of Ballachulish was closely bound together not only by common geographical location and marked similarities in terms of occupation, social structure, living standards, life chances and patterns of residence, but also by cultural values, norms and practices. For, as briefly observed in the Introduction, a shared culture lay at the core of this predominantly working-class community. The nature and significance of this culture will be further explored in Chapters Two and Three. However, at this point I wish to indicate to the reader the importance of the involvement of both Grant, prominent quarrymen's leaders, and many of their allies in the local middle- and working class, in the affairs of the United Free Church of Scotland, the Ballachulish Public School, the Rechabites, and all matters Gaelic in order to preserve and fortify 'everything Celtic and National'.[51]

The United Free Church had its roots in the Disruption of 1843 when, in 'the most spectacular schism in British ecclesiastical history', 'nearly half the adherents and over a third of the clergy walked out of the Established Church of Scotland to form the Free Church of Scotland'. As Callum Brown has written, 'The Gaels took the 1843 Disruption as the cue for virtually total defection to the Free Church'.[52] The latter, promoting 'godly dignity', restraint, respectability, 'strict Sabbath observance', 'distinctive Gaelic psalm-singing' and 'quiet hostility' and social reform rather than outright rebellion against the landowners and other 'oppressors', soon developed close associations in its heartland of the Highlands, and elsewhere, with crofters, workers and others of the 'oppressed lower orders'.[53]

In the 1890s Ballachulish had four churches, the Established, the Episcopalian, the Catholic and the Free Church. The United Free Church was formed in 1900 as a result of the merger of the Free Church and the United Presbyterian Church. The United Free Church was to the fore in providing support for both Grant and the quarrymen, especially in the person of Grant's close friend and ally, the Reverend Duncan McMurchy. Born in 1840, McMurchy had been a minister in south Ballachulish since 1878 and would remain so down to his death in 1921. Some of the men's leaders during the dispute also owed much of their radicalism and strong sense of social and moral purpose to the religious inspiration of the Free Church. For example, Donald McMillan, the elected chair of the Medical Committee who was fluent in English and Gaelic, was an excellent musician and leader of the psalm-singing in McMurchy's church.[54] Much in the manner of the quarrying villages of north Wales and in parts of England, religious dissent in Ballachulish was instrumental in forging a powerful sense of communal togetherness.[55] It also strengthened local determination successfully to resist the actions of the 'upstart', 'tyrannical' and intrusive 'outsider', the Ballachulish Quarries Company Limited. The latter was seen to be untutored in and dismissive of 'local' and 'traditional' or 'customary' ways.[56]

In Ballachulish, as in many other Highland communities, membership of the United Free Church was indissolubly part of a wider allegiance to the Celtic heritage and Gaelic customs and habits. (This paralleled the central importance of the Welsh language and nonconformist Welsh culture to the north Wales quarrymen and their families.)[57] Fairweather informs us that out of a total population of almost 1500 in Glencoe and Ballachulish in the early 1890s, there were 1221 Gaelic speakers.[58] My census samples also demonstrate the central importance of Gaelic. Out of my 1891 sample of 196 individuals, 25 were returned as Gaelic speakers only and 160 as Gaelic and English (returns were not listed for the remaining eleven). In my total of 179 for 1901, Gaelic was listed for nineteen and English and Gaelic for 144 (see Appendix Two and Appendix Three). Thus the vast majority of Ballachulish's population were bilingual. The meetings held between 1902 and 1905 to protest against the actions of the company, were conducted in Gaelic. At one such meeting, in September 1902, while the quarrymen's speeches were translated into English, a Gaelic song was performed for the benefit of the visiting celebrity, Keir Hardie. The latter successfully urged the quarriers to form a trade union.[59] News of 'Gaelic evenings', involving song, readings and lectures and other 'respectable' and 'self-improving' activities, and in which both Grant and many of the quarrymen and their families played important parts, appeared regularly in the local and regional press.[60] The fortunes of Ballachulish's famous shinty team, of which Grant served as president, were also covered in some detail. The team was unique in Argyllshire in having won the Scottish championship. It also provided a rallying point for opposition to the company. In 1903, much to local frustration and anger, it was prevented from taking part in the semi-final of the Scottish championship by the fact that most of its quarrymen players had been forced to leave Ballachulish during the lock-out in search of alternative employment.[61] In addition to Grant, the shinty team received active support from Captain Beresford Drummond and, somewhat ironically in the circumstances of the disputes, Archibald Maccoll who, in April 1902, was reported as being the honorary captain of the club.[62] Maccoll, of course, was the manager of the Ballachulish Quarries Company Limited. He was increasingly seen as a traitor to his local and regional roots – being manager at both the Ballachulish and Easedale quarries and a county councillor – and the dictatorial enforcer of company policy.[63]

So longstanding and deep was local attachment to Gaelic culture that it not only survived, but gained even more strength from enforced transatlantic migration. Thus in October 1907, the *Oban Times* reported that, faced with deteriorating employment prospects at the Ballachulish quarriers, some thirty quarriers had departed 'several months ago' for Canada in order 'to develop the slate industry' at Jervis Inlet, some 30 miles from Vancouver. 'Doing very well' materially, the emigrants had carried their passion for shinty and other aspects of Gaelic culture with them.[64] A concert held by the emigrants in the following month was well received by the locals. In particular,

> The Canadians in the village were greatly enamoured with the Gaelic singing. Every person one meets in the streets is whistling or humming 'Mo Dachaidh' or 'Thainig an Gille Dubh'.[65]

Much closer to home, it was, above all else, their involvement in all things specifically Gaelic and a wider range of Gaelic-influenced or related self-helping and educational activities – the local branch of the Rechabite temperance society, the Ballachulish Public School, the Mechanics' Institute and literary and debating pursuits and the fight for crofter and worker rights in the face of rapacious 'landlordism' and employer 'tyranny' – that brought many of the quarrymen and their leaders into close and friendly contact with Grant, McMurchy and other progressive and social-reforming members of the local middle class.[66] In these ways the Ballachulish experience provided a specific example of the important wider Scottish (indeed British) process in which dissenting, 'improving' and self-denying 'respectables' and reformers from across the class structure developed close cultural, social and political ties.[67]

Carefully structured and self-consciously paternalistic occasions and forces were also evident in the village, especially on the part of local landed-establishment figures. For example, 'Mrs. Beresford Drummond', as 'Lady Superior', provided and gave out the presents for the children at the Public School as part of their annual Christmas 'treat', formally presented each member of the local Volunteers returning from the South African War with 'a splendid gold badge', and asked her household servants 'to invite their friends to a supper and dance at Ballachulish House'. For his part, Captain Beresford Drummond supported the activities of both the Volunteers and, as noted above, the shinty club.[68] These actions were undoubtedly informed by kindly, philanthropic and community-spirited motivations. However, due respect and deference were expected of the recipients, not least because the Beresford Drummonds, along with Lord Strathcona, were among the most prominent and wealthy landowners in the area of Ballachulish and Glencoe. It is, of course, extremely difficult to assess the extent to which positive responses to paternalism on the part of is recipients were either genuine or instrumental, or a mixture of both. But it would appear to be the case, at least so far as the *public* record is concerned, that Grant and the quarriers fully attributed their grievances to the actions of the company rather than in any way to the company's landlord, the Beresford Drummonds. Furthermore, the latter were closely involved with Grant and many quarrying families with respect to the educational and leisure-based activities of the village. The *Oban Times* had no doubt that at least one section of the community, the children at Ballachulish's Public School, were duly grateful for their Christmas 'treat'. For they gave 'Mrs. Beresford Drummond' a 'most enthusiastic reception' and held her 'in the highest esteem for her many acts of kindness on their behalf'.[69]

The marked homogeneity, stability, harmony and cohesion of the community of Ballachulish were also underpinned by the fact that most of its inhabitants depended upon a single industry for their paid employment. By the beginning of my period commercial herring fishing on Loch Leven had expired and the Ballachulish district had become 'more or less dependent' on the roofing slate industry, or 'the sole industry of the village' as it was described by the *Oban Times* in 1907.[70] The quarries, the largest in Scotland, had a long history, the West Quarry having been opened in 1693 and the East Quarry a year later.[71] Macinnes informs us that during the eighteenth century the Scottish roofing slate industry was dominated by the 'Easedale belt', comprising the island of Easedale itself and the 'associated Slate Islands' of the Inner Hebrides. However, the Ballachulish quarries soon constituted the main rival to Easedale. 'By the end of the 18th century', records Macinnes, 'Argyll slate, centred on Ballachulish, was being despatched not only to the main Scottish towns and cities, but also to the Clyde ports and Leith for export to Ireland, England and more distant countries, including America'.[72] At that time the Ballachulish quarries employed over 300 workers, a figure which was roughly the same some 50 years later, and which rose to a high point of 587 men in 1875, according to Fairweather.[73]

As Macinnes observes, 'Intensive urbanisation associated with the heavy industries ensured that slate quarrying entered a golden age from the 1840s to the 1880s'. By the latter date, Ballachulish, successfully geared up to offer a 'more marketable product' than the Slate Islands, 'was clearly established as the foremost quarrying location' in Scotland, a position of pre-eminence that continued up to and including my chosen period.[74] By 1902 the Ballachulish quarries, the largest in Scotland, employed just under 400 manual workers. As noted earlier, at the core of the labour force stood the skilled, experienced and knowledgeable 'quarrymen proper' of rockmen, splitters and dressers. In addition, much like the independent hewers in Scottish coalmining, the 'quarrymen proper', in both Ballachulish and north Wales, took great pride in their independence and control within the workplace.[75] While generally subjected to growing managerial controls over the terms and conditions of their employment, and while the issue of the 'dictatorial' manager was of central importance to the mounting list of worker grievances within the specific context of 1900s Ballachulish, nevertheless the skilled quarrymen continued to view submission to management's untrammelled will and control as craven and 'unmanly'. They continued, for example, to insist upon their established 'rights' to have the majority voice in the appointment of the medical officer at the quarries and to *negotiate* their conditions and terms of work. The latter traditionally took the form of crews of three or four workers, under the direction of the Head of Crew, negotiating the amount to be paid and the length of the contract and the timing of payments (as measured in weeks) with the manager.[76]

Ballachulish's pre-eminent position was, sadly and ironically, gained at a time when the slate industry as a whole, both nationally and in Scotland, was about to enter a period of catastrophic decline. 'Between 1895 and 1914', observes Macinnes, 'the output of Scottish slate dropped from one-twelfth to one-fortieth of the British total'. Macinnes attributes this 'downward spiral' to unsteady demand, government inaction in the face of 'cheap foreign imports', increased competition among Welsh, English, Irish and Scottish slate producers within the Scottish market (the Scottish slate industry was largely dependent upon the home market), and the 'vulnerability of the slate industry to takeovers by city-based conglomerates seeking immediate returns for their shareholders'. Moreover, 'consistently undercapitalised', these conglomerates 'were not prepared to invest in new technology or incur expenditure in order to open up new seams'. As a consequence, concludes Macinnes, 'industrial relations, which were never free from tension under paternalistic landowners, degenerated markedly under the commercial conglomerates'.[77]

This was unfortunately the case at Ballachulish. For much of their history the quarries had been worked by their proprietors, the paternalistic, mostly popular, and 'inventive, flexible and adaptable' Stewart lairds of Ballachulish.[78] They were succeeded by a variety of owners and lessees until the Ballachulish Slate Quarries Company Limited, an archetypal 'commercial conglomerate', took control in 1894. The signs were ominous. The new company was not interested in adopting a paternalistic or 'moral-economic' stance towards its workers and the expressed wishes of the wider community. The maximisation of the company's profits, prerogatives and control within the workplace was to be accompanied by the assertion of its full powers and control over many aspects of the life of the community beyond. Questions of fairness, reciprocity, negotiation and custom were deemed to be, at best, of minor importance in terms of both worker-employer and community-employer relations. Undercapitalised, the company was also determined to realise its goals by the conservative method of cost cutting, especially with regard to labour costs, rather than by the innovative means of new capital investment in machinery and in electricity to power the haulage and pumping operations. Characterised in the past by an absence of strikes and lock-outs, but not complete harmony, workplace relations in the quarries, and between the community and the company, were about to take a serious turn for the worse. Furthermore, the very settled and homogeneous nature of the community, as described above, made it highly likely that the company would meet determined and united resistance. This was the context in which 'The State of War in the Valley of Glencoe' [79], was about to break out. It is to a study of the two conflicts comprising this 'War' that I turn in Chapter Two.

Chapter Two
The Conflicts and Their Consequences, 1902-1907

As noted in the Introduction, the first conflict, from July 1902 to the end of December 1903, revolved, above all else, around the company's dismissal of Dr. Grant from his medical duties in the quarries and in the community. By way of contrast the second conflict, in the summer and autumn of 1905, was concerned mainly with issues of wages and working conditions, although the continuing unpopularity of the quarry manager was also a significant factor. Common to both conflicts, and indeed up to the liquidation of the company in 1907, were contested notions of power, control, authority, reciprocity and 'fairness' and 'right' between, on the one hand, the Ballachulish Quarries Company Limited and, on the other, both the employees of the quarries and the community. My purpose in this chapter is to reconstruct the chronology and nature of the conflicts and their consequences up to the demise of the company.

The First Dispute

In light of the fact that its dismissal of Grant triggered the first dispute, it is appropriate to begin this section with a brief profile of the company. In April 1894 the Ballachulish Slate Quarries Company Limited acquired a 27 year lease on the Ballachulish slate quarries in East and West Laroch. This included not only the works, but also the 'piers and quays, buildings, dwelling houses (including workmen's) and stables', plus stocks of slates, machinery and plant. Its headquarters located in Edinburgh, the company had received its Certificate of Incorporation late in the previous year. It was established with a capital sum of £30,000, broken down into 600 shares at £50 each.[1] Colonel Edward Donald Malcolm of Poltalloch, a Conservative and one of the foremost landowners in Argyllshire, was the company's first chair, while the directors and main shareholders were drawn from the professions and the world of business. They were predominantly males who resided in Edinburgh.[2] Thus, unlike the situation in north Wales, where the most prominent and wealthiest landowners and industrialists, including those in slate quarrying, were 'oppressive' English 'foreigners', the main industrial employer in Ballachulish and district was a compatriot of the locals. However, events would demonstrate that this was no guarantee against being similarly cast as a 'tyrannical outsider'.[3]

Of key importance for the future of workplace relations was the fact that the company contracted Archibald Maccoll, a native of Ballachulish, and Quarrymaster at Port Mary, Easedale, to be the manager of the Ballachulish quarries. Maccoll, the only local shareholder in the new company, was to be paid an annual salary of £300 per year, plus financial bonuses dependent upon the company's attainment of a 10 per cent profit level per annum over a period of three years. Maccoll was also afforded the 'free use and provision' of a place of residence, Laroch House, and allowed to continue to manage the Easedale operation provided that he devoted the vast majority of his working time to the services of the Ballachulish Quarries Company Limited. His appointment was to last indefinitely, 'so long as the Company continues to earn a dividend of five per centum per annum'. In the event of failure to meet this figure, Maccoll would resign his post within three months.[4] From the outset the company, therefore, was keen to highlight both its determination to achieve financial success and the crucial importance of Maccoll, as a local man and a manager with extensive local and regional experience of the slate industry, to the realisation of that success. Lacking any trace of paternalistic or social-welfarist intent, the company charged Maccoll with the responsibilities functionally to 'manage and superintend the operative department of said business (in the) most effective and economical way', and to 'convert into the most marketable and profitable form the materials produced'.[5]

Issues of power and control were also of the essence. While continuing to recognise the time-honoured right of crews to negotiate and receive contracts and to make complaints to the manager, largely through the personage of the Head of Crew, nevertheless, the company placed a high premium upon its 'rights to manage' and its exclusive contracts with *individual* workers. 'Outside' or 'third-party' (usually the code term for trade-union) 'interference' was not to be tolerated. Thus, Rule 3 of the 'Terms and Conditions of Employment', laid down by the company in January 1903, read:

> Any one interfering with the Company's Employees or any of their Officials in the discharge of their duties, or being insubordinate, will render himself liable to instant dismissal from the Works. (See Document One, p. 46)

Similarly, the directors insisted upon their right to punish, by means of suspension and dismissal, 'misconduct', 'incompetence' and 'irregularity' on the part of the workforce, while Maccoll was given full control over the day-to-day affairs of the quarries, including hiring, firing, the payment of wages, dealing with complaints and the continuation or termination of work on 'unproductive rocks' as 'he thinks best for the carrying on of the Works'.[6] In line with the Truck Acts, the workmen' were deemed to be 'free' to buy coal from the company 'or elsewhere', but 'no interference with any workman in the free exercise of this option will be allowed' (see Document Two, p 47).

However, in keeping with the custom dating back 'over forty years', the new company did recognise the right of the Medical Committee, comprising 'the master and seven workmen', to have control over 'all matters pertaining to the medical arrangements', including, crucially, the appointment of the medical officer for the quarries.[7] In accordance with the provisions of the Truck Acts, the medical officer's salary for work undertaken at the quarries had traditionally been met wholly by voluntary deductions from the quarrymen's wages. The new committee, including Maccoll as the company's representative, but with a guaranteed numerical advantage in favour of the men's representatives, agreed to continue this practice. Between 1894 and the end of the century relationships seemed to be relatively harmonious, although there were growing rumours that, as noted earlier, Dr. Farquharson, Grant's predecessor and a critic of the housing and sanitary provisions made by the company for its predominantly quarrying tenants, was forced to resign his post in June 1900 as a result of pressure from the company.[8]

Grant's appointment in August of the same year, nevertheless, met with the unanimous approval of the Medical Committee, including, of course, Maccoll. Although born in Johnstone, Renfrewshire, in 1871, Grant was widely recognised and welcomed as a 'local', a 'true Highlander', fully practised in the Gaelic language and Gaelic traditions, and an extremely able, popular and civic-minded man and medical practitioner. He had been brought up in the Ballachulish district and had worked at the quarries for a while as clerk to the previous lessee of sixteen years duration, Dr. Campbell, before studying medicine with distinction at the Universities of Glasgow and Edinburgh. Prior to his acceptance of the position at Ballachulish, Grant had successfully applied, from a field of approximately sixty applicants, to be medical officer at the Gesto hospital on the Isle of Skye. While there his knowledge and commitment to 'all things Gaelic' had been invaluable to his success in the post. However, Grant had been keen to return to Ballachulish to support his recently widowed mother.[9]

It was within this seemingly promising context – Grant assumed that he was working conscientiously and to good effect – that early in July, 1902, the company suddenly and unexpectedly dismissed Grant – with one month's notice and 'without any reason being alleged or any explanation given' – from his medical duties in *both* the quarries and in the local community.[10] Both Grant and the Medical Committee were incredulous. Grant expressed 'great shock and surprise' at the company's decision – 'no complaint' had been made against him – while the members of the Medical Committee had been neither alerted to, nor consulted about, the company's intentions.[11] Furthermore, according to the Committee, there existed no precedent either for the one month's notice clause in Grant's contract or for the company to have contractual control over his work as Medical Officer for Ballachulish. Acting in good faith, the Committee had left Maccoll to sort out the details of the contract with Grant upon the latter's successful application for the post.[12]

Detailed attention to the extant records, in which silences, ambiguities and self-interest are much in evidence,[13] leads me to offer two conclusions concerning the reasons for Grant's dismissal. First, the three 'reasons' provided by the company, in response to the doctor's persistent requests for a satisfactory explanation, carry little, if any, weight. The 'reasons' given were that some workers had written to the company demanding Grant's dismissal and threatening to strike to achieve that end; that Grant had taken on extra duties 'at a distant granite quarry' detrimental to the satisfactory performance of his work at the Ballachulish quarries, and that 'the directors do not like it'; and that Grant's brother had 'posted notices' in Ballachulish claiming that the company was infringing the Truck Acts. However, it soon transpired that there was little substance in the first two 'reasons'. In all likelihood Maccoll had 'persuaded' two of his relatives working at the quarries to write the letters in order to secure their future employment, while the 'distant' quarry was only four and a half miles from Grant's home and the work involved was minimal. The final 'reason' was entirely false. The posters, in fact, had been put up not by Grant's brother but by Angus Clark, the Secretary of the Medical Committee, and a future leader of the quarriers' trade union.[14] My second conclusion is that both personal and wider issues of rivalry, control and power underpinned the company's decision. Several contemporaries, including Keir Hardie, testified to Grant's 'likeable' and 'unpretentious' character and his great popularity in the community and the workplace. As such, Grant was envied and disliked by Maccoll who was competing for local power, position and influence.[15] Furthermore, as a bright, conscientious, articulate and active young radical doctor, fully in tune with the expressed norms, values, needs and interests of the quarrymen and their families, and not afraid to speak his mind about both workplace issues and matters of health and welfare affecting the community, Grant was a truly critical and independent spirit. He provided an alternative, and potentially competing, point of loyalty and authority to that of the company. As we will see in more detail below, he was regarded as a presence to be removed. 'Evidently what the management want', observed 'Gavroche', 'is some docile, spiritless practitioner who will come to heel at the crack of the management whip'.[16]

In support of this second conclusion, it is important to highlight the facts that the company, and especially its leading light, Colonel Malcolm – an unsentimental 'military man' and a 'master' – expected and demanded both that the quarrymen do their bidding and that the local community accept their dominance. The *Lancet* portrayed Malcolm as the 'head and front' of the company's 'pigheaded attitude', while the *Labour Leader* described Maccoll, a 'trained accountant', as 'virtually the despot of Ballachulish' who was 'universally detested by the people under his control'.[17] It was Malcolm who would keep an invited deputation of the quarrymen waiting for three hours to see him in Edinburgh – 'not even supplied with a seat' – and pass a disparaging comment about 'the men having chains to their watches'. To which, according to the Glasgow United Trades' Council, 'a sturdy Highlander replied – "That they were paid for, and that as long as they were not the chains of slavery they did not object to them"'.[18] The company, as the sole employer of any size, the main owner and lessee of the housing stock and with considerable direct and indirect power over health and welfare, already possessed a massive local presence, whether for good or ill.

Furthermore, and notwithstanding my earlier comments concerning the seeming stability and even harmony of workplace relations during the early years of the company's lease, there is sufficient evidence to suggest that all manner of grievances were beginning to accumulate, some more explicitly than others. According to 'Gavroche', at least, the company's attempt to deprive the quarrymen of their customary right 'to choose and appoint their own medical officer' was 'simply the culminating act in a long series of humiliations and tyrannies which threatened to rob them of every vestige of liberty'.[19] This was an exaggeration. After all, the company had been present in Ballachulish for only six years and, as noted above, Grant's dismissal came as a sudden and unexpected shock to both the doctor, the community and the quarrymen. However, as we will see in due course, the quarrymen and their supporters did express concern during the disputes about numerous 'humiliations and tyrannies' visited upon them mainly, if not exclusively, by the company. In addition to the key issues of the denial of their 'right' of appointment of the medical officer and the company's threatened deductions from the quarrymen's wages to support a medical officer not chosen by the Medical Committee, these embraced many and varied issues and aspects of life. Attention was drawn to the following grievances: the 'exceptional prices' charged by the company to their workers for 'coals, jumper steel, gunpowder, hammer shafts, and other material' and to their tenants and sub-tenants for parish and county assessments; poor housing and sanitary provision; tenants' and sub-tenants' lack of effective rights and defences against being 'turned out' of their homes by the company, 'on a fortnight's notice', and the threatened and actual eviction of labour activists from their homes; 'deprivations' of workers' 'civil and political rights' (including the

victimisation and sacking of dissidents in the workplace, involuntary unemployment, short-time working and, for some, lack of effective voting rights);
inadequate wages paid only on a six weekly basis; and the 'pier dues' imposed
by the 'omnipresent' company upon those wishing to take the boat to Oban
or Fort William.[20] In sum, it was increasingly not only the 'outside' company's intrusive omnipresence, but also its arrogant and unjustified claims to om-
nipotence, both in the workplace and the community, that brought forth loud
and widespread condemnation from the proud and independent-minded local
population. 'On one thing the quarrymen are all agreed', concluded the *Labour
Leader*, 'Their conditions have changed greatly for the worse under the rule of
the present company'.[21]

The immediate incredulity and shock following Grant's dismissal soon gave
way to widespread anger and outrage.[22] The doctor had received a letter from
the company notifying him of the termination of his contract on 3 July. Five
days later a mass meeting, 'representative of all the inhabitants of Ballachulish
and district', was held in the village. The meeting expressed its 'deepest regret'
at the doctor's dismissal, 'at a month's notice', from 'the duties which he has so
ably and faithfully discharged for the past two years', and drew up a petition,
signed by between four and five hundred people, 'respectfully' requesting the
leading members of the company to 'reconsider their decision'. For, although
those present at the protest meeting 'recognise the legality of the present system
of appointment of a medical officer', it was 'a matter of regret' that 'the employees of the quarries should not have some voice in his selection'.

A week later a further mass meeting was held. This was similarly attended by
'almost every man in Ballachulish' and 'several ladies'. Dr. W Dunlop Anderson, a retired medical man and landowner, once again chaired the meeting.
Both Anderson and the Reverend Duncan McMurchy, who declared himself to
have been 'thunderstruck' by Grant's dismissal, spoke very highly of the embat-
tled doctor's abilities and dedication, while Grant himself was pleased to feel
that he enjoyed 'the thorough confidence' of his 'patients and all of you'. Less
pleasing, however, was the news that the company had 'ignored' the petition
and earlier resolution in favour of Grant, and intended 'to put in another doctor under more strict terms'. Yet spirits were high. The meeting passed a vote
of 'entire confidence' in Grant, fully supported his reinstatement and, on the
advice of Anderson, elected nine men, with Donald McMillan as chair, onto
a reconstituted Medical Committee. Extreme concern was voiced, both at the
meetings and by the new committee, that the quarrymen members of the original committee which, of course, had appointed Grant, had not been consulted
about his proposed dismissal. Furthermore, in view of the fact that it was the
quarrymen who paid the doctor's salary at the works, the company, so it was

claimed, 'had no authority to make any agreement whatsoever'. And, in including in Grant's contract, albeit presumably with the consent of the latter but without the knowledge of the quarrymen members who formed an overwhelming majority on the committee, the conditions concerning the company's control over the doctor's appointment in the community and the period of one month's notice of termination, Maccoll 'went beyond the instructions' given by the committee. For 'the manager had no instructions to impose them on Dr. Grant', and 'no such conditions 'were imposed on any of the former doctors appointed by the men'.[23] Thus the essence of the quarrymen's case was that a gross betrayal of confidence and an outrageous and unacceptable attack upon their customary rights had taken place.

It was in this context that the reconstituted Medical Committee resolved to 'assume to ourselves the right of appointing our own medical officer', and that 'we will allow no deductions to be made from our wages on behalf of any doctor not appointed by us'. In August the committee accordingly reappointed Dr. Grant, and collected his salary on the basis of overwhelming support for this course of action among the quarrymen.[24]

They were further strengthened in their resolve by a growing chorus of support. The *Glasgow Herald* accurately observed on 18 July that, 'Dr. Grant has the entire confidence and support of the whole district and that the action of the directors in dismissing him without assigning any reason has aroused feelings of the deepest resentment'.[25] As the cuttings in Grant's volumes from the Glasgow United Trades' Council, the *Oban Times*, *Highland News*, *Glasgow Herald*, *Labour Leader*, the *Lancet* and many other newspapers and periodicals clearly show, this support at district level was not only sustained throughout the dispute, but spread to many other parts of Scotland and, to a much lesser extent, Britain as a whole. Furthermore, it included, but was by no means confined to, organisations of the labour movement. For example, 'clergymen of every denomination' and 'people of all classes' for miles around', and representatives of the 'medical fraternity' nationally, provided strong backing.[26] McMurchy, trustee to the Medical Committee, chair of the local school board, 'one of the ablest classical scholars to be found anywhere' (he had taught Latin and Greek to Grant when the future doctor was a pupil at the Ballachulish Public School), and a very close friend and ally of the doctor, counselled the quarrymen to 'uphold the right and resist the wrong'. For,

> He would tell them who were the real agitators. They were the company, who had so wantonly and shamefully abused their powers in dismissing Dr. Grant, in victimising their men, and in bringing distress and ruin upon a whole community.[27]

Whatever the legal merits of the company's case, the medical press, ranging from the *Lancet* to the *Edinburgh Medical Journal*, also condemned the 'immoral', 'unreasonable' and 'highhanded' nature of its actions. In addition to the considerable merits of the quarrymen's case for proper consultation and due respect for the established authority of the medical committee, it was considered wrong to deprive Grant of the opportunity to continue to gain his livelihood in the community and to fulfil his 'obligations to the poor of the parish'.[28]

These early forms of protest and opposition to the company brought precious few successes. Although the company's two attempt to bring in a doctor to replace Grant were unsuccessful – both the imported doctors leaving Ballachulish within a matter of days after assessing the 'true situation'[29] – it remained undaunted and flatly refused to change its course of action. Moreover, in August, on the day immediately preceding the Medical Committee's reappointment of Grant, the company applied to the Court of Session to 'have Dr. Grant interdicted from practising in the district, or from attending on the men and their families'.[30] During the autumn months it stepped up the pressure on the quarrymen by announcing sackings and evictions, the latter directed particularly against members of the Medical Committee. The men responded by marching, in 'restrained' and 'respectable' fashion, to register their protests at the manager's office.[31]

During autumn and early winter labour issues assumed growing importance. Most dramatically, in September Keir Hardie, taking time off from his holiday in the West Highlands, addressed a large meeting in Ballachulish and advocated the formation of a trade union to 'embrace all the quarriers on the West Coast'. The men responded positively, with the *Labour Leader* reporting in October that a public meeting called by the Ballachulish quarrymen – 'perhaps the most remarkable gathering that has ever been held in the Highlands' – had followed Hardie's advice, at least in terms of the locality.[32] The newly created union was of the 'new', 'catch-all' type: it aimed to include all the workers in the Ballachulish quarries while protecting pay and 'skill' differentials. In addition, the men, with the leaders of the Medical Committee now to the fore in the union, demanded an end to overcharging for the materials supplied by the company and the replacement of six-weekly by four-weekly payments and contracts. The company responded in October by promising to make some concessions on these matters and to reinstate some of the men made redundant.[33]

This first manifestation of a more conciliatory attitude, however, was to prove very deceptive and temporary. There was to be no compromise concerning the position of Dr. Grant. Furthermore, and probably as a result of the hard-line influence of Colonel Malcolm, the company resorted to type in late December when it announced that the men would resume work in the New Year by signing a document concerning 'terms and conditions of employment … generally the same as existed in the Works … after the New Year Holidays, January 1902' . As clearly shown in Document One, 'Terms and Conditions of Employment, 19th January 1903', what this meant was that *no* concessions were to be made by the company, whether in relation to worker grievances concerning over-charging, wages and working conditions and matters relating to housing and sanitation or to their demand to have Grant reinstated. However, this did not mean that the company would simply be satisfied with a return to the *status quo ante* Grant's dismissal. Rather it had a far more radical agenda: to destroy both the time-honoured rights and responsibilities of the men and the Medical Committee and their growing assertiveness and independence – as part of a general strategy to assert full managerial control and power. For example, the company decreed that the traditional voluntary system of funding the salary of the medical officer would be replaced by compulsion. Thus Rule 8 of the 'Terms and Conditions of Employment' bluntly stated that, 'Every Employee will con-tribute to the Salary of the Quarry Medical Officer. The necessary deductions will be made at Pay'. Notwithstanding the qualification that, 'It is not intended to enforce Rule no. 8 until the litigation now in progress between the Company and Dr Grant has been disposed of', there was no reference to the customary rights and responsibilities of the men and the Medical Committee in relation to this matter (see Document One). The decision of the workers and their rep-resentatives to continue to support Grant was simply ignored. Moreover, the question of union recognition was not to be countenanced, while the manager was invested with unambiguous control and decision-making powers over hir-ing and firing, complaints from the men and the effects of rock conditions on prospects of work (see Document One, Rules 1,2,4). The stipulation that con-tracts were to be 'given to Heads of Crews as formerly' (see Document One, Rule 6) carried the implication that negotiation and bargaining were to play second fiddle to increased management 'influence' in this important area.

It is true that the company stated its intention to comply with the law, and especially the Truck Acts, with respect to voluntary 'Deductions from Wages' of 'house rent … the price of any smith work, sharpening and repairing of tools, powder, quarry materials … new tools, or implements supplied to us … the price of coals supplied to us'. Furthermore, the workers' written authorisation of these deductions 'does not form part of the condition of hiring, nor is it a stipulation in our contract of service' (see Document One, Rule 7, Document Two, 'Ballachulish Slate Quarries Company Limited'). However, the very fact that the workers were required to sign the document, 'Terms and Conditions of Employment', in order to be (re-) employed by the company, the widespread suspicion that written agreement to the deductions *was* an essential 'condition

Ballachulish Slate Quarries Company, Limited.

Terms and Conditions of Employment.
19th JANUARY 1903.

1. The terms and conditions of employment will be generally the same as existed in the Works on the resumption of work after the New Year Holidays, January 1902. The rule then existing as to men continuing to work in the Bank Sheds on wet days although the men at work in the Quarries may have to stop work on account of the inclemency of the weather is particularly agreed to. Vacancies in Crews, or Crews vacating rocks, will be filled by the Manager, as was the rule in January 1902.

2. Any individual Workman having a complaint to make will do so to the Manager personally, and any Crew having a complaint to make will make it to the Manager through the Head of the Crew.

3. Any one interfering with the Company's Employees or any of their Officials in the discharge of their duties, or being insubordinate, will render himself liable to instant dismissal from the Works.

4. The Manager will take on and pay off Men as he finds necessary, and will carry on or stop working unproductive rocks as he thinks best for the carrying on of the Works.

5. The regulations affecting such of the Company's Workmen as are in the occupation of dwelling-houses held by the Company, and for payment of Rent and Rates, shall continue as they existed on 1st January 1902.

6. Contracts will be given to Heads of Crews as formerly—one other Member of Crew may be present.

7. Deductions from Wages, as authorised by law, and particularly by the Truck Acts, will be made as in January 1902, but they will be altered from time to time as the law or circumstances may require.

8. Every Employee will contribute to the Salary of the Quarry Medical Officer. The necessary deductions will be made at the Pay.

Note.—It is not intended to enforce Rule No. 8 until the litigation now in progress between the Company and Dr Grant has been disposed of.

Document One
Source: Grant Papers, National Library of Scotland

𝔅𝔞𝔩𝔩𝔞𝔠𝔥𝔲𝔩𝔦𝔰𝔥 𝔖𝔩𝔞𝔱𝔢 𝔔𝔲𝔞𝔯𝔯𝔦𝔢𝔰 ℭ𝔬𝔪𝔭𝔞𝔫𝔶, 𝔏𝔦𝔪𝔦𝔱𝔢𝔡.

AGREEMENT between the Workmen of the BAL-
LACHULISH SLATE QUARRIES COMPANY, LIMITED,
and the said Company as to certain deductions
which it is convenient both for the Workmen
and the Management to have made at the time of
payment of wages.

19th JANUARY 1903.

In terms of the Truck Acts, we, the undersigned, hereby authorise you to deduct from the wages to be earned by us while in your employment, the amount of our house rent (should we occupy any house of which you are the Owner or Lessee), the price of any smith work, sharpening and repairing of tools, powder, quarry materials (including joiner work), new tools, or implements supplied to us; a detailed statement of all deductions to be rendered at each pay. We further authorise you to deduct the price of coals supplied to us. We acknowledge that the above does not form part of the condition of hiring, nor is it a stipulation in our contract of service.

> *Note* —It is to be understood that the Company are prepared to supply coal to work-
> men and others, and that the workmen are free to buy from the Company or
> elsewhere, but no interference with any workman in the free exercise of this
> option will be allowed.

Document Two
Source: Grant Papers, National Library of Scotland

APPEAL to TRADES UNIONISTS.
Ballachulish Slate Quarries' Lock-Out.
A SCOTTISH "PENRHYN" CASE.

FELLOW-UNIONISTS,—We appeal to you on behalf of the Slate Quarry Workers of Ballachulish, who have been Locked-out by their Employers, the Ballachulish Slate Quarry Coy., Ltd., because they made an honest attempt to have what they considered an unjust state of things in relation to their employment remedied.

Payment of Wages.

1st. The Men only received their Wages once every Six Weeks. This they requested to be changed to Payment each 4 Weeks; yet, incredible as it may seem, they were refused.

Charges for Goods Supplied.

2nd. For a number of years exceptional prices have been charged for coals, jumper steel, gunpowder, hammer shafts, and other material—all of which were supplied by the Company to their workmen. For example, hammer shafts were charged at 1/ each, which they are now getting at 3d. Coals were charged 24/ to 26/ per ton, and after much trouble were reduced to 23/. The men, knowing as they did that undue advantage was being taken of their position, took the supply of coals into their own hands, and can get a better quality at 20/ per ton. The Company are now threatening to charge tonnage for beaching the coal steamers on the shore while being unloaded at ebb-tide.

Medical Attendance.

3rd. For this purpose a Committee of Six Men, and the Manager, are appointed to control all matters relating to the Medical Club. The men contribute every penny of the Doctor's salary. In June, 1900, on the then medical man resigning, the Committee appointed Dr. Grant as his successor. He, however, seems to have given offence by reporting on the insanitary conditions of the workmen's houses, which *are owned by the Company*; and for thus daring to speak of their property the Company, who neither paid his salary nor appointed him, dismissed him in July, 1902, without the knowledge or consent of the Medical Committee. The Committee re-appointed Dr. Grant, and declined to permit any interference on the part of the Company in the affairs of the Medical Club. The Company then applied to the Court of Session to have Dr. Grant interdicted from practising in the district, or from attending on the men and their families, even in a private capacity, and have got an interdict granted.

The Men, at the Company's request, sent a deputation to Edinburgh to discuss matters with the Directors. This the men had to do at their own expense. After going to Edinburgh they were kept waiting in one of the rooms for three hours, and not even supplied with a seat. The Malcolm of Poltalloch, who is chairman of the Company, entered and passed some remarks on the men having chains to their watches, to which a sturdy Highlander replied—"That they were paid for, and that as long as they were not the chains of slavery they did not object to them." Malcolm of Poltalloch then informed them that "the Directors could not entertain their complaints."

The Company now refuse to allow the men to work unless they sign an agreement authorising deductions to be made from their wages, the same as when they entered as Lessees of the Quarries. This paper the men refuse to sign, and they believe all fair-minded men will approve of their stand against such tyrannical conditions.

They have appealed against the interdict, and, to raise funds for the legal action and to carry on the struggle which has been forced upon them, we appeal to you, their fellow Trades Unionists throughout the country, who are ever ready to resist oppression and wish to see truth and right prevail, knowing that you will give to this Appeal a hearty response.

We are, Yours in Unity,

COMMITTEE—DANIEL BAIRD.   JAMES MACLAGAN.
GEORGE CARSON.   B. H. SHAW.
CHARLES JACKSON.   WILLIAM GREER, *Convener*.

N.B.—We enclose 6 Gummed Leaflets for you to Paste in Small Pass-Books, if you wish to take that method of Collecting Subscriptions. If more are required, the TREASURER will Supply same on Application.

All Remittances to be sent to Mr. CHAS. JACKSON, Secretary, 137 Caledonia Road.

Document Three
Source: Grant Papers, National Library of Scotland

of hiring' and that, contrary to stated policy, the company itself, rather than an 'outsider', would be the force seeking to prevent the men from using 'free exercise' in their purchase of coal (see Document Two, *Note*), aroused widespread suspicion and anger.

Matters came to a head with the announcement, early in January 2003, that the company's resort to legal action to interdict Grant from practising his profession in Ballachulish, had been successful. In the Court of Session Lord Kyllachy ruled that the doctor was 'bound by the agreement which he had made' with the Ballachulish Quarries Company Limited. Grant was to cease giving 'professional attendance as a doctor of medicine in the village or district of Ballachulish' one month after notice of the ruling.[34] The doctor had thus been deprived of his paid livelihood not only in the quarries, but also as Medical Officer for the Parish Council District of Ballachulish. In terms of the latter, the effect of Kyllachy's order was that Grant's contractual obligations, towards his other employer, the Parish Council of Lismore and Appin, were deemed to be of secondary importance to his contract with the company.[35] As we will see later, this led to widespread charges of wholly unjustified control and 'outside' interference, on the part of the company, in affairs that should, first and foremost, be the responsibility of the Parish Council, its employee, the Medical Officer, and those placed under the latter's charge in the district of Ballachulish. However, this belonged to the future. In the immediate term the company had been greatly strengthened in its determination to 'regain … power over the men, to destroy the newly-formed trade union, and to defeat Dr. Grant'.[36]

Grant and his supporters reacted with outrage and equal determination. Grant decided to appeal against the interdict, while mass meetings resolved to continue their support for the doctor and not to sign 'the document' as a condition of resuming work.[37] This was the context in which the Ballachulish lock-out of January 1903 began. The quarries were brought to a standstill. They were to remain so for the whole year. The *Oban Telegraph and Express* bleakly predicted 'a fight to the death as between masters and men',[38] while the *Labour Leader* concluded that, 'The Christian directors of the Ballachulish company have been driven back to the methods of barabarism', that 'a state of war in the valley of Glencoe' was, indeed, imminent and that 'the Ballachulish question has become a Celtic question'.[39]

The first six months of the lock-out saw little movement on either side and precious few signs that the dispute would be resolved. Impressive solidarity meetings on the part of the quarrymen were accompanied by continuing and widespread support from across the social structure and strong determination on the part of the company to hold out until the men signed 'the document'. In terms of the latter, Colonel Malcolm was to be found unhelpfully 'lecturing' the men's representatives on the wrongheaded and futile nature of their actions at what was supposed to be an informal and conciliatory meeting at Laroch House: a meeting between four of the men's representatives and some of the directors proved to be equally fruitless.[40] Talk of an impending resort to arbitration, under the auspices of the Board of Trade, brought little tangible reward. While a representative from the Board of Trade did confer with the quarrymen's representatives and 'a number of the leading residents' of the district, nothing of consequence, in terms of state intervention, ensued.[41] And the notices of eviction from their homes of 'several members' of the Medical Committee in March further stirred 'great bitterness' against the company.[42]

For their part the quarrymen, Grant and their supporters experienced very mixed fortunes. On the positive side the men remained steadfast in their resolve both to continue to support Grant and in pursuit of improved working conditions. Several large and enthusiastic meetings were held further to endorse these aims.[43] And in March the Medical Committee, having received legal advice, decided to appeal to the law courts to have the original contractual agreement with Grant 'reduced and declared void'. The basis of the appeal was that the doctor had been appointed by the Medical Committee, acting mainly 'on behalf of the quarrymen', and not primarily by the company (although, of course, the company was represented on the committee by its manager). Furthermore, Grant's paymasters were the quarrymen and the Parish Council of Lismore and Appin rather than the company. Yet the committee had been afforded no knowledge of the unprecedented conditions inserted into Grant's contract by the manager, had not been consulted about his dismissal, and its views and rights had effectively been ignored by the manager and the company. The Medical Committee concluded, therefore, that Maccoll had gone 'beyond his instructions' from them in 'imposing the conditions referred to' upon Grant, while the company 'had no authority to make any agreement whatever'.[44]

During the same month the quarrymen put out an 'Appeal for Funds' to 'fellow-highlanders in the north and south who are ever ready to resist oppression, and to all honest, fair-minded people, who wish to see truth and right prevail'.[45] This met with a generous response from workers and sections of the middle class in Scotland and beyond, reaching a total of approximately £900. In addition, there was important labour movement support. As seen in Document Three on page 48, the Glasgow Trades Council sent out a specific 'Appeal to Trades Unionists'. The latter were asked to give 'a hearty response' to the 'Slate Quarry Workers of Ballachulish' who were involved in 'A Scottish "Penrhyn" Case'. Moral and financial support would fortify the quarrymen in their fight against 'oppression' and the 'tyrannical conditions' imposed by the company. In the following month Keir Hardie offered more support by raising the Ballachulish case in parliament and writing to the Secretary of State for the Home Department to suggest that the company's 'Terms and Conditions of Employment' document violated the Truck Acts in its *compulsory*, as opposed to the stipulated *voluntary*, deductions from the quarrymen's wages to pay the salary of the quarries' medical officer.[46]

The men's cause was also helped by three other factors. First, virtually all those employed in the Ballachulish quarries soon found suitable work elsewhere. For example, in mid-February, 1903, the *Oban Times* estimated that out of a total quarry workforce of approximately 400, 180 were already employed in the construction of the new railway line from Oban to Ballachulish, while a further 140 had found work at quarries in the Slate Islands, Aberfoyle and elsewhere in Scotland. Approximately 50 'women and children', previously employed in the quarries, were 'with no regular means of livelihood'. A similar fate had befallen some of the 'older men', while a few among the latter group were employed in 'jobs about the place'. Only a 'few enginemen' remained in the quarries. Six weeks into the lock-out the 'deserted' village of Ballachulish was dominated by its womenfolk, their children and old men. On the occasions when they were able to return home from their new workplaces, the quarrymen continued to form the core of large and impressive meetings of protest and solidarity. In these ways, observed the *Oban Times*, the Ballachulish Slate Quarries Company Limited was deprived of its labour force.[47] Moreover, many of the latter maintained that their newfound jobs were more regular and better paid than had formerly been the case in Ballachulish.[48] In such ways did the forces of supply and demand work strongly in favour of the men, at least for the time being.

Second, while the Ballachulish Slate Quarries Company Limited increasingly conformed to the stereotype of the autocratic and anti-union Scottish employer, many other local and regional employers, with respect to both their behaviour and stated attitudes, did not. For example, several employers in and around Ballachulish and the much wider geographical area of the Highlands and Islands expressed their disapproval of the manner 'in which the Quarries Company have treated Dr. Grant, and then victimised their men', by means of enforced unemployment and eviction from their homes, 'for daring to stand up for truth and right'.[49] Notwithstanding this resort to the language of principle and morality, some of this disapproval may well have been motivated more by self-interest than altruism and beneficence. This was, in all probability, the case on the part of many of those slate quarrying employers in Easedale and elsewhere who were able to employ the Ballachulish men, to both the latter's and their own advantage, at the direct expense of one of their main competitors, the Ballachulish Slate Quarries Company Limited. Yet even among some of these employers, concerns with 'fairness', 'morality' and the mutual rights and responsibilities of employers and workers were by no means either absent or mere smokescreens for baser concerns. This, at least, was the reported perception of the migrant quarrymen. For example, John Macinnes and Alexander McTaggart, both Ballachulish quarrymen employed in quarries on the west coast – with the latter being secretary of the Ballachulish trade union – 'spoke in the highest terms' of the very good wages, working conditions and 'kindness' experienced at the hands of Messers Maclean and Macintyre, their new employers.[50]

Closer to home, examples of employer kindness, sympathy and support for the locked-out men were much in evidence in the press. These ranged, for example, from the local landowner, Mr. Bullough, who paid the unemployed men to build a loch and dam named after himself, to Mr.Best, the railway contractor, who in January 1903 'offered work to older men in the neighbourhood of the village'. The *Highland News* declared of Best:

> Though he is a capitalist himself, he has expressed the strongest disapproval of the manner in which the Quarries' Company have treated Dr. Grant, and then victimised their men for daring to stand up for truth and right.[51]

Best's views were shared by many other members of the local middle class, both employers and professional men, such as Dr. Anderson and McMurchy. Above all perhaps, they detested the 'highhandedness' of the company, its trampling over of customary rights, its usurpation of powers traditionally enjoyed by the quarrymen, their doctor and their community. In so expressing this disapproval, they were confirming their adherence to the notion that the welfare, stability and harmony of the community took precedence over a particular interest's selfish and unqualified pursuit of power and profit. They provided powerful and influential support for the quarrymen's cause.

Third, there was growing evidence of differences and divisions among leading figures in the Ballachulish Slate Quarries Company Limited. Some directors, adopting a more conciliatory approach than Malcolm and Maccoll, expressed a wish to make concessions in order to settle the dispute.[52] Similarly, a leading shareholder, Thomas Shaw, KC, MP, 'expressed considerable sympathy' with the quarrymen's cause, and wrote to the directors in March 1903 urging 'peace and reconciliation'.[53] Even Malcolm at times sought to convince the quarrymen that he had their 'good at heart'. For example, at a meeting with the men in the Public Hall, Ballachulish, in May, Malcolm, while denying that the directors of the company were divided and expressing confidence in Maccoll, nevertheless declared that the company had 'no objection' to a resort to arbitration, involving Board of Trade Representation, in order to resolve the dispute and that, contrary to Keir Hardie's charge, the company had no intention of contravening the terms of the Truck Acts. Moreover, he reminded those present that the company had both made 'liberal subscriptions to get the hospital at Oban started' and insured the lives of 'those who volunteered to fight in South Africa'. Malcolm invited the men to 'come back to our old friendly terms', and indicated that if so persuaded 'you will find the gates open to-morrow, and no papers to sign'.[54]

However, these positive indications brought few, if any, gains to the quarry-men and Grant. *In practice*, and notwithstanding the men's willingness to drop their demand for monthly payments, Malcolm was not prepared to make any substantial and lasting concessions. Managerial prerogatives, control and due worker obedience were of paramount importance to the chair. Malcolm was 'furious' when the men, 'knowing as they did that undue advantage was being taken of their position' by the company (as monopolistic provider), 'took the supply of coals into their own hands' and obtained 'a better quality' at lower cost. In retaliation, 'The Company are now threatening to charge tonnage for beaching the coal steamers on the shore while being unloaded at ebb-tide' (see *Document Three*). Similarly, plans for arbitration came to nought, threats and evictions against union members continued and Malcolm flatly refused to com-promise on the issue of Grant. He was also probably responsible for nullifying the apparent agreement reached by three directors and the men's representa-tives in November 1903 to end the lock-out by means of increasing wages, set-ting up a Conciliation board and not deducting medical charges from wages.[55] Furthermore, the 'people's' cause was badly affected by two major legal de-feats. In June 1903 Lord Kyllachy's earlier judgement was upheld in the face of Grant's appeal, with the latter subsequently considering an appeal to the House of Lords. Two months later the Medical committee's legal action – 'to have it so declared that the company and the manager had no power to enter into the agreement with the medical officer' – was likewise unsuccessful.[56] Grant was compelled to give up his practice in Ballachulish. In September the Medi-cal Committee, while 'still standing by him', 'provisionally' approved the ap-pointment of a temporary replacement for Grant, Dr. Kennedy, another Gaelic speaker and 'located for the time at Ballachulish'. Grant expressed his intention to continue to practice outside Ballachulish until reinstated to his former post, a position with which Dr. Kennedy and his employer, the Parish Council of Lismore and Appin, were in full agreement.[57] But for the quarrymen and Grant losses greatly outweighed gains.

However, in a dramatic turn of events, the losers suddenly became the victors . By December 1903 the works had been closed for almost one year. Trade and the company's business had duly suffered, attempts to bring in 'scab' labour had failed and Kennedy's appointment offered only temporary relief from 'the medical problem'. The company's mounting losses, combined with the continuing resolve shown by the quarrymen, persuaded some of the company's directors to meet with the men's representatives in November in order to end the protracted, bitter and increasingly futile conflict. However, as noted above, this attempt at reconciliation and settlement was probably blocked by Malcolm. In any event, the offer to the men was suddenly withdrawn by the company. Nevertheless, the men and their families continued to weather the storm and even prosper. Some threatened to leave Ballachulish in order to pursue their temporary means of employment on a permanent basis. Moreover, public opinion remained firmly arrayed against the 'autocratic' and 'high handed' actions of the company.[58] Matters could not continue indefinitely in the same way.

The combination of factors outlined above underpinned the sudden and complete capitulation of the Ballachulish Slate Quarries Company Limited in mid-December and the re-instatement of Grant to his posts in the quarries and the community. The interdict against Grant was withdrawn and the men afforded an 'unrestricted choice of doctor'.[59] 'In consideration of Dr. Grant's re-appointment to this district', Dr. Kennedy, tendered his resignation as Medical Officer for the Ballachulish Parish Council from 31 December, whereupon Grant resumed his 'former duties' at 'the former rate of salary and fees'.[60] On the condition of the withdrawal of all legal action against the company, work was scheduled to resume in the New Year, after the Christmas holidays. Furthermore wages were to be increased by between two and three shillings per week for all workers at the quarries, their union recognised, workers' cottages to be built by the company, and a Conciliation Board – designed 'to prevent strikes' and comprising three quarrymen representatives, two directors of the company, the Chair of the Board, and the Sheriff of Perthshire as arbitrator – to be established.[61]

Totally victorious, the men, the community and Dr. Grant were understandably jubilant. The *Labour Leader* claimed that the workers of Ballachulish had 'gained more in eighteen months than in some other parts of the country have been won in as many years'. For they had entered the fray as 'traditional', non-unionised workers, working and living in conditions which, according to the *Labour Leader*, were often far more conducive to deference and fatalism rather than independence and 'agitation'. Yet they had emerged with a greatly enhanced sense of their own capacities and agency, of 'the knowledge of their own strength and the power of union'. The *Labour Leader* concluded that, 'Under a baptism of fire the men of the North have come into the Labour movement'.[62]

However, the resolution of the first conflict in favour of the quarrymen did not mark the end of the 'War'. By the winter of 1904, after months of apparent peace and harmony, conflict resurfaced and formed the prelude to the second dispute of 1905. This time, however, material factors, and especially the worsening economic prospects of the company, would be very much to the fore.

The Second Dispute

Faced with depressed market conditions, the company introduced a five-day working week in December 1904. In February 1905 this became four days. In addition, 150 quarrymen were to be paid off. Mass protests ensued. The quarrymen maintained that, in contrast to Ballachulish, slate quarries and quarriers elsewhere in Scotland were in a prosperous condition, and that, in implementing lay-offs, the Ballachulish Quarries Company Limited would, in keeping with its 'consistent policy' in the past, supply experienced local quarriers to its rivals in Easedale and elsewhere.[63] As a result of these protests, the dismissal notices were withdrawn in March but the four day week remained in place.[64] By this time wages were considerably lower than usual and the company had accumulated a large stock of unsold slates. The *Oban Times* anticipated a 'coming storm'.[65] It was not long in 'coming'.

By the late spring and early summer months the economic situation had deteriorated, not only in Ballachulish, but also in most slate quarries elsewhere in Scotland.[66] Faced with declining demand and sharply increased competition – the Scottish market being 'glutted with slates from the Welsh quarries' – many slate-quarrying employers sought to reduce labour costs. There ensued lockouts at Luing and Balvicar. In both these instances the mainly unionised quarrymen eventually returned to work on reduced wages and a shortened working week.[67]

In Ballachulish itself, the company went so far as to announce the closure of the quarries 'for a time' in mid-June in a desperate attempt to cut its losses.[68] According to the announcement, made through the officials of the trade union and management, it was 'not proposed to lockout the men': the directors would visit the quarries during the following week in order to make a further decision. A week later the directors offered the men's union representatives an agreement involving a resumption of work at four days per week, low wages (with the maximum rate 'not to exceed 25/-'), retained employment for all boys and all those householders who were tenants of the company and a ballot for an additional seventy workers. These employment proposals were both selective and potentially divisive because they amounted to enforced unemployment for many of those who were not tenants of the company, but 'all of whom always had constant employment at the slate quarries'. In an impressive show of unity around the defence of customary employment practices, a mass meeting of the quarrymen 'resolved unanimously' to reject management's proposals.

As in the first dispute, Maccoll was a special target of the men's anger. The manager was seen as the vindictive enforcer, and at times initiator, of discriminatory employment policies and chronic favouritism among the quarrying workforce. Indeed, the mass meeting passed a resolution 'to the effect that work should not be accepted from the present manager', and called, somewhat ominously, upon the company's directors to effect 'a change in the management'.[69] The men were also critical of the company's claims that market conditions fully justified the proposed agreement. The company was said to be underestimating the price of its reserve stock of slates and setting the selling price too high.[70]

The closure of the quarries 'for a time' became, as in the first dispute, for 'an indefinite time'. The *Oban Times* reported a month later, on 15 July, that everything was 'at a standstill' and that, as in early 1903, the men were 'dispersing gradually'. Some were finding employment at Kinlochleven and others further away.[71] However, the peace and quiet attendant upon the 'standstill' were shattered on the very same day when an incident took place that would create 'considerable excitement in the district'.[72] This was the attack on Maccoll's house.

By this time the manager had become the most hated figure in the Ballachulish district. The *Highland News* and the *Oban Weekly News* expressed the common view that the quarrymen had never forgiven the manager for his role in the first dispute. According to the latter newspaper, they blamed Maccoll 'for all their troubles, past and present'.[73] The company's actions in June 1905, and especially an employment policy that gave preferential treatment to its own tenants, as against those from the neighbouring Brecklet estate and that of Lord Strathcona in Glencoe, brought matters to a head. And, as noted above, much of the responsibility for this policy was attached to the 'tyrannical' manager. The *Highland News* observed,

> The men are, rightly or wrongly, convinced that these proceedings are unnecessary and vexatious, and are designed to punish them for their successful strike (sic), and an extremely bitter feeling has arisen against the management, on whom they lay the blame.[74]

On 15 July, several of 'the men', accompanied by 'a number of women', set out to exact revenge by 'visiting' Laroch House, Maccoll's place of residence. In what he described as 'a serious case of mobbing and rioting', the Chief Constable of Argyllshire provided the following report:

> On the afternoon of the date referred to a crowd numbering between two and three hundred persons proceeded in a procession to Laroch House, broke into said house {and} threatened violence towards Mr. Archibald McColl, Quarry-manager residing there, and compelled him by threats to write out a resignation of his position as Quarry manager, and also an undertaking to leave Ballachulish

on the following Monday morning. Mr. McColl, having regards to the serious nature of the threats used towards him by the mob, and the alarms himself and his friends were put to ... left his house by a private road ... on Monday.[75]

What the report did not indicate was the calming influence upon the crowd of 'three influential members of the Union Committee', Angus Clark, Archibald Livingston and John McTaggart. 'Quite ignorant' of the intentions of the crowd, with 'the younger quarrymen' at its core, and the 'extraordinary demonstration' taking place at Laroch House, these three union leaders were alerted just in time for them to arrive, 'pacify' the crowd and induce its members 'to leave the grounds'. The crowd had already broken open the door to Maccoll's house, but Clark and his colleagues managed to converse with the manager through an open window. Maccoll gave them a verbal assurance that he would resign, but this was not acceptable to the crowd. The manager then provided a written resignation. This was accepted and, in the presence of two police constables, the crowd dispersed.[76] However, acting upon a rumour that Maccoll had arranged for 'blackegs' to be brought in by train, members of the crowd proceeded to the station where they 'examined' every arriving passenger. No 'scabs' were found. On their arrival at the railway station, later that night, six police constables, brought in as reinforcements from Oban were, according to the *Oban Times*, 'greeted with hissing and booing'. The Chief Constable, however, pitched his claim much higher, the police being met by 'a howling crowd numbering between four and five hundred persons, who assaulted them by throwing gravel'.[77] Fortunately, Maccoll's departure from Ballachulish saw a return to peace and quiet.

As a result of the crowd's action, twelve local men, all quarrymen and including the three union committee members, appeared in August before Sheriff McClure in Oban. They answered the charge of 'mobbing and rioting'. Of the twelve, eight were convicted and fined sums ranging from £3 to £5, three were found not guilty and the charge against the other was withdrawn. Significantly, 'in restricting these penalties', McClure recognised both the moderate and restraining influence of the union committee members upon the crowd, and 'the good sense that had been shown by the men in front of him and others in Ballachulish since this matter had become public'.[78] Notwithstanding the view expressed by the *Scotsman* newspaper that Maccoll had been 'terrorised' and 'in fear of his life', the local and regional press overwhelmingly continued to portray the quarrymen and the union in a highly favourable light. Usually 'industrious', 'respectable' and 'law abiding', the 'regrettable' behaviour of those involved in the attack on Maccoll's house was seen to have been severely provoked by the 'unfair' and 'despotic' actions of the company and its manager.[79]

Throughout the 'sensational' and 'extraordinary' events of July and August, the quarrymen continued to demonstrate 'a somewhat independent attitude', according to the *Oban Times*. This was largely explained by the plentiful work available at the various 'water works' schemes being developed at Fasnacloich, Glencreran and in other places in the region.[80] However, there were increasing signs that both the men and the company were keen to reach a settlement. In late July a mass meeting of the quarrymen both accepted the fact that the quarries could not be reopened until a considerable number of the massive backlog of slates had been cleared, and requested the company to allocate the reduced amount of work available to one person from each house. In this way the company would be seen to have made a principled decision to abandon its earlier policy and to treat all tenants, and not solely its own, on an equal employment basis.[81]

In addition three very significant changes in personnel took place. First, the resignation and flight of Maccoll signalled to many that 'the only obstacle to a settlement had been removed'. Second, Colonel Malcolm resigned and was succeeded as chair of the company by the far more conciliatory Major Black of Greenock. The latter had 'long connected' with the Ballachulish Volunteers – a local contingent had 'served with distinction' under him in the South African War – and was 'very popular in this district'. Third, 'the respected senior foreman' at the quarries, Hugh Maccoll, was put in charge of the company's affairs locally.[82]

In mid August an agreement was reached between Major Black, representing the company, and Donald McMillan and Angus Clark, representing the men. The agreement stated that immediate arrangements would be made to begin despatching the stock of slates, that pumping would be resumed, that the quarries would reopen once two thirds of the slates had been cleared and that the Conciliation Board would 'adjust the conditions of work'. The agreement was ratified by the quarrymen and the company. Having been closed for ten weeks, it now appeared likely that the quarries would reopen in the foreseeable future.[83]

However, there was no improvement in the short term. Indeed, the continuing backlog of unsold slates, combined with the continuing depression in the product market, meant that by late November work had not yet resumed. The quarries had been closed for five months and the options, as proposed by the stricken company, were very painful – 'considerably reduced' wages, and the resumption of either full-time work for 200 workers or five days work per week for 230 out of a total labour force of approximately 350. In desperation, the quarrymen voted 'narrowly' to accept the latter. In so doing they consciously reversed their earlier inclusive attitude towards employment in the quarries: the available work would now be confined to the company's tenants. The 120 workers denied employment, or even the realistic prospect of employment in the short- to medium-term future, were residents of the excluded Brecklet, Glencoe and North Ballachulish estates. For so long united, both the quarriers and their communities now faced the imminent prospects of division, bitterness and re-crimination. The decision of the meeting had 'aroused the greatest indignation in these districts and has alienated many sympathisers of influence'.[84]

In sum, unlike the first dispute, the second had resulted in a messy com-promise. In very difficult economic conditions the company was enabled to continue its operations, albeit with a reduced workforce. The men had gained union recognition and the promise of a resumption of work at reduced wages for some of them, but others were faced with very bleak employment prospects. The remarkable level of local community solidarity displayed throughout the two disputes, had foundered on the rocks of restricted employment opportuni-ties and the vote in favour of restriction and exclusion. Would this provide the material basis for an upsurge of highly localised 'chauvinism' and 'xenopho-bia'?[85]

Postscript

From time to time during 1906 there were indications of an upturn in the economic fortunes of the company and the quarrymen. However, these were greatly overshadowed by the continuing depression in the industry. The quar-ries reopened in January with Donald McMillan, the popular former chair of the Medical Committee, installed as the new foreman.[86] By March there was 'decided improvement'. The company had received large orders for slates and there was hope that the full-time working, as opposed to what had become the five-day norm, would soon be resumed. However, this situation did not materialise. By August the five-day week was still being worked in the face of 'disappointing' demand.[87] The hope that economic upturn would facilitate the return to 'normal' working not only of the company's tenants, but also those from the excluded estates, had long since died. Men from Glencoe were forced to continue their search for work in Easedale and other locations.[88] 'Good or-ders' were once again announced in September and there was a further 'slight improvement' at the end of the year. But the men were now working four days per week.[89]

The year 1907 started with great promise. The quarries resumed operations in the New Year with the men working full time. This happy state of affairs was still in existence in April, with the added bonuses that new orders were 'in the pipeline' and four weekly contracts had replaced six weekly payments. Moreo-ver, there was an 'abundance of work in the vicinity'.[90] However, renewed opti-mism soon gave way to utter despair. Reports of fluctuating economic fortunes during the early summer months were followed by the devastating news in Au-gust that the Ballachulish quarries were to be 'closed indefinitely'. According to the correspondent of the *Oban Times*, the unwillingness or inability of the company to invest in new production methods, combined with 'the refusal of the men to work on terms which would reduce their present scanty wage (sic) to vanishing point' had inevitably resulted in the closure of the works.[91] In view of their 'considerable' 'concessions' and 'sacrifices' on 'contracts and standard wages' made during the previous two years in an attempt to 'meet the wishes of the Company' and 'keep matters going', the quarrymen were both very disappointed and very bitter at the outcome. In the circumstances their requests for 'steady work for a fixed time if possible' and 'an advance of 1/- per week on skilled wages', had no chance of success.[92] For by this time the company's difficulties had reached crisis point. Its continuing inability to meet its financial liabilities compelled an Extraordinary General Meeting to wind up the company's business and call in the liquidator in August.[93] As in 1903 and 1905, the Ballachulish quarrymen once again sought work elsewhere. The 'works' at Kinlochleven now became an increasingly favoured destination and Ballachulish once more resembled 'a deserted village'. The *Oban Times* reported in August that alternative sources of employment were 'plentiful'. But this could not disguise the fact that the main source of the quarriers' livelihood, the Ballachulish Quarries Company Limited, had gone out of business and that the quarries would remain closed for the rest of the year.[94]

Yet the end of 1907 and dawn of 1908 once again brought renewed hope to this troubled but most indomitable and resilient workforce and community. Otherwise silent on matters concerning the quarries since the dispute of 1905, Grant's clippings carried a notice from the *Glasgow Herald* in October 1907 announcing the sale or lease of the Ballachulish quarries.[95] Two months later the *Oban Times* was pleased to report that the lease on 'the well known slate quarries of Ballachulish' had been secured 'by a new company and that work is expected to commence at an early date'.[96] In January 1908, the new company, the Ballachulish Quarries Limited, under its chair, Mr. Leyland, a landowner from Northumberland and a longstanding friend of the Beresford Drummonds, met with the men's representatives, 'amicably' agreed terms and conditions of work and commenced operations. The *Oban Times* observed that, 'All wish every success to the new Company, and that a new era of prosperity, mutually shared, is in store for Ballachulish'.[97]

Questions concerning whether, and to what extent, that wish was fulfilled in the first two years of the new company's existence will be addressed in the *Afterword* to this study. However, in the meantime I must attend to a series of questions, issues and debates arising out of the disputes and their aftermath, properly set within the wider context of the workplace and the community. It is to this task that I will turn in Chapters Three and Four.

Chapter Three
Questions, Issues and Debates

In the course of reconstructing aspects of workplace and community life and the nature and chronology of the conflicts, I have developed two sets of questions to put to the evidence. The first set comprises three questions concerned specifically with key issues surrounding the disputes and their consequences. They read as follows. Why did the first dispute end in triumph for the quarrymen and Grant and humiliation and defeat for the company? Why did the second dispute result in a compromise between the workers and their employer? And why did this compromise fail both to save the company from liquidation only two years later and to prevent the quarrymen from suffering further cuts in pay and employment? These questions are addressed in Part One of this chapter. I then move, in Part Two, to consider a group of questions and issues that similarly arise out of my specific case study of Ballachulish, but which also relate to, and shed some light upon, wider issues and debates. These comprise the specific and general nature and meanings of 'custom', as applied to both communities and protest, patterns of place and identity, typologies and 'peculiarities' of worker and employer thought and behaviour, the social composition and nature of leadership and the nature and underpinnings of cross-class alliances and movements.

Part One: The Disputes: Questions and Issues

Claimed by 'Gavroche' to have been 'one of the most important conflicts ever fought by Labour and the workers in the north of Scotland',[1] why did the protracted first dispute result in victory for 'the people', 'the workers', 'the community'? The response offered is that a combination of explanatory factors was at work. These cover the issue of support; the fight for both 'customary' and 'modern' freedoms and rights against 'selfish self-interest', outmoded 'despotism' and 'barbarism'; the perceived characteristics of the quarrymen, Grant and the company; the state of the labour market; and the nature of the local community. I will address them in turn.

First, the reader's attention was drawn in Chapter Two to the very impressive depth, breadth and sustained level of support given to the quarrymen and Grant between 1902 and 1904. This support came not only from the local community and the Ballachulish district, but also from across Argyllshire and the rest of Scotland, and parts of England. The high level of local support manifested itself in the mass meetings within Ballachulish itself, the presence at these meetings not only of most of the men, but also many of the women of the village, and the active involvement in the protests of prominent and respected middle-class figures such as McMurchy and Dunlop Anderson, the retired medical doctor. Further manifestations were seen in the criticisms directed at the company and the attempts to provide employment for the locked-out quarrymen by local and regional employers, the unwillingness of other doctors permanently to step into Grant's shoes, and the failure of the company seriously to take on board the option of replacing the men with quarriers from elsewhere.

In relation to 'outside' support, 'Gavroche' both welcomed the news early in 1903 that 'Now the press generally seems to be waking up to the fact that among these hills and lochs something of more than local interest is happening', and declared 'I do not remember of (sic) any Labour dispute in which there was such an absolute unanimity of condemnation for the employer'.[2] For while the workplace 'wrongdoings' of Lord Penrhyn in north Wales met with the unqualified hostility of the labour movement and its supporters nationally, the former, unlike the Ballachulish Quarries Company Limited, was not perceived by such a wide cross-section of society to be interfering so coercively, 'unfairly', and without any due regard to the 'customary' practices and values in the wider affairs of the community. According to 'Gavroche', 'the entire community from Oban to Fort William' was outraged by the company's unjustified and arrogant dismissal of Grant and its total neglect of the 'rights' of the Medical Committee concerning the appointment of the medical officer.[3] The *Oban Times* observed in March 1903, some three months after the start of the lock-out, that, 'All classes in the district and from afar are in full sympathy with the men in the dispute, and applaud the attitude they have taken up'.[4] Among the prominent individuals and institutions from these 'classes' were the Episcopal Bishop of Argyll, Alex Haldane, Mr. Dewar, MP for Inverness-shire, the Glasgow United Trades' Council, the Scotttish TUC, all those who donated in the region of £900 to the quarrymen's appeal fund and the Amalgamated Society of Engineers in London (the latter giving £20 to the men's cause).[5] We have also seen that several newspapers and the specialist medical publications gave their wholehearted and consistent support to 'the cause'. These included the *Oban Times, Oban Telegraph and Express, Highland News,*[6] *Glasgow Herald, Labour Leader, Lancet, British Medical Journal* and *Edinburgh Medical Journal.* There is no doubt that in the absence of such support, and given the reluctance of the state, in the form of the Board of Trade, positively to intervene in the dispute, the cause of Grant and the quarrymen would have been much weakened. The company would have had a much greater opportunity, free from the constraint of adverse 'public opinion', more ruthlessly to pursue and realise its goals.

Second, support for the men and Grant was so strong because they were widely perceived to have the 'righteous' causes of customary morality and justice, and 'modern' rights and freedoms on their side. Opposition to the company was equally strong because the latter, while claiming a 'due legal right', was seen both to be transgressing customary morality, narrowly and 'irrationally' pursuing its own self-interest at the expense of the well-being of the wider community and implementing 'tyrannical' practices from an outmoded past. Instances of these transgressions, pursuits and implementations were noted at various points in my narrative account of the disputes in Chapter Two. However, it is now time to elaborate upon them and bring them together in a more concentrated form. This will enable us more fully to appreciate the force and depth of the main grievances expressed by the men, Grant and their supporters.

As a result of its 'autocratic', unexpected, unexplained and 'totally unjust' dismissal of the doctor, the company was charged with breaking a long tradition of trust, consultation and mutuality with the quarrymen or, more precisely, the latter's representatives on the Medical Committee. 'From time immemorial', declared the *British Medical Journal*, the quarrymen 'have had a say in the appointment of the doctor'. It was consequently wrong and unacceptable for that 'say', in favour of Grant's appointment, to be ignored and reversed by the company without consultation and without heed to the expressed wishes of the Medical Committee.[7] In addition, 'at the time no reason was alleged for the dismissal', while the doctor himself had no inkling that he was about to be sacked.[8] 'Common courtesy' and 'common justice' demanded much better than this. The 'overbearing', 'arbitrary' and 'inconsiderate' treatment meted out by the company were not to be tolerated by 'all fair-minded persons'.[9]

However, the vast majority of critics went beyond the issue of consultation to contest a more fundamental principle: the 'moral right' of the company unilaterally to hire and fire the medical officer. The argument expressed was that, whatever the contractual and legal niceties of the matter, the customary right of appointment and dismissal lay with the committee rather than the company. The committee, of course, contained an inbuilt numerical majority in favour of the quarrymen's representatives. Furthermore, these critics quickly pointed out that it was the quarrymen, rather than the company, who paid the doctor's salary at the quarries. In sum, appropriate respect for the principles and practices of established custom, democratic authority and accountability and financial responsibility, unambiguously demonstrated that far more than a purely contractual employment matter between the doctor and the company was at issue.

As the *Highland News* declared in relation to Grant's dismissal in July 1902, 'Though the company are, we believe, within their legal rights in this matter, still there is another deeper question of common justice to be considered'. And 'common justice' demanded that the company respect the wishes of the appointment committee, the quarrymen paymasters and the local community, and duly overturn its decision.[10] In very similar vein, the *Lancet* maintained that while opponents of the company had to respect the fact that Grant was 'bound by the agreement which he had made', nevertheless, the company had defied accepted practice and the will of the community, to commit 'a moral wrong'. Furthermore, while Grant should have exercised more care in attending to the details of his contract – herein lay a warning to medical professionals nationally – the company was not justified in successfully pursuing and implementing its 'legal right' at the expense of morality, considerable hurt to the workforce and their community and the attempted humiliation and loss of livelihood of a committed and well respected professional doctor.[11] The *British Medical Journal* found it 'remarkable' that 'a company should claim the right ... of choosing a medical officer for their employees while allowing them the privilege of paying for his services',[12] while the *Oban Times* maintained that the real question revolved around 'not so much that of Dr. Grant, or this or that other doctor, as of your right to appoint or dismiss your own medical officer whom you are paying out of your own wages'.[13] For the *Oban Times*, as with most other contemporary observers, the balance of 'right' lay decidedly with the quarrymen and Grant.

The clauses inserted in the doctor's contract concerning the one month's notice of dismissal and the company's right to interdict him from carrying out his medical duties in the district, were also claimed to be unprecedented and lacking in transparency and 'true' or 'moral' legitimacy. Members of the Medical Committee maintained that, while agreed between Grant and Maccoll, the clauses had no basis in past practice and had not been brought to their attention.[14] The proposed interdiction amounted to the extension of the company's powers over hiring and firing beyond the limits of the quarries and their asserted superiority over those exercised by Grant's other employer, the Lismore and Appin Parish Council. Moreover, the interdiction was widely seen by its opponents as the cornerstone of the 'insensitive' and 'outside' company's plan 'arrogantly' and 'immorally' to achieve monopolistic power and control in the locality and to tolerate no opposition. As such, it met with fierce and extensive condemnation. The *Highland News* declared, 'It is surely intolerable that the wishes of the whole community should be set aside by the arbitrary decision of a small body of men non-resident in the district'.[15] A letter from 'A Quarrier' to the same newspaper deemed it to be intolerable, 'in the beginning of the 20th

Century', that 'a tyrannical Company' should dictate 'who is to be our doctor' and 'lord it over us in this manner'. For the interdict was an act of 'unexampled oppression and cruelty', designed to 'rob us of our rights as freemen' and, as such, to be resisted with all moral and legal means. The editor was in complete agreement. For, if the quarriers 'tamely submit', they 'will be willingly allowing themselves to be placed on a level with horses, cattle, sheep and swine'. The 'men of Ballachulish' were exhorted to stand 'shoulder to shoulder' in defence of their rights and freedoms in 'the twentieth century'.[16]

The *Oban Times* 'received a number of letters' expressing the fear that, if successful, the interdict would prevent Grant from carrying out his 'obligations to the poor of the parish'.[17] In the opinion of the periodical *Truth*, the interdict demonstrated that 'the tyranny of the Ballachulish Slate Quarries Company Limited, knows no bounds',[18] while the usually more restrained *British Medical Journal* nevertheless called for an amendment to a law which would prevent a doctor, who 'for whatever reason has made himself obnoxious to the directors', to 'practise his profession within their sphere of influence'. According to the *British Medical Journal,* an 'intolerable injustice had taken place' and 'an oppressive spirit' was abroad.[19]

We have also observed that many of the company's work-place and related actions during the first dispute met with loud and prolonged criticism. These actions included 'overcharging' for materials, the 'unreasonable' length of contracts and pays, evictions, sackings, victimisation, short-time working and unemployment, opposition to 'third-party interference' in relations between itself and its employees, its attempts to replace Grant and the more complete development of 'managerial prerogatives'. However 'rationally' the company may have considered itself to be acting, by the standard of the maximisation of self-interest in the market-place, nevertheless large numbers of those in the local and wider community and the workforce adopted a diametrically opposing viewpoint. The latter once again maintained that the sectional and 'selfish' interest was predominating at the expense of 'the public good'. In the manner of Lord Penrhyn, the company was also seen to be implementing the 'autocratic' methods of a discredited past to ensure its workplace 'rule'. The Glasgow United Trades' Council termed the Ballachulish lock-out 'A Scottish "Penrhyn" Case' (see Document Three). *Truth* declared, in August 1902, that, 'The Directors of the Ballachulish Slate Quarries are seemingly bent upon attaining the same sort of reputation as that enjoyed by Lord Penrhyn by their high-handed treatment of their employees'.[20]

For their part the quarrymen and their supporters presented their demands for consultation, negotiation, mutuality and respect in the workplace not only as being justified by 'custom', but also as the inalienable rights of modern 'freemen' as opposed to 'serfs' or 'slaves'. This emphasis upon the 'modernity' of their cause became even more pronounced once the 'right' to trade-union organisation and recognition became part of their list of demands. The company's attempt to jeopardise 'the right of combination' meant that 'the principle of liberty itself' was 'at stake', according to the *Labour Leader*,[21] while the Scottish TUC congratulated the Ballachulish men upon resisting the 'tyrannical action of their employers in seeking to deny them the ordinary rights of free men'.[22] In a highly racialized comment, the *Lancet* declared the workers in the quarries to be independent Highlanders rather than 'helpless dependents' like the East Indian 'coolies employed in coffee plantations and tea-gardens'.[23] In sum, the implementation of 'tyranny', in whatever form, was to be resisted at all cost.

The position of the Ballachulish Quarries Company Limited may well have been strengthened if it had possessed the wealth, power and the single-mindedness of purpose of Lord Penrhyn and some other quarry owners in north Wales. However, it could not compete in terms of the first two characteristics. In terms of the third, we have seen that initial unity and determination of purpose gave way, during 1903, to increasing evidence of differences and divisions among the directors and influential shareholders. Unlike Penryhn, the company also failed to temper its authoritarianism with selective and effective acts of local paternalism. As a result of this combination of factors, the company's chances of courting popularity and achieving success in the first dispute became increasingly remote.[24]

In complete contrast to the company, both Grant and the quarrymen were highly successful in representing themselves to the public, and being represented in the press, in a highly favourable light. I have indicated earlier in this study that Grant himself was a very able, active, popular and civic-minded doctor and 'local'. 'The men', in contrast to the image of the purely 'selfish' company, were widely deemed to be not only good workers, but responsible and devoted members of their families, their community and their country. As noted above, they adopted the highly successful strategy of presenting themselves both as the fair-minded and wronged defenders of 'custom' and the progressive advocates of modern freedoms. They routinely resorted to the 'legitimising language of custom' – as 'sturdy Highlanders' valiantly fighting against the company's 'chains of slavery' or to the freedom-loving memories of 'Bruce and Wallace' [25] – in order to justify their cause and increase their support. Throughout the first dispute, and notwithstanding their considerable deprivations and injustices at the hands of the company, they were overwhelmingly portrayed in the press as 'respectable', 'upstanding', 'moderate' and 'reasonable'. For the *Highland News* they constituted a 'fine body of stalwart, hard-working, intelligent and respectable Highlanders' who rightly shared 'a deep sense of injustice'. In large measure because of the presence of 'good leaders', they had commendably not risen to 'extreme provocation' and 'not the slightest injury has been done to person or property'.[26] The *Oban Weekly News* raised the scale of praise: 'In all broad Scotland there is no more law abiding, intelligent and thoughtful body of men than are the quarriers of Ballachulish'.[27] McMurchy took it to the national limit: 'He did not know where they could find more intelligent, sober and industrious men and morally and physically finer specimens of the British workman than were to be found among the quarriers of Ballachulish'.[28] Commanding a high level of support, they were increasingly in a strong position to realise their goals. They also constituted confirmation of the hypothesis that 'customary culture' contained within it the potential for the expression of *both* 'traditional', or 'backward-looking', and 'modern', or 'forward-looking', ideas, values, norms and practices.

Yet a high level of support, the general unpopularity of the company, and their own popular representations and discourses were necessary rather than sufficient causes of victory for Grant and the quarrymen. For well into 1903 the company had managed to survive the appearance of differences in its own ranks, strong opposition from the quarriers and some employers, and continuing adverse publicity. However, as observed in Chapter Two, matters could not continue indefinitely along the same course. For the lock-out had been in operation for several months, the company was losing money and its workers to its rivals in an increasingly competitive market, and there was no realistic prospect of recommencing operations in the quarries in the immediate or near future. The main hope for the company was that material deprivation and desperation might drive some or all of the men back to work in the quarries and bring about splits in their united ranks and the community. However, neither of these hopes came to pass. The fact that the quarriers continued to enjoy good employment prospects outside of Ballachulish and that the workforce and the entire community remained steadfast in their unity and determination, combined with the company's growing internal divisions and external economic pressures, effectively tipped the balance in favour of 'the men'. It is to an illustration of the nature and significance of the labour market and the local community that I now turn.

At the outset of the dispute it was expected that the near monopoly enjoyed by the company on local employment opportunities would quickly bring the quarriers 'to heel'. However, events soon took a very different turn. I noted in Chapter two that alternative and relatively well-paid employment opportunities for the locked-out quarrymen soon opened up and remained in abundance throughout 1903. These opportunities ranged from work on the new railway line and provision by local employers, to employment in the quarries of the

Slate Islands and elsewhere in Scotland. In March and April 1903 the *Oban Times* reported that full-time work was 'plentiful' on the railway and that the men who had gone to work in the quarries of Balvicar and Cullipool 'are all well and earning far more money than they were doing at Ballachulish'.[29] The demand for slates had become 'so good' that 'they can hardly keep pace with it'. New quarries were opening up on the island of Luing where conditions in the quarries were reported to be 'the most prosperous ... in living memory'.[30] Throughout the summer, autumn and early winter months the press continued to report favourably upon quarrying employment opportunities and wages 'in the west', for both skilled men and labourers. Wages in general in these quarries were reportedly higher than they had been in Ballachulish under the manage-ment of the Ballachulish Slate Quarries Company Limited, while the pay of labourers in particular was said to be better than that formerly enjoyed by the skilled quarrymen at the Ballachulish quarries.[31] This sharpened sense of rela-tive deprivation duly strengthened the Medical Committee's determination to secure the principles of regional wage comparability and parity in slate quar-rying upon the termination of the lock-out and the resumption of work.[32] The extreme difficulty of finding willing and able substitutes for the skilled quarry-men, and the effective vigilance of the latter and the women of the village in the face of the rumoured importation of 'scab' labour, compounded the company's labour market difficulties. As noted earlier, for most of the period of the first conflict Ballachulish resembled a 'deserted village'.

Tight labour market conditions, and especially continuing opportunities for suitable means of alternative employment, thus played a crucial role in enabling the quarrymen materially to withstand their employer's attempt to 'starve them back to work'. In contrast, faced with the very limited opportunities for alterna-tive employment in their area, the quarrymen of north Wales were usually far less favourably placed to defeat hostile employer actions.[33]

As in north Wales and other parts of Britain and Europe, the unity and strength of the local community in Ballahulish constituted a vital resource in the fight against the 'tyranny' of capital.[34] The reader's attention has already been drawn, in Chapters One and Two, to the nature and importance of a range of 'respectable' institutions and pursuits – Gaelic, the United Free Church, tem-perance, shinty, the Volunteers, the Mechanics Institutes and the Public School – in inducing a very strong sense of togetherness, solidarity and determination on the part of the local community. Furthermore, in Chapter One I highlighted the extremely close correspondence between work, family, neighbourhood and community in Ballachulish. The quarrying labour force consisted of fathers, sons, male in-laws and male neighbours. As in north Wales and elsewhere, the marked familial dimension of the local employment structure greatly reduced the potential for the development of divisions between the skilled and the non-skilled. For such divisions would, of necessity, manifest themselves within and among families, neighbours and other members of the local community. Given the 'closeness' of the local population and the very high incidence of occupational continuity and self-recruitment, the chances of communal solidarity and unity being challenged and undermined by occupational divisions were, especially in the context of the massive solidarity displayed during the first conflict, extremely slim.[35] Moreover, in early 1900s Ballachulish there was an absence of those religious and ethnic divisions and conflicts which were so marked in many Scottish communities.[36] In contrast to the experience of other parts of Britain, including, albeit to a limited extent, the quarrying areas of north Wales, the very fact that the first dispute revolved essentially around the homogeneous labour force of a single, united village, also meant that the employer was unable to exploit feelings of local rivalry and even 'chauvinism' and 'xenophobia' among workers residing in different communities.[37] Finally, much in the manner of Aminzade's artisan communities in nineteenth-century France, the small-scale nature of Ballachulish, combined with the very close ties between organization and protest in the work-place and the community, contributed greatly to the quarrymen's success.[38]

In turning to answer my second question – why did the second dispute end in a compromise between the workers and their employer? – the same combination of factors may be utilized, albeit with some important qualifications, differences and effects. For example, while support for the quarrymen was also strong in 1905, it was less widespread than during the first dispute. Similarly, the second dispute received much less publicity in the press. As an example of the more regular conflict between 'labour and capital', it lacked the unusual publicity, drama and 'human interest' of the company's sudden, unexpected and unprecedented dismissal of the doctor in 1902. For it was very uncommon for a professional man to be dismissed in such a summary, autocratic, humiliating and public way by his employer. This fact, in turn, cast the spotlight upon the characteristics and actions of the company and invited comparisons between the latter and other 'tyrants'.

Notwithstanding the 'mobbing' and 'rioting' incident of July, the quarrymen retained public support for their generally 'respectable' behaviour throughout 1905. Moreover, local and regional support for the union leaders increased as a result of their 'moderate' and 'restraining' influence upon the crowd attacking Maccoll's house, and their desire to negotiate 'fairly' and 'reasonably' with the company. In contrast, we have seen that the company and its manager continued to invite charges of 'unreason', 'autocracy' and the transgression of 'custom' in the press and elsewhere as a result of their attitudes and actions concerning pay, conditions and employment. However, and especially in the wake of Maccoll's flight from Ballachulish, the changes in the personnel of the company conducive to conciliation and negotiation and mounting economic adversity, these charges increasingly declined in frequency and intensity as compared with the period of the first dispute. While the company was still perceived by many of the quarrymen to be attempting to overcome its product market difficulties primarily and unfairly at their expense, there was also a growing and more widespread realisation of the seriousness of these difficulties. Furthermore, the willingness of Major Black to attempt to resolve the problem by means of negotiation with the men and their union, and the active involvement of the Conciliation Board, constituted substantial evidence of a new employer spirit and commanded widespread respect and support. In turn, the negotiating and trade union advances made, and the appointment of a well-respected local manager, induced a far more conciliatory attitude on the part of the labour force. While the availability of alternative employment opportunities underpinned the 'independent' spirit of the quarrymen throughout the summer and autumn months, nevertheless the continuing closure of the Ballachulish quarries in the face of ever worsening market conditions, did not augur well for the future. By the end of 1905 a mood of anxiety and fear, compounded by the vote for selective and divisive employment in the quarries, had replaced erstwhile confidence and optimism. In this situation, the case for a compromise 'solution' was overwhelming.

My third question – why did the compromise fail to save the company and improve the situation of the quarrymen? – may be answered briefly. Set against the general backcloth of the catastrophic decline of the slate industry nationally, the Ballachulish Slate Quarries Company Limited failed to solve its marketing and production problems. In fact, we have seen that, despite periods of optimism, these problems worsened between 1906 and 1907. By the summer of 1907 there was a sense of acute crisis and impending disaster. However, the quarrymen were reluctant to accept yet another round of cuts in pay and employment. The prospect of work at Kinlochleven and elsewhere kept the men's spirits reasonably high.[39] But in August 1907 the inability of the company to meet its financial obligations forced its closure.

Part Two: Wider Issues and Debates

Before proceeding to a consideration of the light shed by my Ballachulish case study upon wider issues and debates, I must offer a brief note of methodological caution and clarification. I am in full agreement with the view that generalisations cannot stand or fall on the basis of the (insufficient) evidence of a single case study. However, along with many other scholars, I subscribe to the view that the evidence unearthed and the views and conclusions reached in the course of studying a specific case can usefully contribute, albeit in duly limited and modest ways, to the advancement of critical knowledge and understanding of relevant general issues and debates. It is on this basis that I explore the significance and relationship between my specific area of study and wider issues and debates.

Throughout this book I have highlighted the key importance of 'custom' to both the culture and protests of quarrymen, Grant and the community in Ballachulish. In view of this emphasis, it is appropriate to begin this section with an examination of the general and specific nature, meanings and significance of custom and culture.

Three general points are of particular relevance to my concerns. First, custom and customary culture are sometimes employed in the scholarly literature to refer not only to values, ideas and norms but also to practices, to the ways in which people behave and communicate in non-verbal ways as well as the ways in which they think and express their ideas in language. When employed in this way, custom and culture necessarily possesses structural as well as cultural characteristics, as residing in *both* experience and consciousness, in the material *and* the mental aspects of life. As E.P. Thompson declared in his work on eighteenth-century English 'customary' 'confrontations and negotiations between patricians and plebs':

> In these studies I hope that plebeian culture becomes a more concrete and usable concept, no longer situated in the thin air of 'meanings, attitudes and values', but located within a particular equilibrium of social relations, a working environment of exploitation and resistance to exploitation, of relations of power which are masked by the rituals of paternalism and deference. In this way (I hope) 'popular culture' is situated within its proper material abode.[40]

As I noted in the Introduction, and as manifest in the course of my narrative, I have adopted Thompson's approach to the study of 'customary culture'. I have also attempted closely to follow his advice both clearly to define and firmly to set 'culture' and 'custom' in their proper historical contexts of time and place and, while exploring the inextricable connections between them, to avoid seeing cultural matters as simple expressions of economic structures and processes.[41]

Second, 'custom' is closely associated by historians and sociologists with the defence of established or 'traditional' 'rights', especially when these 'rights' are placed under threat. Furthermore, more often than not these 'rights' are observed to reside more within 'culture' – in memory, folklore and in community-based sanctions of approved and disapproved forms of action and thought

– than more narrowly within legal statute. However, the former by no means necessarily precludes legitimising resort (whether pre-, simultaneous, or post-) to the latter. Once again, much depends upon the precise *historical* context.[42] As indicated in my Introduction, these 'customary rights' often involve notions of fairness, reciprocity, mutuality and legitimacy – a 'moral economy'- appropriately set within a particular place and a period in time. Finally, in opposition to a 'compartmentalist' approach to the study of history and society, appeal to these 'rights' may empirically be shown to have influenced not only the cultural, but also many other facets of life, including economic ones.

Third, there has been marked and continuing debate as to whether custom and customary forms of protests have been essentially backward-looking phenomena, characteristic of the pre-industrial and industrialising ages, or whether they have both possessed more complex and fluid characteristics, both backward- and forward-looking in character, and persisting well into the modern industrial age. Charles Tilly and Craig Calhoun have been prominent among advocates of the former position. Tilly, for example, has traced an epochal shift, with the rise and development of industrial capitalism, international markets and modern (especially liberal-democratic) nation states being accompanied by a marked decline in 'reactive' 'customary' movements, such as food riots, and the rise of 'proactive' protests, such as strikes, demonstrations and organised and ideologically-based political parties. For Tilly increases in the scale of social organization brought about the 'modernization' of forms of collective action.[43] Calhoun developed the interesting and challenging thesis that early nineteenth-century protesting 'artisans and others' in England were, in opposition to E.P. Thompson's celebrated thesis, far less the forward-looking agents of a working class 'in the making', than 'reactionary radicals', seeking to restore those community-based solidarities and customs being torn apart by the onrush of individualistic and competitive industrial capitalism.[44]

Critics have, in agreement with Tilly, acknowledged the importance of broad shifts in the nature and character of social protest – for example, in England from the more defensive, limited and conservative concerns of eighteenth-century rioters to the more radical, forward-looking, and well organised concerns of later nineteenth-century trade unionists and political radicals.[45] However, they have argued that the historical sociology of Tilly and Calhoun has been unduly schematic and one-sided in character, too insensitive to the contingency and complexity of historical experience. For example, a long line of historians – from Thompson himself to George Rudé and, most authoritatively, Dorothy Thompson – have clearly demonstrated that radical movements during the 1830s and 1840s contained *both* 'reactive' and 'proactive' elements, with appeals to 'custom' increasingly constituting the legitimising basis for the establishment of *new* and forward-looking radical demands and rights for working people, such as trade union recognition and universal manhood suffrage. Indeed, rooted in increasingly *independent* and *radical* working-class cultures, forward-looking demands and popular movements rapidly assumed dominance within British popular protest.[46]

The geographer David Gilbert has criticised Tilly for the 'generality' of his model and his 'too homogeneous a view of the impact of capitalism on social geography'. In his study of the South Wales and Nottinghamshire coalfields and their communities between 1850 and 1926, Gilbert encountered, *pace* Tilly, the continued importance of small social units, such as local communities possessing strong traditions of place and rights, and 'strikes with a mixture of proactive and reactive claims'.[47] Raphael Samuel similarly noted the importance of 'customary rights' and the defence of 'a particular way of life' to the miners involved in the strike of 1984-5.[48]

The Ballachulish experience lends itself to a number of conclusions relevant to these general areas of debates about custom. For example, in endorsement of a key tenet of the general literature, the appeal of the quarrymen, Grant and their allies to custom was undertaken to legitimise their actions in the conflicts on the basis of past rights and responsibilities. Furthermore, these rights and responsibilities were perceived to be severely threatened by an 'innovative' force. The latter, of course, took the form of the Ballachulish Quarries Company Limited, 'rationally' seeking to maximise its self-interest, power and control both in the workplace and the wider community. We have observed that the quarrymen, Grant and their supporters reacted by accusing the company of breaking established 'moral-economic' norms and sanctions in relation to its dismissal of the doctor and its generally unprecedented 'immoral', 'selfish' and 'tyrannical' actions. The resulting conflicts revolved not around the unhelpful dichotomies of 'market' versus 'anti-market' or 'rational' versus 'irrational' values and practices. For the quarrymen were fully-fledged industrial proletarians who had long derived their livelihoods from market-based activity, but, as we have seen, whose notion of 'rationality', embracing customary or 'moral' notions of fairness and reciprocity, stood in marked contrast and opposition to the unfettered 'entrepreneurial' 'rationality' of the company. As noted in the Introduction, and in opposition to rational-choice theory, the conflicts issued from *competing* notions and practices of 'rational' behaviour in the market-place and beyond, of 'human nature' in general', and of how best to serve 'the public interest' and achieve 'the public good'. As such, the disputes constituted an early twentieth-century Scottish version of Thompson's observed 'succession of confrontations between an innovative market economy and the customary moral economy of the plebs' in eighteenth-century England.[49]

Yet much more than a 'reactive' or 'backward-looking' resort to custom or a form of 'reactionary radicalism' was at work in Ballachulish. For in the course of their 'customary confrontations' with the company, the quarrymen also developed new 'proactive' or 'forward-looking' 'modern' habits, views and goals. For example, we have seen that they not only continued to insist upon their time-honoured right to elect their own representatives onto the Medical Committee, but also departed radically from past practice in forming a trade union, and a 'new', inclusive union to boot, to which they elected, at mass meetings, very able and articulate local men as leaders. While some of the latter had acquired leadership, reading and speaking skills in the United Free Church, in the course of the conflicts all of them quickly developed the confidence, independence and ability to speak at large public meetings, to publicly articulate the men's demands and to attempt patiently and respectfully, but determinedly, to negotiate with an unresponsive company and an arrogant and dismissive chair who had the 'bad taste' to 'comment on the clothes' worn by them, saying 'they could have little to complain of when they could dress so well'.[50] They had very quickly become 'modern' trade union leaders, versed, as seen in their influence in the Maccoll incident of 1905 and in the compromise reached with the company in the same year, in the arts of moderation and restraint as well as militancy. Partly as a result of their influence, but probably more so as a direct consequence of mass struggle and conflict, a 'traditional' workplace, characterised predominantly by non-unionism and 'dictatorship' in 1902, was remarkably transformed, by 1905, into an extremely 'modern' one in which institutionalised collective bargaining had taken root and a far more conciliatory atmosphere prevailed between workers and employers. The quarrymen and their leaders also registered some radical political gains. In the autumn of 1902 a meeting of the men asked Maccoll to resign as the community's representative on Argyll County Council because he had 'forfeited their confidence'.[51] It is also possible that their identification and exposure of the close ties between Colonel Malcolm and the Tory candidate for Argyll in the 1903 by-election, Stewart, played a part in the latter's defeat at the hands of the Liberal, Ainsworth. Liberalism was the dominant political force in Ballachulish and district. However, Labour and socialist politics continued to exert minimal influence upon politics in the Highlands.[52]

In sum, the specific case of the protesting Ballachulish quarrymen provides clear endorsement of the abovementioned criticisms directed at Tilly and Calhoun. My observed customary protests were more complex, fluid, and forward-looking in character than the labels 'reactive' or 'reactionary radicalism' would suggest.

The Ballachulish experience contributes to wider issues and debates in other ways. Some of these may be inferred or stem logically from what I have written in the previous two pages. For example, my evidence fully supports Thompson's thesis that the 'resort to custom' occurred not only in relation to 'meanings, attitudes and values', but also with regard to questions of power, authority and material issues. We have thus seen that, from the point of view of the quarrymen all manner of issues, including questions of company, worker and communal rights, responsibilities and spheres of autonomy and influence, housing, employment and pay, came within the proper brief of 'custom'. As suggested by many contributors to debate, we have also observed that the customary culture of the Ballachulish quarrymen derived its authority and legitimacy primarily from within the experiences and traditions of the community. As such, it was 'invented' by the community, by agents of civil society, rather than by the law or the state. Accordingly, as shown in both Ballachulish and more widely, it was representatives of the community who acted as the arbiters and guardians of the principles of customary thought and practice. However, it is significant that both Grant and the quarrymen's Medical Committee resorted to law in attempted confirmation of their customary rights and actions. As briefly noted above, this resort was by no means unusual among customary communities. However, it is important to record two additional factors. First, the defeats suffered by their 'morally justified' cases at the hands of the law, did not deter Grant and the quarrymen from the continued and even more resolute pursuit of their 'righteous' causes. Second, the legal judgements passed down in favour of the Ballachulish Slate Quarries Company Limited perhaps demonstrated the full extent to which the law had become firmly rooted in contractual 'rights' by the beginning of the twentieth century. By this time, any previous (especially pre-nineteenth century) confusions and ambiguities concerning the relative legal rights and claims of 'moral' and 'contractual' contestants, had surely been decided firmly in favour of the latter.

The Ballachulish case also lends itself to future research into four much neglected areas of study. The first of these, as implied in the previous paragraph, revolves around the developing relationships among customary 'moral economy', orthodox political economy and the law from the eighteenth century to the late twentieth century. The second area concerns the developing nature and character of customary culture itself. For the very presence and formidable strength of 'custom' in early twentieth-century Ballachulish strongly lends itself to the argument, advanced by Gilbert and Raphael Samuel, that the subject area of 'custom', broadly defined, merits much further research in its twentieth-century manifestations. It has in all probability declined in importance and appeal in the face of the remorseless, if uneven, advance of 'the market' and 'market-embedded' individualism, competition, commodity-consciousness and all the other accoutrements of industrial capitalism. However, its continuing presence, both in Britain but more so in much of the 'developing' world, is of obvious historical and contemporary interest and significance, especially with reference to the ongoing engagement between 'moral economy' and 'political economy'.[53]

This moves us logically to a key point raised in Introduction and confirmed by the Ballachulish experience: the historically *contested* nature of economic rationality and 'human nature'. My study of Ballachulish, of course, has brought into sharp relief the competing claims of rational choice theory rooted in the maximisation of self-interest and the 'social choice' alternative offered by customary moral economy. This third avenue of potentially rewarding research is simply listed at this point. I will revisit it in more detail in the final chapter.

Fourth, my case study will hopefully help to stimulate a renewed research into the complex *connections*, the degrees of correspondence, between 'culture' and 'structure'. As matters currently stand in the humanities and social sciences, old-fashioned and largely discredited modes of structural*ism* have largely been superseded by fashionable postmodernist concerns with representation and subjectivity. However, just as structuralism largely and unsatisfactorily ignored questions of 'culture' – of purposive agency, consciousness and meaning – so postmodernism has, in an equally lopsided and unsatisfactory manner, abandoned 'structure', or at least material as opposed to discursive 'structures' and 'systems', in its obsession with 'culture'. I maintain that in the process the necessary and fruitful, but irreducible, historical reconstructions and engagements of 'culture' and 'structure' have unfortunately, but hopefully temporarily, been marginalized or forgotten. For however useful it might be, for abstract and logical purposes, to examine the independent and separate properties of 'culture' and 'structure', nevertheless, in historical practice they are often, and have frequently been shown to be, intimately connected. For example, we have seen that while economic relationships, processes and structures in Ballachulish undoubtedly possessed an independent existence and major effect upon people's health and welfare, irrespective of their conscious expression, nevertheless in many instances questions of meaning and value, of 'reason', 'fairness' and so on, and of authority and power, were placed upon and became inseparable from 'the economic' itself. In this sense 'the cultural' and 'the economic' were inextricably connected. More extensive and intensive research into the nature and extent of these connections, over time and in many places, is to be greatly welcomed.[54]

In moving to a consideration of patterns of place and identity, reference to the Ballachulish experience and its significance in terms of the relevant wider literature and national picture, lends itself to four main conclusions. First, and

contrary to an approach which posits the supremacy of a single form of identity and consciousness among working people in modern Britain – for example
'the people' or 'populism' over 'class' or vice versa'[55] – my, albeit limited, study
highlights the importance of the *complex* and *multiple* identities and attachments held by the same people living in the same place at the same period in
time. These included an extremely strong male quarrier identity with all things
'local' and 'respectable' – the community and its very close and settled population, the shinty team, Gaelic 'habits and customs', education, 'improvement',
temperance, the Volunteers and so on. They also embraced opposition to those
'outsiders' unsympathetic and hostile to 'local ways', most obviously the company. There was also a commitment to predominantly radical and progressive
causes and evidence of an emergent labour and even class consciousness. At the
same time class-based equality was limited by strongly gendered limitations and
boundaries. Finally, I have detected strong attachments to both Scottish and
British forms of patriotism, including radical patriotism.

Many examples of these multiple, complex and, I may add, developing and
shifting, identities, attachments and entanglements have been observed in the
sources and already reproduced in my text. As such I do not need to rehearse
them in full. However, it may be useful to bring together a few cited examples
and some new ones at this juncture in order more coherently to demonstrate
the strength of my case.

As observed earlier, the quarrymen drew widespread praise for being 'intelligent, sober and industrious men'. They were seen to be 'respectable, upstanding
and moderate' members of the local community and committed family men.
They had demonstrated their 'moderation' and 'restraint' in the face of 'extreme'
provocation' from the 'outsider', 'absentee' company. As such they could be
counted among the 'morally and physically finer specimens of the British workman'.[56] In addition, as Alex McClaren, one of the leaders, declared at a mass
meeting of the quarrymen, they were 'all free-born Britons' and 'Britons never
would be slaves'.[57] They were also 'independent' and 'sturdy' 'Highlanders'. In
the past manner of 'Bruce and Wallace', they would 'stoutly' defend their 'rights
as 'modern freemen'. The 'chains of slavery' were to be smashed, whether 'in
South Africa', 'Siberia' or as practised by the company in Ballachulish itself.[58]
Their patriotism also assumed more conventional forms. For example, many
Ballachulish quarrying families and other members of the local community gave
a rousing welcome home, in August 1902, to those returning members of the
Volunteers who had fought in the Transvaal.[59] The same month saw impressive
and enthusiastic coronation celebrations for Edward VII. These involved virtually the entire community and consisted of a parade by the local Volunteers,
school sports and prize giving by Mrs. Beresford Drummond, a procession to

Lord Strathcona's home in Glencoe, the lighting of bonfires, and the decoration of 'nearly every house in the village'. The 'vast crowd' which gathered in the public square of Ballachulish sang and toasted the King's health.[60] A month later the *Oban Times* warmly congratulated King Edward upon his visit to Loch Leven in the Royal Yacht. The keen interest displayed by the monarch in the welfare of both the locals and the other Highlanders in the course of his visit had 'created a new attachment to his person among his Highland subjects'.[61]

Significantly, unlike attachments to the locality, respectability, radicalism and patriotism, identities of gender – the ways in which male and female identities were constructed and reconstructed – were very rarely mentioned, at least in an *explicit* manner, in the sources concerning the disputes, the workplace and the community. We have seen that the valuation rolls, the census and, to a much lesser extent, the press contain important information on occupations and households, including family, kinship and occupational structures and the sexual division of labour. Yet the roles and thoughts of women within their families, neighbourhoods and in relation to the disputes, the male quarrying work-place, Dr. Grant and the crucial issues of health and welfare, barely figure in the sources. As noted earlier in this study, there are brief references in the press to the fact that women were present in the protesting crowds, that they took part in the 'mobbing' action against Maccoll, and that, in the enforced absence of most of their male partners, they assumed added responsibility for detecting any attempt on the part of the company to import 'scabs' into the quarries.[62] However, in keeping with much of the traditional literature on social protest movements, women are afforded only a supportive and shadowy role and presence.[63]

Yet, somewhat paradoxically, in contrast to the position and thoughts of women the wider issue of gender, and especially the highly gendered *assumptions* of the key protagonists in the disputes, permeate, however implicitly, the sources. It was thus widely assumed, or 'taken for granted', that the public sphere, including the world of paid work, 'skill', independence, control, power, authority, politics, public meetings and so forth, was the 'natural' preserve of men and 'manliness'. It thus followed automatically that women belonged to the private world of the home, the family and their immediate surroundings. As such they would not figure largely as participants in work-place and 'public' disputes. There was perceived to be little or no need to write these 'obvious' 'facts of life' into accounts of the disputes. As a result, the roles and voices of Ballahulish's women are largely lost to us. We are left with a very incomplete picture of conflict between, on the one hand, male workers and a male doctor, and, on the other hand, the male-dominated company. In turn, conflict is set

against the backgrounds of a largely male-dominated 'community' and predominantly male supporters.

Second, while fully attentive to the forces of complexity and multiplicity, I
wish to draw the reader's attention to two increasingly important points of
identity in Ballachulish. These were the attachment to the locality as a predominantly radical place and space, and the closely related phenomenon of emergent
labour-movement consciousness, including class feeling and expression. I will
deal with these in turn.

As observed in Chapter One, manual workers and their families in Ballachulish shared, along with many of their national counterparts, strong attachment
to 'the local'. However, it is also important to highlight the fact that this attachment in Ballachulish was of an increasingly radical kind. It is true that backward-looking and more conservative aspects of community thought and action
did not disappear. However, they were increasingly overshadowed by forward-
looking elements. The reasons for this are to be located in socio-structural and
cultural factors as well as in the flow of events during the disputes.

In several communities in nineteenth- and early twentieth-century Britain
conservative and Conservative notions of local 'place' and 'local patriotism'
prevailed. These communities ranged from modern industrial towns such
as Blackburn, Bolton and Wolverhampton, to traditional farming villages in
Shropshire and Essex.[64] They tended to be dominated by (often large) paternalistic Conservative industrialists or landed gentry and aristocracy who owed
allegiance to established religion. These ruling groups and their subordinates
enjoyed a strong and immediate presence in both the work-place and the life of
the community. They were particularly important in setting, 'from above', the
culture, tone and style of their particular 'locales'. In many cases popular deference was expected in return for 'the gift' of employer and/or landed paternalism. Support for established religion was frequently combined with opposition
to dissenters and Roman Catholics, especially immigrant Catholics. However,
it is not my purpose here to incorporate the aspect of religious divisions and
conflicts into my examination of the politics of a sense of 'local place'.[65]

It is the case that the literature also reveals some examples of paternalism
and attachment to mainstream religion on the part of Liberal employers. They
too sought to 'rule' their local communities 'from above'.[66] However, in the
majority of cases radical notions of 'local place' were set within very different
social and cultural contexts than those of their Conservative counterparts. For
example, the radical locale was frequently characterised by the strong presence
and influence not only of fully-fledged proletarians, but also of intermediate
strata, especially 'producerist' artisans and skilled workers and the more independent–minded and progressive among the 'middling sort' of people– shop-

keepers, booksellers, publicans, some (mainly small) employers, professionals and the like– who formed a cushion between the top and bottom social layers. Moreover, these groups joined together to form political and other alliances and coalitions across the class structure. They created cultures, often rooted in respectability, educational improvement, the 'rights of man', temperance and religious dissent, which owed much to the notions of independence and self-help (both individual and collective in character) and little or nothing to paternalism, deference and direction 'from above'. These independent and radical cultures, prevailed in many quarrying and mining communities in north and south Wales, the cotton centres of Burnley and Nelson in England, in parts of London and the 'great manufacturing centres' in England, and in mid-nineteenth century Edinburgh, and areas of Glasgow, Aberdeen and elsewhere in Scotland.[67]

Ballachulish also conformed to this type of radical 'place'. The reader's attention has thus been drawn to the importance in the quarrymen's lives of the dissenting Free Church – 'locked out of the corridors of power' and adopting a predominantly critical and radical stance towards 'the status quo and to the dominant institutions of Scottish society'[68] – and of respectability, independence, educational improvement and temperance. I have also described the development, during the course of the disputes, of a strong and highly successful local alliance between, on the one hand, the increasingly determined and radical quarrymen and, on the other, Grant and his fellow middle-class progressives and Liberals, drawn mainly from the ranks of professionals but also including some sympathetic employers. Their combined radical and egalitarian definitions of 'Highlandism', 'Scottishness' and 'Britishness', including respect for the 'popular touch' of the monarchy, stood in marked opposition to organic, hierarchical and paternalist/deferential Scottish Tory notions of 'Highlandism' and 'Balmorality'.[69] In addition, the aggressive and hostile stance adopted by the company during the disputes was a significant factor in the generation of popular radicalism.

The latter, of course, manifested itself not only in relation to the perceived interests of the local community, but also with respect to the interests and actions of the quarrymen within the work-place. We have seen that in the course of conducting and legitimising their struggles against the company the quarrymen not only appealed to customary rights and practices, but also developed new goals and patterns of behaviour. As noted above, the latter manifested themselves most clearly in the formation of the trade union, the demands for union recognition and institutionalised collective bargaining and the emergence of a group of able labour leaders. Prominent in the work of the Medical Committee, Donald McMillan, Alexander McClaren , Angus Clark and James and Alexander McTaggart, also took an active part in the trade union. McClaren, fluent in English and Gaelic, a freemason and president of the local Liberal Association, had the courage to rebuke the 'laird of Poltalloch' for the company's 'tyranny' in dismissing Grant. 'Sir', declared McClaren directly to Colonel Malcolm, 'this action is not like the conduct of intellectual men but more like the petty spitefulness of a gang of schoolboys.' McClaren, a future leader of the crofters' union established by Grant, was, along with other labour leaders, targeted for eviction from his home.[70] Angus Clark, Secretary of the Medical Committee and Grant's future brother-in-law, played a prominent part in the campaign to raise funds for Grant's law suits against the company. Later in life he became a successful quarry owner, President of the Gaelic Society of London, founder member and first President of the Highland Club in London, a committee member of Grant's Highland Development League, and a founder member of both the National Party of Scotland and the Scottish National Party.[71] As Grant observed, the quarrymen thus had amongst themselves, 'many men possessed of good brains and quite capable of wisely advising them'.[72]

Most of these leaders and the quarrymen were committed to the Liberal cause. Notwithstanding some support among the quarrymen for tariff protection for their industry in the face of decline and mounting competition, most seemingly shared Grant's beliefs that protection was 'a doubtful remedy' (only a 'small' amount of slates being imported from abroad in relation to the total quarried nationally) and that progressive Liberalism offered the best hope for the advancement of both the working classes and the wider society. Attention was drawn to Liberalism's support for trade unionism, conciliation and arbitration and the belief that the demonstrable advantages of free trade, and especially that of the 'cheap loaf', greatly outweighed the asserted and unproven benefits of protection.[73] Moreover, as seen in Keir Hardie's welcome presence in Ballachulish and Grant's Liberal leanings towards socialism and his friendship with socialists, including William Stewart ('Gavroche') of the Labour Leader, this was a flexible and capacious form of Progressivism, capable, as argued by Knox for Scotland and Howell, Thane, Biagini and Reid for England, of embracing a wide range of radicals, including many members of the Labour Party and some socialists.[74]

In sum, alongside their attachments to custom and local community, there was also a growing consciousness among the Ballachulish quarrymen that they were also organised workers, part of a wider labour community and movement, informed by keen senses of class grievances, pride and the search for social justice. The case of Ballachulish thus offers support for Mike Savage's claim that, 'class formation is a spatial process, in which local identities and class identities can merge and mingle together'.[75]

My study of Ballachulish also casts some light on the general thesis that the existence of particularly deep and enduring working-class divisions (around skill, respectability, ethnicity and religion) in Scotland, created a weaker and less developed labour movement than in England.[76] While taking due cognisance of the limitations and weaknesses of 'the movement' in England, it is important to note that during my period both mass or 'new' trade unionism and Labour politics made far more headway in England than in Scotland. Moreover, and once again taking into account the serious problems faced by the labour movement in establishing a significant presence in rural areas nationally, there is no doubt that, outside of the coalfields, the Scottish labour movement was particularly weak in the Highlands and other rural areas.[77] As reflected in the late arrival of its quarrying trade unionism, the continuing rule of Liberalism and the seemingly non-existent presence of Labour and socialist politics locally, the case of Ballachulish provides further evidence to support the case of Scottish, and especially Highland, absolute and relative weakness.

However, when considered in its entirety, the Ballachulish evidence suggests that this conclusion of weakness must be qualified in important ways. For example, we have clearly seen that while arriving 'late', trade unionism developed very rapidly among not only the 'skilled' but also the whole of the quarrying labour force in Ballachulish. (This was also the case in Easedale and elsewhere among quarriers in the Highlands and Islands.) The transformation from non-unionism to a strong union presence and collective bargaining conducted by able labour leaders within the space of three years was remarkable by any standard of organised labour's development. Furthermore, the homogeneity of the local community and the very close correspondence between, on the one hand, work and, on the other, family and community, effectively undermined the potential for the development of serious cultural and other divisions among the quarrymen and their families. There is also evidence of growing political awareness and tactical sophistication, For example, in their support for Ainsworth and their opposition to Stewart in the 1903 by-election, the Ballachulish quarrymen, acting as both workers and members of the local community, were seeking to 'reward their friends' and 'punish their enemies'. Although especially marked in the Highlands, the weakness of the Left politically in this period was a Scottish and national rather than a purely local or rural phenomenon.[78]

Lastly, the Ballachulish evidence concerning worker consciousness and the fortunes of the labour movement acts as a useful reminder that there is no automatic reason why those industrial workers living and working in remote rural areas should 'naturally' be more 'backward' or 'deferential' than those urban workers situated more centrally. For we have seen that revealed patterns of behaviour and consciousness are heavily shaped by the specific historical contexts in which they arise – the nature of the local community, the workplace, and the attitudes and behaviour of the key participants constituting key objects of study – and the ebb and flow of events over time. The evidence also invites us more actively and extensively than in the past to explore the engagements between custom and conflict, and change and continuity, among and within a wide range of remote communities in Britain.

Third, the Ballachulish experience lends itself to a similarly cautious and qualified conclusion in relation to a further purported 'peculiarity' of Scotland capitalism – that trade union weakness owed much to employers who were more united, more anti-union and more successful in their pursuit of the 'open shop' than the majority of their counterparts in England.[79] On the one hand, we have seen that the Ballachulish Quarries Company Limited fully conformed to the picture of the ruthless Scottish capitalist employer. The company was de-termined to maximise its profits, power and control, to tolerate no interference and opposition from a 'third-party' – whether Grant, the Medical Committee, the union or the community – and to minimise labour and other costs. Local feelings and traditions and general issues of morality and fairness were deemed, at best, to be secondary to the 'rational' pursuit of its own self-interest. There was simply no place for 'custom' in the company's 'modern'/ 'entrepreneurial' view of the world. On the other hand, one of the most significant aspects of the Ballachulish disputes was the perceived weakness and, in important re-spects, *defeat* of capitalist 'political economy' at the hands of customary 'moral economy'. After all, the first dispute resulted in an unqualified success for the quarrymen, Grant and their customary supporters, and the second in a com-promise. While adverse market conditions and entrepreneurial failures were primarily responsible for the demise of the company in 1907, nevertheless the continuing independence and struggles of the quarrymen against managerial 'dictation' also constituted important contributory factors. Significantly, Grant and the quarrymen drew support from local and regional employers, including slate quarrying employers, who were far more attuned to the importance of 'lo-cal ways' and the issues of social stability, harmony and mutuality in relation-ships between workers and employers, than was the 'outsider' Ballachulish Slate Quarries Company Limited single-mindedly pursuing its 'selfish' aims. In sum, the events at Ballachulish demonstrate the continuing and substantial power of 'custom' to 'the people' in a modern industrial-capitalist context.

In practice, therefore, the Ballachulish case was far more complex, far more evenly contested and involved much greater elements of compromise and con-cession on the part of the employer, than a one-dimensional and static portrayal of united and successful anti-union Scottish employers would suggest. To argue in this way is to support the balanced conclusions of Arthur McIvor in relation to the 'peculiarities' debate. Many Scottish, and especially Clydeside, employers undoubtedly displayed militantly anti-union *attitudes*, but *in practice* their behaviour and industrial relations outcomes were often constrained and significantly modified by workplace struggles, the power of trade unionism, market conditions and so on. Pragmatism could overshadow ideology to promote, at least in some instances, trade union recognition and collective bargaining rather than widespread and sustained non-unionism of the north- American kind.[80]

Fourth, my study of Ballachulish highlights the importance of not only working-class, but also progressive middle-class leaders to the development of radical movements. As such, I endorse the conclusions reached by those historians, such as Knox for Scotland and Reid and Biagini for England, concerning the key role played by middle- and working-class 'respectables' and 'improvers' in the development of radical Liberalism nationally.[81] These middle-class 'friends of the people' were, in many cases, also vital to the development of Chartism and socialism.[82] In terms of Ballachulish, I have drawn the reader's attention at various points to the nature and importance of the cultural and political bonds and alliances developed between the quarrymen and Grant, McMurchy, and other local members of the progressive middle class, and the widespread nature of support for their cause, including many middle-class people. My final task in this chapter is further to illustrate and substantiate my case with reference to the specific case study of one of the key protagonists in the disputes: Dr. Grant.

As briefly noted in the Introduction and in Chapter Two, Lachlan Grant, a 'local' and 'true Highlander', developed a wide-ranging and impressive radical curriculum vitae .[83] As revealed especially in his press cuttings, he was active in several discrete, but closely related, kinds of public activity. I have already documented his overriding commitments to 'the land of the Gael', 'the preservation of everything Celtic and national', and his pursuit of many Gaelic cultural and sporting activities. Within this overarching framework, he became a hard-working, well respected and radical doctor, an advocate of educational and land reform, a Justice of the Peace, and an 'advanced' Progressive or Liberal who prized reasoned scrutiny and professionalism, public responsibility and service and the causes of diversity and humanity over those of the utilitarian maximisation of individual self-interest and gain and social uniformity and regimentation.

At the time of the first dispute Grant's medical record was already impressive. He gained prizes during his years as a medical student at the Universities of Glasgow and Edinburgh, and graduated with distinction from the latter in the mid 1890s. Having visited hospitals in the USA and Canada, he returned to Scotland and was appointed assistant to a Dr. McCalman in Oban. He was subsequently successful, at the age of 25, in his application for the post of Medical Officer to the Gesto Hospital on the Isle of Skye. In 1900 he applied, and was 'unanimously chosen', for the vacant post of Medical Officer for the Parish Council District of Ballachulish. Thus Grant was able to return 'home', both to comfort his recently widowed mother and devote his services to the quarrymen and the local community.[84] Beyond the mid-1900s, Grant more than fulfilled the promise of his early career. For example, he wrote scholarly medical articles for the Lancet and the British Medical Journal, became a life Member of the Psychological Association of Great Britain and Ireland, a Fellow of the Royalty Faculty of Physicians and Surgeons, Glasgow, bacteriologist to Argyll County Council and Consulting Medical Officer to British Aluminium, Kinlochleven.[85]

As a medical man with 'intimate knowledge of the conditions of life in the Gaelic-speaking parts of Scotland' (the Lancet [86]) and a strong social conscience, Grant advocated and publicised, in his writings and speeches, the benefits of a healthy balance between mental and physical activity, legislation and compulsory inspection to improve sanitary and housing conditions, the 'proper feeding' of schoolchildren and their regular and compulsory medical inspection, including hearing and eye tests. He was also strongly in favour of the replacement of the system of the individual payment of fees for medical attendance with 'a comprehensive scheme of medical aid constructed on a basis similar to that of the rate-supported fever hospitals or lunatic asylums'. While the former, market-based, system was demonstrably inefficient, inadequate and uneven in both its funding and coverage, and while 'spasmodic charity' was 'wrong … behind the times and unworthy of a self-respecting commonsense people', the introduction of the state-based system would result in improved efficiency, health and a more comprehensive and socially-just system. In Grant's view, the efficiency and adequacy of medical treatment 'should not depend on the wealth or poverty of a district; it was a question of general efficiency throughout the country', and the 'well-to-do sections of the country should pay for the poorer parts'. For in the Highlands and elsewhere 'every family should be entitled to medical attendance as a simple right of citizenship'.[87] Furthermore, under the state system 'good medical men could then be had to attend the more remote parts of the Highlands without any wish of leading a starvation existence'. For Grant, sections of the Scottish press and the medical journals nationally were extremely critical of the poor financial reward of many Highland doctors and the 'harsh' and 'autocratic' treatment 'they have been subjected to by Local Boards'.[88] Grant further proposed that all hospitals, infirmaries and nursing homes should progressively be placed under local authority control.[89]

Grant also saw an increased role for the state, combined with education and a developing sense of common purpose and commitment to the public good, as crucial elements in a strategy designed effectively to tackle the wider problems of the Highlands. As against the common, easy, and mistaken resort to emigration – designed merely to empty the Highlands of their best resource, the people – Grant proposed land nationalisation (with ample compensation), improved access to the land for smallholders, the formation of a crofters' union and state-supported development of natural resources and industries (such as forestry, farming and fishing).[90] The more widespread development of a system of education designed to produce not 'machines all of the same pattern' but 'to draw out the best' in children and 'the flowering and development of the heart', would create a more civilized and large-hearted citizenry– committed to the notions of 'common humanity', 'comradeship' and the 'universal spirit of friendship and brotherhood between man and man'. This was seen as a necessary guarantee of future prosperity and peace, not only in the Highlands, but also nationally and internationally. These were the values that the Ballachulish Public School and Grant, McMurchy and others connected with it, were seeking to instil into the local children in order to make them not only able, healthy and efficient, but also generous, co-operative, altruistic and idealistic, 'a credit to their race'.[91]

In these various ways Grant expressed his commitment to an advanced form of Liberalism, to a Progressivism which, as at the national level, incorporated an increasingly collectivist dimension into a political and moral philosophy traditionally rooted in voluntarism, independence and individual freedom and responsibility. In both Ballachulish and nationally many Liberals and socialists shared the belief that unbridled individualism and the single-minded pursuit of self-interest, however 'rational', would no longer secure 'the public good', rooted in continued and accelerated economic growth, restored national efficiency, social harmony and peace. Rather, a new form of 'collectivist idealism', harnessed to, rather than a substitute for, individual freedom, had become the required order of the day.[92] Under the broad reforming umbrella of Progressivism, Grant became an increasingly active figure in Argyllshire Liberalism. By 1909 he had become President of the Argyllshire Liberal Council and a tireless advocate and campaigner for Ainsworth, the sitting Liberal MP.[93] He had also come to symbolise what Harold Perkin has termed 'The Rise of Professional Society' – the growing prominence in British society of middle-class professionals committed to expertise, selection by merit and an enhanced role for a reforming state to promote a more regulated, efficient and just society. This was in marked contrast to the dominance of Victorian society by the 'entrepreneurial ideal', as reflected, above all, in the pursuit of private interest and the identification of the private with the public good by self-made men.[94]

Finally, it was not only as a respected professional and social reformer that Grant attracted the support of the local community. For he was also an extremely warm, likeable and helpful man. According to the *Highland News*, he was 'a young man of exceptional ability and of the highest personal character'.[95] The *Oban Telegragh and Express* likewise saw him as 'a most admirable young man', capable of filling 'a much higher position than local doctor at Ballachul-ish … but he loves the place, and is liked by and likes the men'. 'No dema-gogue or firebrand', he was nevertheless motivated by a strong sense of right and wrong.[96]

In sum, both as an able, articulate and wronged professional and an active, likeable and well-respected individual and member of the community Grant was a charismatic local figure and leader. As a result there was a very strong chance that his plight and cause would attract considerable sympathy and sup-port. But development of the latter was neither an inevitable nor a purely spon-taneous matter. The building of a movement of support for the doctor required much intellectual and practical time, effort and ability on the part of Grant himself and his professional and other friends and allies. It necessitated pur-posive agency, as manifested especially in organisational ability and leadership skills. Furthermore, we must not forget that the key role over the two disputes as a whole was played by those at the very core of activity, the quarrymen, and their leaders. The latter, 'organic intellectuals',[97] emerged from the quarrying workforce itself. As such, they had a practical and intimate connexion with 'the men', their families, their traditions and their aspirations. Skilled organisers, they were adept at articulating and practically advancing their constituents' per-ceived interests, grievances and aims. They were also democratic rather than bureaucratic leaders: their authority derived from a dialogue with, and their election by, the quarrymen and by votes cast at the mass meetings rather than from appointment to positions within a hierarchical chain of command.[98] They successfully developed close ties with Grant and other middle-class leaders. In the absence of this *combined*, inter-class leadership, it is, of course, extremely doubtful whether the quarrymen and Grant would have achieved the successes they did.

The nature and importance of cross-class leadership in the Ballachulish dis-putes invites us to consider its significance for the much neglected question of social-movement leadership in general.[99] It also invites us to widen our terms of reference further in order to examine the overall implications of my case study for the study of social movements and social movement theory. I undertake these tasks in the fourth and final chapter.

Chapter Four
Ballachulish and the Study of Social Movements

The movements which developed around the disputes at Ballachulish may usefully be set within the wider context of, and in turn cast some new light upon, the historical and sociological study of social protest movements. Particular relevance and interest reside in the following: the issues of rationality, spontaneity, organisation and leadership; the role of industrial workers, and particularly 'skilled' and independent-minded workmen, in rural protest movements; and the case to be made for a holistic and 'social choice' approach in preference to that of resource mobilization and rational choice.

The issue of 'rationality' can be properly addressed only when set within the context of recent trends in the study of social movements. The decades of the 1970s and 1980s witnessed the declining influence of 'collective behaviour' approaches to social movements and the rise to dominance, especially within the USA, of the 'resource-mobilization' paradigm.[1] Those adhering to the former had put most of their energies into descriptions and explanations of the grievances underpinning social movements. While an attempt was made to locate the socio-structural roots or 'strains' underlying these grievances, it was widely assumed that psychological factors, and especially 'irrational' feelings of 'panic', 'disturbance', 'anxiety, fantasy, hostility' and 'paranoia' were to the fore.[2] Much time and effort was spent in analysing the 'spontaneous', 'fickle' and largely 'disorganized' and 'destructive' behaviour of a wide array of protesters – 'the aggressive mob' or 'rabble'; 'the residuum' or 'rags and tatters' of society; 'the hostile outbursts' of strikers, rioters and revolutionaries; and the 'conspiracy theories' of US Populists and other agrarian (and urban) radicals.[3] These protesters were often portrayed in the 'collective behaviour' literature as simple and plain folk, ill equipped to undertake what has recently been defined by Amartya Sen as the true test of rationality – the 'reasoned scrutiny' of their thoughts and actions.[4] As a corollary, they were seen to be largely incapable of locating the 'true' or 'objective' causes of their grievances. Hence they resorted to explanations based upon 'fantasy', 'panic' and 'false conspiracy', and were the 'easy' or 'passive' victims of 'manipulative' and 'self-interested' 'demagogues' and 'foreigners'.[5] It was the dual task of social scientists to put the historical and sociological records straight and, especially for those influenced by the 'struc-tural-functionalism' of Talcott Parsons, to investigate the ways in which the 'disturbance-symptoms' manifested by protesters had historically been 'han-dled and channelled' by those in authority and others 'rationally' to promote contentment, social harmony, inclusion and integration.[6] The blatant ideologi-cal and social-engineering characteristics of the Cold-War induced 'collective behaviour' project – with protest and opposition often being labelled as 'ir-rational', conformity as 'normal' and 'rational', the social-scientist as 'truly ob-jective' and the desired end of personal and social life being acceptance of and commitment to the 'common values' binding society together – provoked two major counterblasts. These were resource mobilization theory, located centrally in the United States; and the left-wing 'socialist-humanist' response of histori-ans and others scholars based in Britain and Europe, but whose influence soon spread to the USA and elsewhere.[7]

Proponents of resource mobilization theory argued that what mattered most in the study of social movements was not the socio-psychological issue of griev-ance, but 'resources, formal organisation, tactics, political opportunities', out-comes and the 'rational' weighing on the part of potential participants of the costs and benefits of involvement. They shifted the focus, at least in many so-ciological studies, from 'irrational' to 'rational' concerns and from 'the cultural' to 'the structural'.[8]

Socialist-humanist historians of social movements strongly challenged the claim that their subjects were 'irrational' or 'pathological'. For example, in *The Making of the English Working Class* (1963), Edward Thompson presented the thesis that between the end of the eighteenth century and the Reform Act of 1832, most English working people developed a reasoned and impressive form of class consciousness which combined an appeal to custom with demands for the radical transformation of English society. In a direct challenge to Neil Smelser, a prominent collective behaviour theorist and 'a colleague of Professor Talcott Parsons', Thompson presented his notion of oppositional class con-sciousness, rooted in conflict and struggle, as both developing out of the his-torical evidence (rather than issuing from his own preconceptions) and as being a rational phenomenon rather than a symptom of 'disturbance'.[9] For it was Thompson's view that, rather than being the misguided or knavish 'objects of study' of 'objective' social-scientists, his working-class subjects had fully dem-onstrated their ability to make sense of, and to apply 'reasoned scrutiny' to, their own lives and those of others and to exert their agency upon their largely unwilled structured conditions of existence. In sum, when viewed within their proper historical context of the rapid and unsettling changes associated with the period of the Industrial Revolution and the American and French Revolutions and in terms of their own value systems, ideas and norms, Thompson's working-class subjects did not merit pity or 'the condescension of posterity'. Rather they were proud, able, independent-minded and creative historical actors and agents in their own right.[10] In sum, they passed Sen's 'rationality' test.

From the 1960s onwards Thompson's emphasis upon the rationality of participants in modern popular movements was shared by a relatively small, but highly influential, grouping of left-wing historians in Britain and the USA embracing, *inter alia*, the key figures of Dorothy Thompson, George Rudé, Eric Hobsbawm, Herbert Gutman, David Montgomery and Eugene Genovese .[11] For example, contrary to the view of Gustave Le Bon, 'the founding father of modern crowd psychology', and many other conservative writers, Rudé showed that between 1730 and 1848 the protesting crowd in England and France was increasingly characterised more by its powers of reason and 'discriminating purposefulness' than its fickle, irrational, destructive and primitive behaviour.[12] More specifically, Rudé and Hobsbawm pioneeringly demonstrated that the protests by agricultural labourers and others against poor wages and the introduction of the threshing machine during the 'Swing Riots' of 1830 constituted, within the context of the period, a perfectly rational response to the decline of paternalism and 'the full triumph of rural capitalism' in the English countryside. [13] The birth and development of the nationally-based Chartist movement for political democracy and social justice during the following two decades, signalled a marked advance in the scale, organisation and sophistication of popular movements. As Dorothy Thompson observed, Chartism's predominantly forward-looking character and its 'basic belief in the possibility of success' imposed on it 'a discipline and a rationality in which it differed from earlier popular movements'. For, while it 'produced within itself older forms of demonstration and protest', yet 'these were almost always controlled by a sense of longer-term purpose than the older and more traditional forms of riot or conspiracy'.[14] Likewise, Genovese's study of slavery, Gutman's work on the slave family and a wide range of ethnic and occupational groups within the labouring population, and Montgomery's books and articles on mainly industrial workers in the post-bellum years, did much to rescue the American 'people', and especially its workers and their social movements, from traditional historical neglect and condescension. Much in the manner of what Edward Thompson showed for England, these historians clearly demonstrated the importance of slave and 'free' worker agency and reasoned preference and choice to American history. In company with their like-minded colleagues across the Atlantic, they also clearly showed that not only narrowly self-interested but also altruistic, cooperative and moral considerations and values underpinned a wide variety of popular movements.[15]

The Ballachulish evidence lends its full support to the criticisms directed by resource mobilization theorists and social-humanist historians against collective behaviourists. For example, the movements at Ballachulish were not spontaneous and disorganized.[16] While rooted in a variety of economic, social and cultural grievances, the campaigns to reinstate Grant and improve the workplace situation of the quarrymen did not arise automatically – by means of a visceral and compulsive 'stimulus-response' mechanism[17] – out of these grievances. Rather, they had to be built, planned and directed by both 'rank-and-file' participants and leaders as self-conscious, reasoning and self-activating human agents.

As such, the organization and mobilization of resources were of obvious and necessary importance to 'movement building' and the outcomes of the disputes at Ballachulish. Once the company had made public its dismissal of Grant, both the quarrymen and the doctor acted quickly and successfully to mobilize the considerable resources of the community and the workplace. They were greatly aided in their task by the small-scale and tightly-knit character of the local community, the close familial and organisational ties between work, home and community life, the large size of their 'natural' support base and the favourable opportunities for alternative sources of paid employment for men. Furthermore, they made a conscious and highly successful attempt to recruit supporters from across the entire social structure. While appealing to specific occupational, gendered and class-based groups, they enlisted support from representatives of most social strata, including employers, religious leaders, politicians and other influential members of the middle and upper classes. They demonstrated a good awareness of the importance of 'public opinion', and especially press opinion, to the success of their cause. As we have seen, they were careful to present themselves and their actions as considered, intelligent, restrained, law abiding and respectable. They resisted the temptation to react violently to provocation and so invite adverse publicity and repression. In short, they took great pains to portray themselves and be seen as rational and temperate human beings pursuing a just cause, rather than as a desperate, disorganized and mindless mob. They received their reward in their outright victory at the end of 1903 and in the compromise of 1905.

In contrast, the company neglected its public image and paid a heavy price. We have seen that it was widely portrayed as being totally insensitive to local traditions and feelings and concerned solely to ruthlessly pursue its own power and self-interest. It also suffered badly as a result of its 'outsider' status and the fact that its local representative, Maccoll, was highly unpopular. It made little or no attempt to establish a sympathetic basis of support among the locals – for example, by means of cultural and leisure-based initiatives and activities – and alienated significant elements of the propertied elite by its lack of respect for the traditions of paternalism and mutuality.

Leaders played a key role in the process of resource mobilization. As Barker, Johnson and Lavalette have reminded us, 'pure spontaneity never exists, for there are always leaders and initiators, even if many remain nameless figures who leave few traces in historical records'.[18] In support of this proposition, we have seen in Chapter Three that the local leadership, both working- and middle-class in character, played a crucial role in building and organising widespread support for Grant both locally and more widely. The elected quarrymen leaders called mass public meetings, played a major part in creating and developing a trade union, related extremely well to their constituents on the basis of mutual trust and respect and negotiated impressively with the company's representatives Yet, along with those peasant, artisan and worker leaders rescued by Rudé – as against the prevailing orthodoxy of the crowd as 'an abstract phenomenon without face or identity'[19] – the leaders at Ballachulish have for too long been lost to the historical record.

As in many other modern popular movements, the working-class leaders at Ballachulish were male – I found not a single instance of a female leader – strongly independent-minded and recruited from the ranks of the more skilled and regularly employed. This is not to argue that women, the non-skilled and the casual were incapable of organisation and leadership, but it is to suggest that local employment, community and family structures and dominant values and norms worked against their involvement at the leadership level, as opposed to a supporting role. As we have seen, work in the dominant local industry, slate quarrying, was traditionally regular and long term in character. In addition it was male and family dominated, with about half the jobs being seen as 'skilled' – the preserve of predominantly proud, respectable and articulate autonomous workmen. Many of the latter were also prominent and respected figures in the religious, sporting, military and educational life of the community. In many ways, therefore, it was entirely predictable that they would act as the main leaders and spokespersons during the disputes. Women, as observed earlier, were widely expected to perform household duties and offer support to their male partners, dependants and relatives in times of strife. This was consistent with the established pattern of gender relations in working-class families. It is also one of the main reasons why women had usually occupied secondary and supportive, but not passive or totally dependent, roles in those nineteenth-century popular protest movements in which they were involved.[20]

As we have observed, the quarrymen leaders at Ballachulish were joined by, and enjoyed good relations with, middle-class leaders. The latter were mainly professional in character. This was predictable in view of Grant's professional standing and his close working relations and friendships with other doctors and with similarly minded educators, ministers of religion and others within the professional ranks. However, it is also indicative of a wider pattern of involvement of 'the middling sort' and alliances between mainly middle-class and upper-working class men, in numerous progressive popular movements throughout the nineteenth and early twentieth centuries. These ranged from Chartism in localities such as Birmingham, Edinburgh and parts of London (where the social divide between the top and bottom groups was softened by a strong middle-class presence), to mid- and late-Victorian and Edwardian radical-Liberal and socialist organisations and, albeit in far more limited and uneven ways, to areas and instances of rural protest.[21] Furthermore, many of the 'middling sort' involved in, or sympathetic to, popular movements enjoyed the relative independence, freedom and autonomy conferred on them by their occupations as publicans, shopkeepers, newsagents, coffee-house keepers, booksellers, dissenting ministers, professional men and some skilled and craft workers. They were far less directly and immediately 'in the boss's eye' and so vulnerable to victimisation and dismissal, as many within the working class. They also enjoyed levels of income and stability and regularity of employment which enabled them, in contrast to many non-skilled and casual workers, to have the time and opportunity to do more than constantly eke out a living.[22] We have seen that one of the major reasons why the Grant case occasioned so much interest in the press was because it highlighted the uncommon vulnerability and dependence of a middle-class professional man upon the wishes of his employer.

In support of the socialist-humanist case, and in opposition to *both* classical collective behaviourism and the dominant resource mobilization approach rooted in rational choice theory,[23] the Ballachulish case also clearly shows that, within historically- and socially-situated terms of reference, it was perfectly rational or 'natural' for the individual to join others in social movements rather than to opt out of collective action and to 'free ride' on the backs of protesting others. Indeed, in view of the strength and cohesion of the local community at Ballachulish, and the fact that individuals and families were so deeply embedded in it, the decision to 'free ride' would have been seen as irrational, as being against 'commonsense'. For it would have entailed major costs, such as rejection and ostracism by family, friends and the community as a whole. To be sure, the quarrymen fully realised that involvement in collective action also carried potential and actual costs in terms of employment, wages and eviction from their homes. However, these risks and costs were deemed to be highly preferential to non involvement, and in all probability necessary to the successful achievement of both individual and collective goals. In the event, of course, their choices and calculations turned out to be largely justified.

Thus the Ballachulish case usefully reminds us that people are deeply embedded within social structures, practices, norms and values at particular points in and over time, and that their thoughts and actions are informed by complex and multiple factors. As such, the historically constituted subject must form the starting point of historical and sociological analysis rather than the *a priori*, free-floating, narrow and deterministic abstraction of 'rational economic man' beloved of rational-choice and many resource-mobilization theorists alike.[24]

In moving to a more concrete level, the Ballachulish experience holds considerable significance for the study of an important, but much neglected, area of historical research: the role of industrial workers in rural protest movements. My case study fully reveals the key importance of such industrial workers, and especially 'skilled' and in many ways independent and autonomous workers, to the development of one such rurally-based protest movement at a particular moment in time. In a community so heavily dependent upon a single industry, it would, of course, be surprising if the skilled quarrymen had not been at the very centre of the Ballachulish disputes. However, it transpired that their radical influence was by no means confined to their home village. For those Ballachulish quarrymen who left the quarries from 1907 onwards to take up employment, whether temporary or permanent, at the aluminium works at Kinlochleven, were undoubtedly involved in attempts to organise the latter along the lines of mass 'new unionism'. This was seen most prominently in the early autumn of 1910 when the aluminium plant was brought to a standstill by a strike involving the vast majority of the workforce of between seven and eight hundred men, including migrants from the Ballachulish quarries. The dispute revolved centrally, as in the earlier Ballachulish disputes, around control issues. However, this time it was not the dismissal of a doctor but rather the alleged victimisation and the dismissal of two local trade-union officials of a branch of the National Union of Gasworkers and General Labourers, 'formed in the town some months ago', that triggered the conflict. The company had 'no intention of being dictated to by any trade union as to how they should carry on their business'. However, in the face of mass solidarity on the part of the largely Gaelic-speaking workforce, the company backed down. Union recognition and negotiation ensued.[25]

'Hidden from history', the strike at Kinlochleven demonstrates the ways in which the unionised Ballachulish quarrymen helped to spread the labour-movement faith to another remote, but hardly economically backward, part of rural Scotland. As members of a close community and with past experience of regular employment, they had acquired the trade union habit largely denied to the army of predominantly unskilled, casual and itinerant navvies of Patrick MacGill's acquaintance. However, the Kinlochleven strike provided a good illustration not only of the ways in which independent-minded industrial workers transmitted the values and practices of trade unionism, but also of the manner in which a new workforce, consisting of both 'old hands' and men new to the rigours of factory production, could very rapidly work together to promote organised labour's cause. For the aluminium workforce was made up not only of quarrymen from Ballachulish, but also some of those 'rough' labourers previously employed alongside MacGill and 'Moleskin Joe' and rural migrants from Skye and other Scottish Islands.[26] The very fact that this new and heterogeneous labour force could act with such immediate and impressive unity in 1910 acts as a caution against the adoption of the stereotype that unskilled and rural workers and migrants were necessarily and fixedly poor social-movement, and especially labour-movement, material. In truth, whether or not such people participated in social movements depended upon the precise historical context, the nature and mix of the personnel involved, their traditions, values, ideas and habits and their relations with other workers, employers and the state.

Thus the cases of Ballachulish and Kinlochleven demonstrate the importance of developing a future Scottish labour and social history research agenda in which it is not only the activities of crofters, coalminers and urban workers that command attention. The more intensive and extensive examination of remote rural locations in the Highlands and elsewhere in Scotland may well bring to light other 'hidden' disputes in which the presence of industrial workers and their relations with other members of their local communities were of crucial importance.

There are also implications for the national picture and the national research agenda. For the importance of industrial workers in Ballachulish to the spread of radical ideas and practices was mirrored at the national level. For example, railway workers, coal miners, skilled craftsmen and artisans and their allies within 'the middling sort', provided important 'outside' inspiration, leadership and support to several campaigns to organise farm workers, both industrially and politically. These campaigns ranged from 'The Revolt of the Field' in the 1870s, the revival and second phase of agricultural trade unionism, centred upon East Anglia, from the end of the nineteenth century to the First World War and beyond, and attempts to organise farm servants in East Lothian and elsewhere in Lowland Scotland from 1900 to 1939.[27] As observed by Howkins for East Anglia, Mansfield for Shropshire and Cranstoun and Anthony for East Lothian, these 'outsiders' were political radicals and trade unionists who usefully brought their organisational and ideological skills to bear upon an agricultural workforce which in many cases was not especially noted for its strong labour-movement traditions and allegiances.[28] Simultaneously, however, these authors are careful to point out that the agricultural workforce was far less uniformly unskilled, deferential and fatalistic than 'the stereotype of the British farm worker' would suggest.[29] As in the case of Ballachulish, questions concerning the presence and influence of industrial workers upon the fortunes of the labour- and wider social movements, and their relations with other workers and social strata within the British countryside have for far too long been totally neglected or insufficiently pursued. They merit urgent and detailed scholarly attention.

In turning to a more concentrated examination of the question of methodology, the case of Ballachulish suggests that a holistic approach, based upon social choice theory, constitutes a more fruitful approach to the study of social movements, and especially popular forms of social protest, than the approaches of either the collective behaviourists or the resource mobilization theorists. I have already answered the charge made by the former that social-movement participants are irrational. As noted above, resource mobilization theorists have usefully drawn our attention to the concrete and important issues of the organisation of material and ideological resources and political opportunities and conditions facing social movements. However, and notwithstanding some attempts to pay more attention to the social psychology of those involved in social movements, most practitioners of resource mobilization theory continue to weigh their accounts far too heavily in favour of resources at the expense of grievances, values and ideologies. As such their approach is too selective and partial, being too excessively 'structural' and too insufficiently 'cultural' in character.[30]

For example, the mobilization of resources was an important aspect of the Ballachulish disputes, but it was only one of many significant features. I have argued strongly throughout this study that it is impossible fully to understand and explain the events at Ballachulish without reference to the grievances expressed by the participants. We have observed that these grievances revolved centrally around different and conflicting notions of rationality, as expressed most acutely in the running battle between the customary 'moral economy' of the quarrymen and their supporters and the 'entrepreneurialism' of the company. In the manner of 'new social movement' approaches, I have attempted both to explore grievances as being rational, in opposition to many collective behaviourists, and, in contrast to resource mobilization theorists, to pay due attention not only to the ways in which social movements are organised, but also the reasons why they take place.[31]

I have also demonstrated that the grievances and conflicts at Ballachulish were not confined to either the 'structural' or the 'cultural' aspects of life: they pervaded material existence as well as traditions, ideas, value systems and norms. A non-reductionist exploration of the engagements and levels of correspondence between 'structure' and 'culture' has been at the core of my investigation. My aim, shared with many of the 'new social movement' scholars, has been to 'explain meanings linked to structural factors behind a collective action'.[32]

Moreover, my exploration has been set within a particular context and sequence of events. For explorations of 'structure' and 'culture' are largely empty of *historical* meaning unless related to time, place and change and continuity over time. As Ron Eyerman and Andrew Jamison have written, 'Social movements express shifts in the consciousness of actors as they are articulated in their interactions between activists and their opposition(s) in historically situated … contexts'.[33] My attempt to integrate into my analytical framework the issues of 'structure', 'culture', time, place, chronology and human agency may lack something in terms of theoretical precision and tidiness, but it has hopefully enabled us to understand and explain both 'how structural change is transformed into collective action'[34] and the patterned, but complex and contingent, nature of the disputes at Ballachulish.

I wish, finally, to return to the important matter of the *kind* of consciousness, of rationality, displayed by the quarrymen. As Myra Marx Ferree has maintained, while formally eschewing a concern with grievances and the social psychology of participants, nevertheless most practitioners of resource mobilization theory have 'imported' the key tenets of the microeconomic theory of rational choice (Mancur Olson's notion of the 'free-rider' and the view that 'individuals will always act to maximize their personal benefits and reduce their costs') into their studies of social movements.[35] As Ferree further argues, this imported and assumed view of rationality constitutes 'a Trojan horse' on the grounds that it 'is not a testable proposition' ('since the theory offers no rules for measuring preferences independent of the choices made'), it does not take into account the socially-embedded nature of human beings and their complex and changing motivations and that it neglects 'value differences and conflicts'.[36] Furthermore, my study of Ballachulish has demonstrated the deeply flawed empirical character of rational choice theory. We have seen that rationality at Ballachulish was contested rather than consensual, was by no means concerned *exclusively* with the maximisation of self-interest, and, as such, was not of a single type.

This brings me to the issue of social choice theory. The latter, 'pioneeringly formulated in its modern form' by the economist, Kenneth Arrow, counts among its most distinguished practitioners, the economist and philosopher, Amartya Sen. As noted in the Introduction to this study, social choice theory, as expressed by Sen, presents a fundamental critique of rational choice theory. The latter is seen as being unduly narrow, exclusive, essentialist, formulaic, empirically flawed, deterministic and contradictory. As Sen writes,

The belief that the pursuit of some prespecified aims must be taken to represent the essence of rationality is disputed, and this includes challenging the allegedly peerless status of self-interest as the exclusive navigator of rational behavior ... the insistence on the pursuit of self-interest as an inescapable necessity for rationality subverts the 'self' as a free, reasoning being, by overlooking the freedom to reason about what one should pursue ... even as it privileges self-interest, it also undermines self-reasoning ... our ability to reason and undertake reasoned scrutiny.[37]

Sen proceeds to offer an alternative, social-choice, view of rationality, one rooted in 'true' freedom and rationality, in which people, both as individuals and members of society, exercise their powers of agency, their genuine 'freedom to reason about' the range of preferences and choices concerning their own welfare and interests and those of the wider society.[38] Sen defines the 'central question' of social choice theory as being, 'How can it be possible to arrive at cogent aggregate judgments about the society ... given the diversity of preferences, concerns, and predicaments of the different individuals *within* society?' In response, Sen argues that social choice theory offers the possibility to 'understand the demands of rational decisions for a society when all members of the society have the freedom to participate, directly or indirectly, in the decisional process, and this involves respect for their voice, influence and rights'.[39]

Thus, in contrast to rational choice theory, social choice theory places the active, thinking individual, scrutinising a range of options in the light of his or her social situation, values and preferences, at the centre of its analysis. As such it is far more flexible and sensitive to complexity, contestation, historical context and continuity and change than rational choice theory. For example, it allows for the possibility that people's observed thoughts and actions may be underpinned by a complex and contingent array of factors – involving a possible mixture of co-operative, competitive, self-interested and altruistic motivations – rather than exclusively by self-interest.

Of manifest importance to those theoretically and practically concerned with *policy* matters, nevertheless social choice theory holds out great potential importance and relevance for historical study. British historians, largely wedded to an empirical tradition heavily resistant to social theory, have remained unaware of this potential. Yet the case of Ballachulish, however small in scale and limited in importance, demonstrates this potential. For what we have observed at Ballachulish is a practical expression of social choice theory – of how individuals living in a particular community at a particular point in time, scrutinised past and present experiences to make reasoned decisions about the private and public good. The key decision reached by the quarrymen, of course, was that both their own and the wider public interest would be better served by continuing abidance by the largely co-operative and community-based tenets of 'moral economy' and customary practice than by an embrace of the company's rational-choice philosophy of competition, individualism and self-interest. Furthermore, this decision was reached on the basis of a high degree of direct, but highly gendered, participation in the democratic decision-making forums of the mass meeting and elections for members of the Medical Committee and trade-union representatives. The small size and highly integrated character of the local community greatly facilitated the democratic process of decision making.

The quarrymen's 'customary' perspective, while primarily local in character, also reflected their outlook on the wider world. This perspective is of continuing interest to historians and other scholars because it reveals the existence of alternative minority traditions, albeit often forgotten and defeated, in the face of the seemingly inexorable triumph of 'modernization', of a market-based society of the self-interested type. In the future historians and sociologists may wish to set the insights of social-choice theory into engagement with the experiences of those communities, predominantly small-scale in character, in which, in the manner of Ballachulish, moral-economic and customary views of the world are in conflict with the 'modernizing' impulse of self-interest.

This chapter has described the ways in which my specific study of Ballachulish contributes to the wider study of social movements and the stimulus it hopefully provides to the investigation of new and neglected areas of historical and sociological research. Above all, perhaps, it has sought to indicate some of the ways and areas in which the largely abstract concerns of social theorists and the more empirical interests of historians may productively be brought together to advance the study of social movements.

Afterword

The commencement of quarrying operations by the new company, the Balla-chulish Quarries Limited, in January 1908, signalled new hope for the workforce and the community. As briefly observed at the end of Chapter Two, the company sought both to restore good relations with the quarrymen and to modernise production methods in the quarries. It started life with a capital of £12,000 in £1 shares. The chair was a Mr Leyland, a landowner in Northumberland, with a keen interest in the welfare of Ballachulish as a result, according to the *Oban Times*, of being a 'life-long friend of the late Sir George de la Poer Beresford and Lady Beresford, and Captain and Mrs. Beresford Drummond'. Messers Kemp and Mitchell of 'one of the largest firms of slate merchants in Scotland', were also involved in the new company.[1]

As an indication of their 'good faith', the directors of the company met with the men's representatives early in the New Year and came to an 'amicable' ar-rangement concerning the 'terms and conditions of work'. The crew-based contract system would continue, monthly payments would prevail and fixed wages were arranged 'on failure of contracts'.[2] Work started at the end of Janu-ary. Three months later the *Oban Times* commended the new company on its 'liberality' and 'enterprise'. For, 'in depressed times like the present', the com-pany had made a successful attempt to keep on 'the full complement of men' (around three hundred in total), had produced 'large quantities of slates ... of the finest quality' and was arranging 'to put in new machinery of the most up-to-date type'.[3]

However, by the mid-summer of 1909 it appeared that renewed hope and promise of the previous year would founder on the familiar rock of the in-dustry's continuing, in fact accelerating, decline. In August the chronically de-pressed demand for slates, continuing cut-throat competition among producers and the surplus stock of slates at Ballachulish, moved the company to propose a reduction in the labour force. The men reacted by condemning 'overproduc-tion' and holding out for full employment. The quarries were once again closed and the quarrymen resorted to the familiar tactic of seeking work elsewhere, this time at the aluminium works in Kinlochleven.[4] Nevertheless, in marked contrast to the recent past, and as a further indication of the company's wish to promote a more cooperative and consensual atmosphere within the workplace, it agreed to refer the dispute to arbitration. The company also accepted the men's demand that the existing stock of slates be loaded by local quarriers and that the 'outside men' be withdrawn.[5] The process of arbitration took place in Glasgow. It involved two representatives each from the ranks of the company and the men and a Board of Trade representative, and resulted in a compromise solution. While the company retained the right to have total control over hiring and firing, some concessions were made to the men concerning wage and employment levels.[6]

Work resumed and the company pressed ahead with its plans to mechanise parts of the works. In March 1910 the *Oban Times* once again praised the company upon its forward-looking attitude. The proposed electrification of haulage and pumping operations in the quarries represented 'the first instance of electrification being applied to slate quarrying work in Scotland', and 'speaks much for the public spirit and enterprise of the Company'. The latter had made 'extensive improvements' in its first two years'.[7] Electric power was introduced in the late summer. All that was needed to complete the company's good work and improvements in workplace relations was an upturn in trade.[8]

The period between 1908 and 1910 thus saw a conscious attempt by the new company to cultivate a 'new spirit' of harmony and cooperation within the workplace. In the wake of the disastrous results of the pursuit of complete power and unmitigated self-interest by the previous employer, it made perfectly rational sense for the new company to *combine* the profit motive with a more caring and reciprocal attitude towards the labour force. I suggest that this represented an attempted reconciliation between the concerns of 'moral economy' and those of 'political economy'. The company's policies probably involved the desire to return to a more 'laird-like' style of paternalist management and control. But we must not forget that this was set within the very 'modern' context of enhanced worker independence and an acceptance of trade unionism and institutionalised collective bargaining. The contrast with the policies and attitudes of the Ballachulish Quarries Company Limited was marked. For 'modernization' in the workplace did not involve the total defeat of 'custom'. Both the 'customary' and the 'modern' would, as in many other places and aspects of twentieth-century life, continue to coexist in the Ballachulish quarries.[9]

In conclusion, it is sad to record that good intentions on both sides of the quarrying industry in Ballachulish were not enough to save it. The quarries closed down at the beginning of the Great War 'through lack of trade and men'. After the war the government took a ten year lease on them. All the employees became £20 shareholders and two of the workmen sat on the board of directors. Production continued between 1922 and the 1950s, while Ballachulish was characterised by 'a strong socialist awareness amongst the workers, a flourishing branch of the Communist Party in the 1930s and 1940s, a good production record and almost no strikes'.[10] Yet competition from 'more modern, factory made substitutes' eventually forced the closure of the Ballachulish quarries in 1955. The important story of developments between 1914-1955 and beyond, including the life histories and memories of the quarrymen themselves and the women of the village, remains to be told.

Notes

Introduction

1. *Labour Leader,* 7 March 1903.
2. Myra Marx Ferree, 'The Political Context of Rationality: Rational Choice Theory and Resource Mobilization', in Aldon D. Morris and Carol McClurg Mueller (eds.), *Frontiers in Social Movement Theory* (New Haven and London, 1992), p. 30.
3. Ferree, 'Political Context', pp. 29-36. See also the Introduction by Carol McClurg Mueller, 'Building Social Movement Theory', to Morris and Mueller (eds.), *Frontiers,* pp. 3-25.
4. Ferree, 'Political Context', pp. 36-40.
5. Ferree, pp. 40-48. My *historical* approach, which seeks to explore the complex and non-reductionist engagements between 'social consciousness' and 'social being', owes a great deal to the 'historical materialism' of Edward Thompson. See, for example, E.P. Thompson, *The Making of the English Working Class* (London, 1991), Preface, Postscript; idem., 'The Poverty of Theory: or an Orrery of Errors', in his *The Poverty of Theory* (London, 1995), especially the Introduction by Dorothy Thompson and pp.1-5, 59-68 and the Postscript to Edward Thompson's essay.
   For a convincing critique of the view that 'rationality demands the maximization of "self-interest" to the *exclusion* (my italics) of other reasons for choice' see Amartya Sen, *Rationality and Freedom* (London, 2002), Sen sees rational choice theory as too narrow, arbitrary, formulaic, essentialist and involving a 'basic denial of freedom of thought' (pp. 4-7,22-37, Ch. 4).
6. For the classic exposition of the 'moral economy', with specific reference to the market-based context of eighteenth-century food rioting, see E.P. Thompson, 'The Moral Economy of the English Crowd in the Eighteenth Century', and 'The Moral Economy Reviewed', in his *Customs in Common* (London, 1991). For the extended notion of an 'industrial moral economy' – the view that 'where the community's economic well-being was concerned, market forces and the profits of individuals should be subdued to custom' (Thompson, *Customs,* p.338), see Adrian Randall, 'The Industrial Moral Economy of the Gloucestershire Weavers in the Eighteenth Century', Chapter two in John Rule (ed.), *British Trade Unionism 1750-1850: The Formative Years* (London, 1988). For the considerable socio-political impact of the 'the legitimising language of community, custom and rights' in early modern England, see Andy Wood, *Riot Rebellion and Popular Politics in Early Modern England* (Basingstoke, 2002), p. 14.

While utilising, and highlighting the importance of, the notions of 'custom' and 'moral economy' to the Ballachulish conflicts, I am cognisant of two important facts: that my chosen context was very different from that of eighteenth-century relations between patricians and plebeians; and that the precise term, 'moral economy' (but not 'custom') did not form part of the language of the participants themselves at Ballachulish. Attentive to the nuances, complexities and differences of historical context, and Thompson's cautions against imprecise and decontextualised usage of the term, 'moral economy', and the 'danger of confusing the historical evidence with the terms of interpretation which we have ourselves introduced' (*Customs*, pp. 336-351), I, nevertheless, maintain that the terms 'moral economy' and 'custom' may be fruitfully applied to the Ballachulish case. Above all, they constituted 'an alternative "economics" (*Customs*, p. 340), with respect to *both* values and behaviour *in general* – an alternative 'whole way of life', within a particular material situation of conflict and struggle, to that espoused by the company.

7.   Ferree, 'Political Context', pp. 32-6, 40-3.

8.   *Report by the Chief Constable of Argyllshire for Quarter (year) to 7 September, 1905.* Argyll and Bute Council Archives, Lochgilphead, CA/3/79/25. Courtesy of Murdo MacDonald, archivist at Lochgilphead.

9.   For the sad catalogue of events between 1906 and 1908 see *Oban Times*, 10 March, 18 August, 22 September, 22 December 1906, 26 January, 20 April, 3 August, 14 December 1907, 4, 18 January, 21 March, 1908; Chapter two below.

10.   Barbara Fairweather, *A Short History of Ballachulish Slate Quarry* (Glencoe, 1974), p. 4, 'although for a few years some of the older men carried on'; *The Herald*, 23 June, 2005.

11.   *Report on Strikes and Lockouts in the United Kingdom in 1903 and on Conciliation and Arbitration Boards*, Strikes and Lockouts, Board of Trade (Labour Department), (London, 1904), cd. 2112, p. 26.

12.   R. Merfyn Jones, *The North Wales Quarrymen 1874-1922* (Cardiff, 1983), Chs. VII and VIII for the Penrhyn Lock-Outs, p. 106 for the reference to Ballachulish.

13.   See, for example, H.A. Clegg, Alan Fox and A.F. Thompson, *A History of British Trade Unionism since 1889*, Vol. 1, *1889-1910* (Oxford, 1964); Sidney and Beatrice Webb, *The History of British Trade Unionism* (London, 1920); Henry Pelling, *A History of British Trade Unionism* (Basingstoke, 1992); W. Hamish Fraser, *A History of British Trade Unionism 1700-1998* (Basingstoke, 1999); J.T. Ward and W. Hamish Fraser (eds.), *Workers and Employers: Documents on Trade Unions and Industrial Relations in Britain since the Eighteenth Century* (Basingstoke, 1980); Eric J. Hobsbawm, *Labouring Men: Studies in the History of Labour* (London, 1974); idem, *Worlds of Labour: Further Studies in the History of Labour* (London, 1984); E.H. Hunt, *British Labour History 1815-1914* (London, 1988); Chris J. Wrigley (ed.), *A History of British Industrial Relations 1875-1914* (Amherst, 1982); Alan Fox, *History and Heritage: The Social Origins of the British Industrial Relations System* (London, 1985).

14. By 1910-11 Scotland ranked second only to England and Wales in terms of European urbanisation (towns and cities of more than 20,000). The proportion of the population engaged in agriculture fell from 'around 25 per cent in the mid-nineteenth century to 11 per cent in the early twentieth century'. See R.J. Morris, 'Urbanisation and Scotland', in W. Hamish Fraser and R. J. Morris (eds.), *People and Society in Scotland, Vol. II, 1830-1914* (Edinburgh, 1990), p. 74; R.H. Campbell and T.M. Devine, 'The Rural Experience', in Ibid., p. 46.

15. As William Kenefick has kindly indicated to me in private correspondence (9/03/2005), 'Scottish industry was highly localised ... and so too were the small and very independent Scottish trade unions'. Kenefick also pointed to 'the central and unifying role' of the trades councils in stimulating the development of trade unionism in Scotland. On these matters see also Hamish Fraser, *History British Trade Unionism*, pp. 37-8, 92-3; W.W. Knox, *Industrial Nation: Work Culture and Society in Scotland 1800-Present* (Edinburgh, 1999), Ch. 17.

16. William Kenefick and Arthur McIvor (eds.), *Roots of Red Clydeside 1910- 1914? Labour Unrest and Industrial Relations in West Scotland* (Edinburgh, 1996); Alan Campbell, *The Scottish Miners 1874-1939*, 2 Vols (Aldershot, 2000). W.H.Marwick, *Labour in Scotland: A Short History of the Scottish Working Class Movement* (Glasgow, 1949); idem, *A Short History of Labour in Scotland* (Edinburgh, 1967); Catriona M. M. MacDonald, *The Radical Thread: Political Change in Scotland. Paisley Politics 1885-1924* (East Lothian, 2000); Jim Smyth, *Labour in Glasgow 1896-1936: Socialism Suffrage Sectarianism* (East Lothian, 2000). For industrial workers in a rural context see, for example, Mark Freeman, 'Employment in the Islay Distilleries, 1841-1914', *Scottish Labour History*, 35 (2000), pp. 55-67. The following three sources greatly facilitated my search of the Scottish labour history literature: Ian MacDougall, *A Catalogue of some Labour Records in Scotland and some Scots Records outside Scotland* (Edinburgh, 1978); *Journal: Scottish Labour History Society, 1-17, 1969-82*, held in the National Library of Scotland at HJ4.1745 (courtesy of Alan Bell); Arthur McIvor (compiler), 'Cumulative Index to the Scottish Labour History Society Journal, Numbers 1 to 24, 1969-1989', *Scottish Labour History Society Journal*, no. 25 (1990), pp. 88-102. I also checked back issues of the *Scottish Historical Review*. Particularly informative in terms of the latter is the *Index to the Scottish Historical Review*, vol. LXXV, no. 200 (October 1996, supplement), compiled by Alison E. Grant.

17. *Labour Leader*, 24 October 1903. See also W. H. Fraser, 'Patterns of Protest', p. 270, and Tony Clarke and Tony Dickson, ''The Birth of Class?', pp. 292-309, in T.M. Devine and Rosalind Mitchison (eds.), *People and Society in Scotland*, Vol. 1, *1760-1830* (Edinburgh, 1988).

18. T.M. Devine, *Clanship to Crofters' War: the Social Transformation of the Scottish Highlands* (Manchester, 1994), Chs. 3, 4, 5; Allan I. Macinnes, 'Scottish Gaeldom: The First Phase of Clearance', in Devine and Mitchison (eds.) *People and Society*, pp. 70-90; Campbell and Devine, ' Rural Experience'.

19. Charles W.J. Withers, 'Rural Protest in the Highlands of Scotland and in Ire-land,1850-1930', in S.J. Connolly, R.A. Houston and R.J. Morris (eds.), *Conflict Identity and Economic Development: Ireland and Scotland 1600-1939* (Preston, 1995), p.173; Devine, *Clanship*, Ch. 14; Hamish Fraser, 'Patterns of Protest', pp. 268-91; Eric Richards, *A History of the Highland Clearances*, Vol. 2, *Emigration Protest Reasons* (London, 1985); Campbell and Devine, 'Rural Experience'.

20. Duncan Clark kindly alerted me to the existence, and supplied a copy of Missel-brook's articles; Fairweather, *Short History*, p. 3. There is no mention of the 1905 dispute in either Misselbrook or Fairweather. Allan Macinnes, 'Good Days, Bad Days: The Story of Scottish Slate', *Sunday Mail Magazine, The Story of Scotland*, Vol. 42 (1989), pp. 1146-8. The Glencoe and North Lorn Folk Museum houses, to the rear, a small room containing models of the quarry and a quarryman, photo-graphs, quarrying tools, a short written account of 'The Trouble' at 'Ballachulish Quarry' (no date given) and an extract from the *Highland News* (no date) an-nouncing 'Another Great Meeting of the Men' and 'Shoulder to Shoulder. All for Dr. Grant'. The written account incorrectly states that the company was dissolved in 1903. No references to Dr. Grant and the disputes are to be found in either the Ballachulish Visitor Centre's written wall display, 'Great Days of Slate', or the in-formation panels in the quarry opposite. My article, 'A State of War in The Valley of Glencoe: The Ballachulish Quarries Disputes, 1902-1905', *Scottish Labour His-tory*, Vol. 38 (2003), pp. 14-36, attempts to fill some of the gaps in the literature.

21. Barbara Fairweather, *Highland Heritage* (Glencoe, 1984), p. 20.

22. I first made contact with Sheena Roddan and Duncan Clark, courtesy of Roddy Macleod, in July 2005. All three have patiently and generously answered my que-ries. Duncan Clark has sent me relevant material.

23. The National Library of Scotland holds microfilm copies of the Minutes of the Par-liamentary Committee of the Scottish Trade Union Congress, Mf MSS 136 (Acc. 4682/1-4). See, for example, 18 April, 20 June, 16 August 1903. The Minute Books of the Lismore and Appin Parish Council are held in the Argyll and Bute Council Archives, Lochgilphead. See, for example, 9 October 1903 (CA/7/30/4),for notifi-cation of Grant's interdiction 'from practising his profession in Ballachulish'.The Chief Constable's Reports are also held at Lochgilphead. See, for example, note 8 above.

24. I consulted these newspapers at the National Library of Scotland and at the British Library's Newspaper Library, Colindale. Extensive press cuttings are to be found in Grant's press cuttings in the National library of Scotland. See *Papers*, 1902-93, of or concerning Dr Lachland Grant, MD. Acc. 12187. Hereafter, Grant, *Papers*.

25. 'Gavroche', and 'Cosmopolitan' were the pseudonyms of William Stewart, a Scot-tish member of the ILP, and the author of publications on Keir Hardie, Robert Burns and Scottish radicalism and socialism. See MacDougall, *Catalogue*, p. 523.

26. For examples of 'Gavroche's' articles see *Labour Leader*, 28 July, 4 August 1905.

27. See the letter from James Meldrum of Renfrewshire, *Clarion*, 17 April 1903, and the reference to Ballachulish in W. Stewart's article, 'Socialism in the Highlands', *Clarion*, 1 September 1905.
28. I consulted *Forward* for 1906 and 1907 in Colindale.
29. See, for example, the *Lancet*, 2 August 1902, pp. 3000-1, 24 January 1903, pp. 249-50, 21 March 1903, pp. 823-4, 27 June, 1903, pp. 1821-2.
30. See Grant, *Papers*, Vol. 1 (July 1902-March 1903), Acc. 12187/1, Vol. 2 (March 1903-November 1903), Acc. 12187/2, Vol. 3 (November 1903-February 1908), Acc.12187/3.
31. Grant, *Papers*, Vol. 3, 22 March 1907.
32. See Grant, *Papers*, Vol. 3, October 1907.
33. See Grant,Papers, Vols. 4-12; idem, *A New Deal for the Highlands*.
34. The 1891 and 1901 census returns for Ballachulish were consulted at the General Register Office for Scotland, New Register Office, Edinburgh, and on the internet at www.ScotlandsPeople.gov.uk. Access to the latter is by name only rather than by place. The valuation rolls, collected annually, provide important information about property values (rateable value) and patterns of ownership, tenancy and occupancy of that property. The rolls for Ballachulish, 1901-1906, were consulted at the National Archives (Historical Search Section), Ref. VR89/46-52, *Valuation Rolls for Argyll, 1901-1906* (7 volumes), and the National Library, Shelf Mark L225-226.
35. See Board of Trade Papers, National Archives,(West Search Room), Ref. BT2 2609 (3 files).
36. I consulted the *Slate Trade Gazette* in Colindale for the years 1902-1907. There are very brief references to the disputes at Ballachulish in 1903 (Vol. IX, pp. 111, 213) and 1905 (Vol, XI, p. 212).
37. For the importance of community, locality and the relationship between work and community see David Gilbert, *Class Community and Collective Action: Social Change in Two British Coalfields 1850-1926* (Oxford, 1992), especially Chs. 2, 7; Ronald Aminzade, *Ballots and Barricades: Class Formation and Republican Politics in France 1830-1871* (Princeton, 1993); Craig. J. Calhoun, 'Community: Toward a Variable Conceptualization for Comparative Research', *Social History*, 5,1 (1980), pp. 105-129; Donald M. MacRaild and David E. Martin, *Labour in British Society 1830-1914* (Basingstoke, 2000), Ch. 4.
38. Thompson, *Customs*, Introduction, IV, V. See also George Rudé, *The Crowd in History 1730-1848* (London, 1964), Introduction, Ch. 14; Charles Tilly, *From Mobilization to Revolution* (Reading, Massachusetts, 1978); Craig J. Calhoun, *The Question of Class Struggle: The Social Foundations of Popular Radicalism during the Industrial Revolution* (Chicago, 1982).
39. See, for example, Mike Savage, 'Class and Labour History', and Eileen Yeo, 'Gender in Labour and Working-Class History' in Lex Heerma van Voss and Marcel van der Linden (eds.), *Class and Other Identities: Gender, Religion and Ethnicity in the Writing of European Labour History* (Oxford, 2002), pp. 55-72, 73-87; Neville

Kirk (ed.), *Northern Identities: Historical Interpretations of 'The North' and 'North-erness'* (Aldershot, 2000). See the very useful thematic section on local history and labour history in the Australian journal, *Labour History*, 78 (May 2000), especially the articles by Patmore, Taksa, Strachan, Jordan and Carey, Eklund, Ellem and Shields, and Faue.

40. W.W. Knox, 'The Political and Workplace Culture of the Scottish Working Class,1832-1914', in Fraser and Morris (eds.), *People and Society*, especially pp. 149-50, 155-6; idem, *Industrial Nation*.

41. Knox, 'Political and Workplace Culture', pp.150-1; idem, *Industrial Nation*, Ch.16; Arthur McIvor, 'Were Clydeside Employers More Autocratic? Labour Manage-ment and the "Labour Unrest", c1910-1914', in Kenefick and McIvor, *Roots*, es-pecially pp. 42-4; Ronnie Johnstone, *Clydeside Capital 1870-1920* (East Linton, 2000).

42. Calhoun, *Question of Class Struggle*; Savage, 'Class and Labour History'; Gilbert, *Class Community*, Ch. 7 For an illuminating study of labour and community con-sciousness among Guatemalan-born workers in the modern-day US New South see Leon Fink,*The Maya of Morganton: Work and Community in the Nuevo New South* (Chapel Hill, 2003), especially Ch. 7.

43. Knox, 'Political and Workplace Culture', pp. 156-61; idem, *Industrial Nation*, Ch. 18; E.F.Biagini and A. Reid, *Currents of Radicalism: Popular Radicalism Organised Labour and Party Politics in Britain 1850-1914* (Cambridge, 1991).

44. Sen, *Rationality* , p. 66, Chs. 2, 20, 21, 22. See also Ch. 4 below.

Chapter One

1. Grant, *Papers*, Vol. 2, March 1903; *Labour Leader*, 7 March 1903.

2. Barabara Fairweather, *Living in Old Glencoe: A Social History of the Glencoe and Ballachulish Areas* (Glencoe, 1971), observes (p. 3) that, 'Usually Glencoe and Ball-achulish are taken together for numbers of population', with the latter falling from 2500 in 1875, 'with the Quarry working fully to capacity', to 1444, 'due to emigra-tion', in 1881, and standing at 1480 in 1891. A figure of 1,800 for the population of Ballachulish in 1907 is given by the *Oban Times*, 3 August 1907.

3. Barbara Fairweather, *A Short History of Kinlochleven* (Glencoe, 1984), pp. 4-5; idem, *Living in Old Glencoe,* p. 5.

4. *Oban Times*, 3 August 1907, 18 January 1908.

5. *Oban Times*, 23 May 1908.

6. Patrick MacGill, *Children of the Dead End: The Autobiography of a Navvy* (London, 1914), pp. 176-7. I am grateful to Mike Winstanley of Lancaster University for first bringing MacGill's autobiography to my attention.

7. MacGill, *Children*, pp. 187, 227, 232-3, 250.

8. MacGill, *Children*, Chs. XXV, XXVI, 225-6, 251-2.

9. See, for example, Grant, *Papers*, Vol. 4, December 1908, March 1909, *Oban Times*, 6 March 1909 for lectures on 'Books and Reading' and 'Mutuality and Generosity of Spirit' at Kinlochleven.

10. Cameron McNeish, The *Munros: Scotland's Highest Mountains* (Edinburgh, 1996), pp. 61-7. The Scottish Munros are named after Sir Hugh Munro who, in 1891, first compiled the list of 3,000 ft. mountains in Scotland (McNeish, *Munros*, p. 7).

11. Jones, *North Wales Quarrymen*, pp. 1-2.

12. However, we must be wary of presenting too uniform a distinction between the categories 'casual' and 'rough', on the one hand, and 'steady' and 'respectable', on the other. In practice, the boundaries were often flexible and overlaps were much in evidence. For example, in October 1910 the Chief Constable reported a 'serious disturbance' at 'the works' in Kinlochleven in which 'several hundreds of the company's employees', 'being refused drink' in the canteen, attempted to 'wreck the building by means of stonethrowing', and subsequently 'set upon' the constables who were apprehending 'two of the ringleaders'. Yet these 'rioters' who constituted an 'unruly mob', were part of the more regular and (at least self- ascribed) 'steady' and 'respectable' labour force employed 'at the works'. During late August and September of the same year the vast majority of this same labour force (contemporary estimates varied from over 600 to 800 workers) had gone on strike against the company's refusal to recognise a union and its alleged victimisation of two local trade union officials. However, on the latter occasion there was 'no disturbance nor any attempt to interfere with the Company's property', and 'the strikers gave no trouble to the police'. See *Chief Constable's Reports*, 12 October, 21 December 1910, Argyll and Bute Council Archives, Lochgilphead. See also the letter from Neil Miller of Kinlochleven to the Chief Constable, dated 24 February 1908, in which he draws attention to the 'exceptionally rough' behaviour of Kinloclhleven's 'navvies' and suggests an 'increase in the Police Staff'. I am grateful to Murdo MacDonald for copies of both the Reports and the letter. See also *Oban Times*, 3 September 1910.

13. Captain and Mrs Beresford Drummond were not only wealthy landowners, but also heavily involved in the educational, social and cultural life of Ballachulish. The former took a keen interest in the fortunes of Ballachulish's very good shinty team, while the latter provided an annual Christmas 'treat' for the children in Ballachulish's public school. Both were friends of Dr. Grant and Reverend McMurchy. For examples of the Beresford Drummonds' activities in the community see *Oban Times*, 2 January 1904, 26 January 1907, 5 March 1910, Grant, *Papers*, Vol. 4, January 1909 and Chapter three below.

14. Fairweather, *Living in Old Glencoe*, pp. 4-5.

15. Jones, *North Wales Quarrymen*, p. 25.

16. See Mike Savage and Andrew Miles, *The Remaking of The British Working Class 1840-1940* (London, 1994), pp. 30-40. Based on Miles's sample of 10,835 marriage registers, the authors conclude that between 1899 and 1914 'more than 60 per cent' of skilled workers' sons and about 50 per cent of those of unskilled workers

were to be found 'following in their father's footsteps' (pp.30, 34, 37). It should be noted that Miles's sample is based upon the occupational experiences of fathers and sons in England, and that it covers a diverse range of occupations. In contrast, my focus also embraces brothers and male in-laws, but is restricted to a sample of one Scottish locality dominated by a single industry. The fact of the latter, and the very limited nature of alternative sources of employment, largely explain the unusually high level of occupational self-recruitment among both males and females in Ballachulish. The same conclusion may be drawn for the slate-quarrying communities of north Wales and some other communities dominated by a single industry. See Jones, *North Wales Quarrymen*, pp. 22, 48, 73, 97; Jean Robin, *Elmdon: Continuity and Change in a north-west Essex Village* (Cambridge, 1980), 75-91. Future research will hopefully build upon and geographically extend the pioneering quantitative foundations set by Savage and Miles. Unlike the USA, the important subject areas of working-class occupational and social mobility in Britain have been much neglected. See Savage, 'Class and Labour History', pp. 62-4.

17. While people were most commonly grouped in nuclear families in Ballachulish, it was by no means unusual to live in extended family units. In terms of the latter, the census often lists brothers, sisters, nephews, nieces and brothers- and sisters-in-law as residing with the head of family and his nuclear unit. As one would expect, mothers and fathers of the head of the family are listed far less frequently. For examples, see Appendix Two, Appendix Three. For the 'considerable resilience' of the working-class extended family at the national level, see John Benson, *The Working Class in Britain 1850-1939* (London, 1989), pp. 121-2; and the classic Study by Michael Anderson, *Family Structure in Nineteenth Century Lancashire* (Cambridge, 1971), Ch. 5.

18. Jones, *North Wales Quarrymen*, pp. 97-8.

19. *Oban Times*, 14 February 1903.

20. Jones, *North Wales Quarrymen*, p. 41.

21. Savage and Miles, *The Remaking*, pp. 23-4.

22. Fairweather, *Short History of Ballachulish Slate Quarry*, p. 3.

23. This was less the case in the 1891 census. See Appendix Three.

24. Jones, *North Wales Quarrymen*, pp. 41-3.

25. Jones, *North Wales Quarrymen*, pp. 75-77.

26. Grant, *Papers*, Vol. 1, February 1903.

27. *Labour Leader*, 30 August 1902, 16 January 1904; *Oban Times*, 17 October, 19 December 1903.

28. *Labour Leader*, 16 January 1904; *Oban Times*, 14 February, 28 November 1903.

29. *Labour Leader*, 30 August 1902.

30. See Knox, *Industrial Nation*, p. 135.

31. *Labour Leader*, 30 August 1902.

32. *Oban Times*, 25 July 1903; idem, 18, 25 April, 17 October 1903.

33. See Grant, *Papers*, Vol. 2, March 1903, Glasgow United Trades' Council's 'Appeal to Trades Unionists. Ballachulish Slate Quarries' Lock-Out. A Scottish "Penrhyn" Case' (reprinted as Document 3, p. 48) and pp. 44-48.

34. See Grant, *Papers*, Vol. 3, especially December 1905, January 1906 and December 1906, and his *A New Deal for The Highlands* (1935), for his advocacy of compulsory state inspection to tackle the overcrowding and insanitary conditions and poverty endemic in the Highlands, for the proper feeding, clothing and medical inspection of schoolchildren, and for legislation to promote access to the land and so ease the chronic poverty of, and migration's drain upon, the region's most vital resource, its people; *Labour Leader* , 6, 20 September 1902.

35. Although 'Gavroche' himself claimed conditions in Ballachulish to be as 'acute' as in 'any of the congested districts of our large towns', *Labour Leader*, 6, 20 September 1902.

36. Grant, *Papers*, Vol.1, December 1902, January 1903.

37. *Labour Leader*, 20 September 1902, Grant, *Papers*, Vol. 2, March 1903.

38. Christine MacKay, an MSc student at Edinburgh University, is currently conducting research into patterns of labour migration between slate quarrying communities in Scotland during the period from 1891 to 1911. Christine is particularly interested in Luing, one of the slate islands which attracted to its quarries some of the locked-out Ballachulish men and which, in April 1903, was reported to be enjoying the 'most prosperous conditions' in living memory . See *Oban Times*, 25 April 1903.

39. Jones, *North Wales Quarrymen* (pp. 21-25, Chs. III, IV), observes that although 'many men ... travelled significant distances to work' and that many of the labourers in the larger quarries in north Wales migrated from Anglesey and elsewhere 'abroad' and 'continued to live the life of migrant workers', nevertheless, by the last quarter of the nineteenth century the vast majority of those working the quarries formed a very settled local workforce with a strong sense of both occupational 'calling' and pride in, and belonging to, their local communities and their wider Welsh culture. See also Robin, *Elmsdon* (pp. 75-8), for a picture of 'remarkable homogeneity' in terms of the local origins of Elmsdon's male farm workers and their wives.

40. Anderson, *Family Structure*, pp. 41-2; David Holding,' Assimilation and Conflict: Irish Communities in Bolton and Preston, 1840-1914'. Unpublished PhD, Manchester Metropolitan University 2002, especially Ch. 3. For wider aspects of labour migration see Anderson, *Family Structure*, 34-41; MacRaild and Martin, *Labour in British Society*, Ch. 3; Benson, *The Working Class*, Ch. 5; Colin G. Pooley and Ian D. Whyte (eds.), *Migrants Emigrants and Immigrants: A Social History of Migration* (London, 1991), especially Introduction.

41. *Valuation Rolls for the County of Argyll* (National Library of Scotland), 1901-2 (pp. 419-420), 1902-3 (pp. 426-427), 1905-6 (pp. 445-446).

42. *Valuation Rolls for the County of Argyll* (National Library of Scotland), 1901-2 (pp. 420-422), 1902-3 (pp. 427-429), 1905-6 (pp. 446-448).

43. *Valuation Rolls for Argyll 1901-1906* (National Archives of Scotland), VR 89/47, p. 414, VR89/48, p. 421, VR/51, p. 440.

44. As Higgs usefully reminds us, the census enumerators for England and Wales were sometimes inconsistent in altering 'the boundaries of ... enumeration district in line with local administrative changes', and in their entry of houses 'in their books in the order in which they appeared in the streets'. Both these inconsistencies were present in the Scottish returns. See Edward Higgs, A *Clearer Sense of the Census* (London, 1996), pp. 12-13, 59. See also M.W.Flinn et. al., *Scottish Population History from the 17ᵗʰ Century to the 1930s* (Cambridge, 1977).

45. For example, reference to the valuation rolls for 1901-2 allows us to see that the McClachlan family, returned as living on Ballachulish Rd. in the 1891 census, is listed for West Laroch in both the valuation rolls and the 1901 census. The quarrying district of West Laroch included Ballachulish Rd. (see Appendix One, p. 420, no 11 West Laroch; Appendix Two, p. 6; Appendix Three, p.3; *1891 and 1901 Census.Glencoe and Ballachulish, Preliminary Reports, Enumeration District 001*. The reader will observe that my samples of the census for both 1891 and 1901 take the McClachlan family as the starting point for comparison (see Appendix Two, p. 6, Appendix Three, p. 3).

46. Benson, *Working Class*, Chs. 4,5; MacRaild and Martin, *Labour*, Ch. 4; Knox, *Industrial Nation*, Chs. 3,9,15; Nicholas Mansfield, *English Farmworkers and Local Patriotism 1900-1930* (Aldershot, 2001), Ch. 7.

47. Robin drew the same, highly localised, conclusion for farmworkers in the Essex village of Elmsdon (*Elmsdon*, p. 77). For the national picture see Benson, *Working Class*, pp. 120-1; MacRaild and Martin, *Labour*, pp. 84-; Anderson, *Family Structure*, pp. 34-41; Richard Anthony, *Herds and Hinds: Farm Labour in Lowland Scotland, 1900-1939* (East Linton, 1997) for regular but relatively short distance mobility among farm workers.

48. Benson, Working Class, p. 119; MacRaild and Martin, *Labour*, pp. 69-70; Knox, *Industrial Nation*, pp. 37, 93; T. M. Devine (ed.), *Scottish Emigration and Scottish Society* (Edinburgh, 1992); M. Anderson and D.J. Morse, 'The People', in Fraser and Morris (eds.), *People and Society*, Ch. 1; Charles W.J. Withers, *Urban Highlanders: Highland-Lowland Migration and Urban Gaelic Culture 1700-1900* (East Linton), 1998, Ch. 4.

49. Fairweather, *Ballachulish Slate Quarry*, p. 2. See also Gordon Lyall, 'Day They Wiped the Slate Clean', *Weekend Scotsman*, 21 November 1981.

50. Jones, *North Wales Quarrymen*, pp. 15, 22.

51. Grant, *New Deal; Oban Times*, 2 January 1904 (Grant's speech at the school treat).

52. Callum G. Brown, 'Religion, Class and Church Growth', in Fraser and Morris (eds.), *People and Society*, pp. 313, 316-17, 319; idem, *Religion and Society in Scotland Since 1707* (Edinburgh, 1997).

53. Brown, 'Religion, Class and Church Growth', pp. 319-20.

54. *Highland News*, 13 June 1903. Murdo MacDonald has kindly supplied me with the details of McMurchy's birth, death and period as a minister in Ballachulish. Notwithstanding Grant's close friendship with McMurchy, I have not discovered a record of Grant's membership of the United Free Church. However, Sheena Roddan believes that he 'must have been a member'. While having 'absolutely no recollection' of Grant 'ever going to … church', Duncan Clark maintains that 'it is almost impossible to believe that he was not a member of the church, however nominally'. E-mail from Duncan Clark to Neville Kirk, 2 August 2005.

55. Jones, *North Wales Quarrymen*, pp. 43-6, 62-4; Hugh Macleod, *Religion and Society in England 1850-1914* (Basingstoke, 1996).

56. In north Wales the quarrymen's opposition to the 'outsider' usually took the form of opposition to those English families who derived great wealth from the ownership of most of the land and the enormously profitable slate quarries in Gwynedd. See Jones, *North Wales Quarrymen*, pp. 15-16.

57. Jones, *North Wales Quarrymen*, pp. 15, 47, 55-71.

58. Fairweather, *Living in Old Glencoe*, p. 3; Lyall, *Weekend Scotsman*, 21 November 1981.

59. For Hardie's visit see *Labour Leader*, 20 September, 11 October 1902; Grant, *Papers*, Vol. 1, September 1902 (*Highland News*. 20 September 1902).

60. See, for example, Grant, *Papers*, Vol. 1, September 1902, Vol. 3, December 1907, Vol. 4, May 1910; *Highland News*, 6 December 1902; *Oban Times*, 26 March 1910.

61. See the letter by 'Caman' in the *Highland News*, 7 March 1903; *Oban Express*, 28 February 1903; Grant, *Papers*, Vol. 1, July 1902 (*Oban Telegraph and Express*, 25 July 1902). For the popularity of shinty see the 'great ovation' given by the 'hundreds crowding the platform' to the championship-winning junior team upon their return to Ballachulish railway station in 1907 (*Oban Times*, 20 April 1907).

62. *Oban Times*, 4 January, 12 April, 1902, 5 March 1910.

63. *Oban Times*, 12 April, 1902. In the autumn of 1902 a group of quarrymen asked Maccoll to resign his position as county councillor because he had forfeited their trust (Grant, *Papers*, Vol.1, cutting from the *Highland News*, 4 October 1902).

64. *Oban Times*, 5 October 1907.

65. *Oban Times*, 30 November 1907. Roughly translated into English as 'The Home I Left as a Sad Young Man'.

66. See, for example, *Oban Times*,14 March 1903, 1 January, 10 September 1910.

67. See the references in footnote 40, Introduction. See also Geoffrey Best, *Mid Victorian Britain 1851-1875* (London, 1971); Neville Kirk, *Change Continuity and Class: Labour in British Society 1850-1920* (Manchester, 1998), Chs. 4, 8.

68 . *Oban Times*, 4 January, 23 August 1902, 2 January 1904, 26 January 1907, 5 March 1910; *Highland News*, 13 June 1903; Grant, *Papers*, Vol. 4, January 1909 (the school). The local Volunteer Company of the Argyll and Sutherland Highlanders was very active in Ballachulish. Many members were quarrymen. See, for example, Grant, *Papers*, Vol. 2, May, June 1903; *Highland News*, 13 June 1903; *Oban Times*, 4 October 1902, 19 January, 1904,18 May 1907.

69. *Oban Times*, 26 January 1907.
70. *Oban Times*, 13 August 1907.
71. Fairweather, *Short History of Ballachulish Slate Quarry*, p. 1.
72. Macinnes, 'Good Days, Bad Days', pp. 1146-7.
73. Fairweather, *Short History of Ballachulish Slate Quarry*, p. 2.
74. Macinnes, 'Good Days, Bad Days', p. 1147.
75. Jones, *North Wales Quarrymen*, Ch. IV; Alan Campbell and Fred Reid, 'The Independent Collier in Scotland', in Royden Harrison (ed.), *Independent Collier: The Coal Miner as Archetypal Proletarian Reconsidered* (Hassocks, 1978), pp. 54-74. For the classic study of the 'autonomous craftsman' see David Montgomery, *Workers' Control in America: Studies in the History of Work, Technology and Labor Struggles* (Cambridge, 1986), Ch. 1.
76. See *Terms and Conditions of Employment, 19th January 1903*. This appears as Document One, p. 46. In north Wales the attempted replacement of the crew-based bargaining system by a contract system in which the quarrymen became the employees of middlemen sub-contractors, was 'consistently opposed' by the 'quarrymen proper'. The contract system was seen as a major threat to the quarrymen's independence, control and earning power. It was an important factor in the disputes of the period. See Jones, *North Wales Quarrymen*, pp. 73-4, 85-6, 217.
77. Macinnes, 'Good Days, Bad Days', p. 1148. See also Lyall, *Weekend Scotsman*, 21 November 1981.
78. Macinnes,'Good Days, Bad Days', p. 1147; Fairweather, *Short History of Ballachulish Quarry*, pp. 2-3.
79. This phrase was coined by 'Gavroche' in the *Labour Leader*, 17 January 1903.

Chapter Two

1. *Certificate of Incorporation. The Ballachulish Slate Quarries Company Ltd., 29 December 1893*, National Archives of Scotland, BT2 2069.
2. Malcolm belonged to the Scottish Conservative Club, located in Edinburgh. See Edward Donald Malcolm, *Letters and Correspondence*, MS 1738, 88, National Library of Scotland. The names and addresses of the company's directors and shareholders are listed in the company's records from 1894 onwards. Women's involvement was minimal. For example, the *List of Shareholders*, 24 April 1894, included only two women, Sara Alston of Bothwell (no occupation listed) and Miss Christina Nisbet of Edinburgh (no occupation given) out of a total of twenty five. BT2 2069.
3. Jones, *North Wales Quarrymen*, pp. 15-16, 61-2.
4. See *Minutes of Agreement between Edward Bruce Low on behalf of the Proposed Company and Archibald Maccoll, Quarrymaster Easedale, 29 December 1893*. National Archives of Scotland, BT 2 2069.
5. Loc. cit.
6. Loc. cit.

7. *Labour Leader*, 7 March 1903.
8. *Labour Leader*, 20 September 1902.
9. Sheena Rodden and Duncan Clark have kindly provided biographical details of Grant (e-mails from Duncan Clark to Neville Kirk, 2, 3 August 2005). See also *Highland News*, 13 June 1903; *Glasgow Evening News*, 28 August 1902. Grant died in 1945. He is buried in beautiful surroundings in the cemetery at Duror.
10. For the events surrounding the appointment and dismissal of Grant see Grant, *Papers*, Vol. 1, July and August 1902; Grant, *Papers*, Vol. 2, March and April 1903, especially Keir Hardie's letter to Akers-Douglas, Secretary of State for the Home Department, 6 April 1903; *Labour Leader*, 26 July, 9, 16 August 1902, 7 March 1903; *Lancet*, 2, 16 August 1902.
11. Grant, *Papers*, Vol. 1, July 1902.
12. Loc, cit.
13. The records range from those of the company, in which there are no references to Grant's appointment and dismissal, to Grant's press cuttings, which contain material overwhelmingly favourable to the doctor's case, to the *Labour Leader*, in which, some might argue, 'Gavroche' presented an exaggerated critique of the Ballachulish Slate Quarries Company Limited in our to make a predetermined case for socialism. The most balanced account is probably to be found in the pages of the *Lancet*. The latter did not have a particular ideological axe to grind, apart from safeguarding the interests, and especially the contractual rights and responsibilities, of medical professionals such as Grant. Significantly, the *Lancet* was unreservedly critical of the company's belatedly 'lame' and 'feeble' efforts to justify Grant's 'summary' and 'morally wrong', if 'legally correct', dismissal, and its 'pigheaded' and 'dictatorial' attempt to curtail the doctor's employment in 'the locality in which they happen to carry on business'. See the *Lancet*, 16 August 1902, 24 January, 21 March, 13, 27 June, 5, 12, 19, 26 December 1903.
14. *Highland News*, 13 June 1903; Grant, *Papers*, Vol. 1, July 1902, Vol. 2, Hardie to Akers-Douglas, 6 April 1903; *Lancet*, 16 August 1902, 24 January 1903.
15. Grant, *Papers*, Vol. 1, September 1902, especially the press cutting of Hardie's view in the *Labour Leader*, 27 September 1902.
16. *Labour Leader*, 20 September 1902.
17. *Lancet*, 5 December 1903; *Labour Leader*, 16 August 1902.
18. See Document Three, *Glasgow United Trades' Council*.
19. *Labour Leader*, 23 August 1902.
20. *Labour Leader*, 23, 30 August, 6, 13, 20 September 1902; *Oban Times*, 31 January 1903, 6 May 1905; Grant, *Papers*, Vol. 1, December 1902; Document Three, Glasgow United Trades' Council.
21. *Labour Leader*, 23 August 1902.
22. The following description of the key chain of events during July and August 1902 is based upon Grant, *Papers*, Vol. 1, July and August 1902; the *Lancet*, 2 August 1902, pp. 301-1 (leading article), 16 August, pp. 449-50; and the *Labour Leader*, 26 July, 9, 16, 23, 30 August 1902.

23. Grant, *Papers*, Vol. 1, July 1902, Vol. 2, March 1903 ('Appeal for Funds'); *Lancet*, 2 August 1902; *Labour Leader*, 16 August 1902, 7 March 1903.
24. *Lancet*, 2 August 1902; Grant, *Papers*, Vol. 1, July and August 1902; *Labour Leader*, 7 March 1903.
25. Grant, *Papers*, Vol. 1, July 1902.
26. *Labour Leader*, 26 July, 9 August 1902.
27. For McMurchy see *Oban Times*, 31 January 1903; *Highland News*, 13 June 1903.
28. *Lancet*, 2 August 1902.
29. Grant, Vol. 1, July, October (for *Edinburgh Medical Journal*)1902; *Oban Times*, 19 July 1902; *Highland News*, 13, 20 September 1902.
30. *Labour Leader*, 7 March 1903.
31. *Highland News*, 11 October 1902.
32. *Labour Leader*, 20 September, 11 October 1902.
33. *Labour Leader*, 18 October, 6 December 1902.
34. *Lancet*, 10 January 1903; *Highland News*, 3 January 1903; *Oban Times*, 3 January 1903.
35. See *Correspondence* and *Minute Books of the Lismore and Appin Parish Council*, October 1903 and 1904, Argyll and Bute Council Archives, Lochgilphead, CA/7/30/4, CA/7/30/5, CA/7/30/30. Courtesy of Murdo MacDonald.
36. *Labour Leader*, 17 January, 1903.
37. *Labour Leader*, 17, 24, 31 January, 21 February 1903; Grant, *Papers*, Vol. 1, December 1902, January 1903; *Labour Leader* , 17 January 1903.
38. For the *Oban Telegraph and Express* for 9th January, see Grant, *Papers*, Vol. 1, January 1903.
39. *Labour Leader*, 17 January 1903.
40. Grant, *Papers*, Vol. 1, February 1903, Vol. 2, April, May 1903; *Oban Times*, 2 May 1903.
41. *Oban Times*, 9, 23 May 1903; Grant, *Papers*, Vol. 2, May 1903.
42. Grant, *Papers*, Vol. 2, April 1903; *Oban Times*, 21 March, 18 April, 9 May 1903.
43. See, for example, *Oban Times*, 14, 21 February 1903, Grant, *Papers*, Vol. 2, April, May 1903; Highland News, 2 May 1903.
44. *Oban Times*, 21, 28 February 1903; Grant, *Papers*, Vol. 1, February 1903, Vol. 2, March 1903.
45. Grant, *Papers*, March 1903.
46. Grant, *Papers*, April 1903.
47. *Oban Times*, 14, 21 February 1903.
48. *Oban Times*, 31 January 1903; *Labour Leader*, 21 February 1903.
49. *Highland News*, 17 January, 16 May 1903; Grant, *Papers*, Vol. 1, January 1903.
50. *Highland News*, 23 May 1903; Grant, *Papers*, Vol. 2, May 1903.
51. *Highland News*, 17 January 1903.
52. *Labour Leader*, 11 April, 2 May 1903; *Oban Times*, 2 May, 19 September 1903.
53. *Labour Leader*, 11 April 1903; Grant, *Papers*, Vol. 1, for Shaw's comments in the *Border Advertiser*, 10 February 1903.

54. *Oban Times*, 23 May 1903; Grant, *Papers*, Vol. 2, May 1903.
55. *Labour Leader*, 31 January, 2 May 1903; Grant, Vol. 2, March, April 1903, Vol. 3, November, December 1903; *Oban Times*, 21 March, 2, 9 May, 21, 28 November 1903; *Lancet*, 5 December 1903; *Highland News*, 14 November 1903.
56. *Lancet*, 13, 27 June, 18 July, 22 August 1903; *Labour Leader*, 27 June, 8 August 1903; Grant, *Papers*, Vol. 2, June, August 1903; *Oban Times*, 8 August, 1903.
57. Grant, *Papers*, Vol. 2, September 1903; *Lancet*, 19 September 1903; *Correspondence and Minute Books: Lismore and Appin Parish Council, 9 October 1903, 1904*, Argyll and Bute Council Archives, Lochgilphead, CA/7/30/4, CA/7/30/5, CA/7/30/30.
58. *Lancet*, 12 December 1903.
59. *Oban Times*, 12 December 1903; *Labour Leader*, 16 January 1904; Grant, *Papers*, Vol. 3, December 1903, January 1904.
60. The post of Medical Officer for the Parish Council District of Ballachulish was subsequently advertised. Grant applied, and in April 1904 the half yearly meeting of the Parish council of Lismore and Appin under the Poor Law 'unanimously' approved his appointment. Significantly, in acknowledging receipt of the Council's decision, the Secretary to the Local Government Board in Edinburgh, declared, in a letter dated 26 April, that the latter, 'specially wish to know … whether any outside authority has a right – as formerly – to come between the Parish Council and the Medical Officer as regards the engagement of the latter'. In the event, the question of this 'right' was never again put to the test. See *Correspondence, Lismore and Appin Parish Council*, CA/7/30/30; *Minute Book: Lismore and Appin Parish Council, 1904*, CA/7/30/5.
61. Oban Times, 19 December 1903; *Labour Leader*, 19 December 1903, 16 January 1904; *Lancet*, 12, 19, 26 December 1903, 23 January 1904; Grant, *Papers*, Vol. 3, December 1903, January 1904.
62. *Labour Leader*, 16 January 1904.
63. *Oban Times*, 18, 25 February 1905.
64. *Oban Times*, 11 March 1905.
65. *Oban Times*, 18, 25 February 1905.
66. For an exception, and the opening of new workings at Easedale, see *Oban Times*, 10 June 1905.
67. For the course of these disputes see *Oban Times*, 6 May, 10 June, 15, 22 July, 5 August 1905; Grant, *Papers*, Vol. 3 (1905, nd. – for comments concerning market conditions).
68. Oban Times, 17 June 1905.
69. Grant, *Papers*, Vol. 3, June 1905 (especially the cutting from the *Oban Weekly News*, 20 June 1905); *Oban Times*, 24 June 1905; *Highland News*, 22 July 1905.
70. Grant, *Papers*, Vol. 3, 1905 (nd.)
71. Grant, *Papers*, Vol. 3, July 1905 (for *Oban Times*, 15 July 1905).
72. *Highland News*, 22 July 1905.
73. Grant, *Papers*, Vol. 3, July 1905.
74. *Highland News*, 22 July 1905.

75. *Report by the Chief Constable of Argyllshire for Quarter to 7 September 1905*, Argyll and Bute Council Archives, CA/3/79/25.
76. Grant, *Papers*, Vol. 3, July 1905; *Oban Times*, 22 July 1905.
77. *Oban Times*, 22nd July 1905; *Report by the Chief Constable … to 7 September 1905*.
78. Grant, *Papers*, Vol. 3, August 1905; *Report by the Chief Constable … to 7 September 1905*; *Oban Times*, 19, 26 August 1905.
79. Grant, *Papers*, Vol. 3, July (for *Scotsman*, 19 July), August; *Highland News*, 22 July 1905.
80. *Oban Times*, 22 July 1905.
81. *Oban Times*, 29 July 1905.
82. *Oban Times*, 11 March, 29 July, 19 August 1905; Grant, *Papers*, Vol. 3, March, August 1905.
83. *Oban Times*, 19 August 1905; Grant, *Papers*, Vol. 3, August 1905.
84. *Oban Times*, 25 November, 16 December 1905.
85. Jones (*North Wales Quarrymen*, pp. 115-16) maintains that divisive 'local chauvinism' operated with 'some', but limited, force among in the quarrying communities of north Wales. For a pioneering and fascinating study of 'local xenophobia' see Keith D.M. Snell, 'The Culture of Local Xenophobia', *Social History*, Vol. 28, 1 (January, 2003), pp. 1-30. For further discussion of the importance of 'the local' to the residents of Ballachulish see Ch. 3 below.
86. *Oban Times*, 13 January 1906.
87. *Oban Times*, 10 March, 18 August 1906.
88. *Oban Times*, 17 February 1906.
89. *Oban Times*, 22 September, 22 December 1906.
90. *Oban Times*, 26 January, 20 April 1907.
91. *Oban Times*, 3 August 1907.
92. *Oban Times*, 3 August 1907.
93. Board of Trade Papers, National Archives (West Search Room), Ref. BT2 2609, 25-27.
94. *Oban Times*, 10 August 1907, 4 January 1908.
95. Grant, *Papers*, Vol. 3, October 1907.
96. *Oban Times*, 14 December 1907.
97. *Oban Times*, 18 January 1908.

Chapter Three

1. *Labour Leader*, 16 January 1904.
2. *Labour Leader*, 31 January 1903.
3. *Labour Leader*, 17 January 1903.
4. *Oban Times*, 7, March 1903.
5. *Oban Times*, 21 March 1903; Grant, *Papers*, Vol. 2 (2 May 1903) for Scottish TUC; *Minutes of the Parliamentary Committee of the Scottish TUC 1900-6* (letters to Ball-

achulish quarrymen 18 April, 20 June, 16 August 1903), Mf.Mss 136 (Acc. 4682/1-4) National Library of Scotland.

6. Writing his/her column, 'Loch Leven Echoes', in March 1903, 'Sgur Dearg' thanked the *Highland News* for 'its consistent and valued support' for the quarrymen and Grant. See Grant, *Papers*, Vol. 2, March 7 1903.
7. Grant, *Papers*, Vol. 1, 17 January 1903 (for the *British Medical Journal*).
8. *Lancet*, 2, 16 August 1902, pp. 300-1, 449-50, 21 March, 1903,pp. 823-49.
9. Grant, *Papers*, Vol. 1, 31 July 1902 (for the *Glasgow Herald*).
10. *Highland News*, 26 July 1902.
11. *Lancet*, 27 June 1903, pp. 1821-2, 18 July 1903, p. 183, 19 December 1903, p. 1740.
12. Grant, *Papers*, Vol. 1, 10 January 1903 (for the *British Medical Journal*).
13. Grant, *Papers*, Vol. 1, 16 August 1902 (for the *Oban Times*).
14. *Labour Leader*, 7 March 1903.
15. *Highland News*, 26 July 1902.
16. *Highland News*, 3 January 1903.
17. Grant, *Papers*, Vol. 1, August 1902 (for the *Oban Times* and the *Lancet*).
18. Grant, *Papers*, Vol. 1, 22 January 1903 (for *Truth*).
19. Grant, *Papers*, Vol. 1, 10, 17 January 1903 (for *British Medical Journal*).
20. Grant, *Papers*, Vol. 1, 14 August 1902 (for *Truth*).
21. *Labour Leader*, 31 January 1903.
22. Grant, *Papers*, Vol. 2, 2 May 1903.
23. *Lancet*, 16 August 1902, pp. 449-50.
24. For the paternalism of Penrhyn and other slate quarry owners in north Wales see Jones, *North Wales Quarrymen*, pp. 120-1.
25. *Highland News*, 31 January, 14 February 1903; Grant, *Papers*, Vol. 1, January, February 1903.
26. *Highland News*, 11 October 1902.
27. Grant, *Papers*, Vol. 3, 23 August 1905 (for the *Oban Weekly News*).
28. Grant, *Papers*, Vol. 1, January 1903 (see the clipping from the *Highland News*, 31 January 1903 for McMurchy's eulogy).
29. *Oban Times*, 14 March, 18 April 1903.
30. *Oban Times*, 25 April 1903.
31. *Oban Times*, 25 July, 28 November 1903.
32. Oban *Times*, 17 October, 28 November 1903.
33. Jones, *North Wales Quarrymen*, pp. 17-25, 115-6.
34. For the importance of places and spaces, and especially those of a local character, to the study of identity, social relationships and social movements see, for example, Jones, *North Wales Quarrymen* Chs. 1,2, 3; Gilbert, *Class Community*; Aminzade, *Ballots and Barricades*; Calhoun, *Question of Class Struggle*; Savage, 'Class and Labour History'; MacRaild and Martin, *Labour*, Ch. 4; Benson, *Working Class*, Ch.5; Stuart Macintyre, *Little Moscows: Communism and Working Class Militancy in Inter-War Britain* (Cambridge, 1980).

35. Jones, *North Wales Quarrymen*, pp. 48, 73-4, 97 108, 118-9.
36. Knox, *Industrial Nation*, Ch. 15; Alan Campbell, 'Honourable Men and Degraded Slaves: A Comparative Study of Trade Unionism in two Lanarkshire Mining Communities, c. 1830-1874', in Harrison (ed.), *Independent Collier*, pp. 75-113.
37. Snell, 'The Culture of Local Xenophobia'; Jones, *North Wales Quarrymen*, p. 115; Mansfield, *English Farmworkers*, , pp. 199-200.
38. Aminzade, *Ballots and Barricades*; idem, 'Capitalist industrialisation and Patterns of Industrial Protest: A Comparative Urban Study of Nineteenth Century France', *American Sociological Review*, 49 (1984), pp. 437-453; Gilbert, *Class Community*, pp. 24-5.
39. *Oban Times*, 3 August 1907, 18 January 1908.
40. Thompson, *Customs*, p. 7.
41. Thompson, *Customs*, pp. 13-14 (especially Thompson's quote from anthropologist, Gerald Sider).
42. For a study of 'Custom, Law and Common Right', see Thompson, *Customs*, Ch. 3; idem, *Whigs and Hunters: The Origins of the Black Act* (London, 1975).
43. Tilly, *Mobilization*; Gilbert, *Class Community*, pp. 26-8.
44. Calhoun, *Question of Class Struggle*.
45. Rudé, *Crowd in History*, Intro., Chs. 11, 12, 14; Harold Perkin, *The Origins of Modern English Society 1750-1880* (London, 1972), Chs. VI, VII; John Rule, *The Labouring Classes in Early Industrial England 1750-1850* (London, 1987), Conclusion.
46. E.P. Thompson, *The Making of the English Working Class* (London, 1980), pp. 887-915, 937-9; Rudé, *Crowd in History*, pp. 233-4; Dorothy Thompson, *The Chartists: Popular Politics in the Industrial Revolution* (Aldershot, 1986), pp. 111-2, 251, 336-9; idem, *Outsiders: Class Gender and Nation* (London, 1993), Chs. 1,2; Gilbert, *Class Community*, pp. 42-4.
47. Gilbert, *Class Community*, pp. 26-8.
48. Raphael Samuel, B.Bloomfield and G.Bonas (eds.), *The Enemy Within: Pit Villages and the Miners' Strike of 1984-5* (London, 1986), especially the Introduction.
49. Thompson, *Customs*, p. 12.
50. Grant, *Papers*, Vol. 1, January 1903 (for the *Highland News*, 14 January 1903).
51. Grant, Papers, Vol. 1, September, October 1902; Highland *News*, 4 October 1902.
52. *Labour Leader*, 15 August 1903, 10 March, 1 September 1905, 16 February 1906; *Highland News*, 15 August, 5 September 1903; *Glasgow Herald*, 7 September 1903; *Oban Times*, 5 September 1903; Grant, *Papers*, Vol. 2, August, September 1903.
53. See, for example, Thompson's reference in *Customs* (pp. 341-51) to the important work of James C. Scott on the notion of a 'moral economy' among the peasants of South-East Asia. See also Adrian Randall and Andrew Charlesworth (eds.), *Moral Economy and Popular Protest: Crowds Conflict and Authority* (Basingstoke, 2000).
54. Welcome attempts to break down the dualism between 'structure' and 'culture' may be observed in the work of Thompson(see, for example, *Customs*) and Savage (see, for example, 'Class and Labour History'). See also John Walton's splendid es-

say, 'Cannery Row: Class, Community and the Social Construction of History', in John R. Hall (ed.), *Reworking Class* (London, 1997), Ch. 8.

55. For a review of some of the relevant literature see Neville Kirk, 'Decline and Fall, Resilience and Regeneration: A Review Essay on Social Class', *International Labor and Working Class History*, 57 (Spring, 2000), pp. 88-102; David Cannadine, *Class in Britain* (London, 1998).

56. *Labour Leader*, 23 August, 11 October 1902; Grant, *Papers*, Vol. 1, January 1903, Vol. 3, August 1905; *Highland News*, 11 October 1902, 24, 31 January 1903.

57. Grant, *Papers*, Vol. 2, September 1903 (clipping from the *Highland News*, 12 September 1903).

58. *Highland News*, 31 January, 14 February 1903; Grant, *Papers*, Vol. 2, March, September 1903.

59. *Oban Times*, 23 August 1902.

60. *Oban Times*, 23 August 1902.

61. *Oban Times*, 6 September 1902.

62. For these references see above, pp. 56-57.

63. However, for relatively recent attempts to integrate women more fully into this literature see, for example, Thompson, *Customs*, pp. 305-336; Wood, *Riot Rebellion*, pp. 95-111, 192-4; Thompson, *Chartists*, Ch. 7; idem, *Outsiders*, Ch. 3; Malcolm Thomis and Jennifer Grimmett, *Women in Protest* (London, 1982); Anna Clark, *The Struggle for the Breeches: Gender and the Making of the British Working Class* (London, 1995); Eleanor Gordon, *Women and the Labour Movement in Scotland 1850-1914* (Oxford, 1991); Sonya O. Rose, *Limited Livelihoods: Gender and Class in Nineteenth Century England* (Berkeley, California, 1992); Karen Hunt, *Equivocal Feminists: The Social Democratic Federation and the Woman Question 1881-1911* (Cambridge, 1996); M.L. Bush, 'The Women at Peterloo: The Impact of Female Reform on the Manchester Meeting of 16 August 1819', *History*, 89, 294 (April, 2004), pp. 209-232.

64. Patrick Joyce, *Work Society and Politics: The Culture of the Factory in Later Victorian England* (Brighton, 1980); Jon Lawrence, *Speaking for the People: Party Language and Popular Politics in England 1867-1914* (Cambridge, 1998); Mansfield, *English Farmworkers*, pp. 30-6, 43-6, 49-50, 168-71, 181-6, 193-8; Robin, *Elmsdon*, xvi.

65. To do so would unduly widen my specific framework of reference. For the importance of religious conflict in the Scottish context see Knox, *Industrial Nation*, Ch. 15, pp. 298-9 and the review of Knox's book by John Foster in *Scottish Labour History*, Vol. 35 (2000), pp. 91-3; Alan Campbell, 'Honourable Men', in Harrison (ed.), *Independent Collier*. In an article in the *Labour Leader,* 16 February 1906, entitled, 'Why Does Scotland Lag Behind?', 'Gavroche' set the longstanding Scottish concern with 'sentiments and symbolism' against the 'practical' bent of the English. An aspect of the former lay in the high number of votes cast for 'an orange flag or a green banner'.

66. See, for example, Joyce, *Work*, Chs. 4, 5, 8.

67. Gilbert, *Class Community*, Chs. 3,4; Stuart Macintyre, *Little Moscows*; Neville Kirk, 'Traditional Working-Class Culture and "The Rise of Labour": Some Preliminary Questions and Observations', *Social History*, 16, 2 (May, 1991), pp. 203-16; Geoffrey Crossick, *An Artisan Elite in Victorian Society: Kentish London 1840-1880* (London, 1978); Robbie. Q. Gray, *The Labour Aristocracy in Victorian Edinburgh* (Oxford, 1976); Knox, *Industrial Nation*, Ch. 9; idem, 'Political and Workplace Culture', in Fraser and Morris (eds.), *People and Society*, especially pp. 152-161.

68. Knox, 'Political and Workplace Culture', pp. 154-5.

69. Neville Kirk, 'The Conditions of Royal Rule: Australian and British Socialist and Labour Attitudes to the Monarchy, 1901-1911', *Social History*, 30,1 (February, 2005), pp. 64-88; Alex Tyrrell, 'Scottishness and Britishness: From Scotland to Australia Felix', *Humanities Research*, Vol. XIII, no. 1 (2006), pp. 17-26.

70. *Highland News*, 13 June 1903; Grant, *Papers*, Vol. 2, March 1903, June 1903, Vol. 3, 22 March 1907 (McLaren) ; *ObanTimes*, 16 August 1902.

71. E-mail from Duncan Clark to Neville Kirk, 27 July 2005.

72. Grant, *Papers*, Vol. 1, January 1903.

73. Grant, *Papers*, Vol. 4, February 1909 (speech at the meeting in support of Ainsworth, the Liberal MP for Argyllshire, in Ballachulish, reported 9 February, 1909). For the case in favour of tariff reform see the letter entitled, 'Slate Quarries and Tariff Reform', from a 'Patriot', in the *Oban Times*, 11 January 1910; *Highland News*, 15 August, 5 September 1903; *Oban Times*, 5 February, 26 November, 24 December 1910.

74. Knox, 'Political and Workplace Culture', pp. 158-162; idem, *Industrial Nation*, Chs.12, 18; David Howell, *British Workers and the Independent Labour Party 1888-1906* (Manchester, 1983), Ch. 1;Pat Thane, 'Labour and Local Politics: Radicalism, Democracy and Social Reform 1880-1914', in Biagini and Reid (eds.), *Currents*, Ch. 1, pp. 244-70; John Belchem, *Popular Radicalism in Nineteenth Century Britain* (Basingstoke, 1996), Ch. 9.

75. Savage,' Class and Labour History', p. 67.

76. Knox, 'Political and Workplace Culture'; idem, *Industrial Nation*, especially pp. 31-3, 81-4 129-31.

77. For contemporary identification of the weaknesses of organised labour and socialism in Scotland in general and the Highlands in particular see, for example, the articles by 'Gavroche' in the *Labour Leader*, 6 January, 10 March, 1 September, 10, 17 November 1905, 16 February 1906. See also Knox, *Industrial Nation*, Chs. 17,18.

78. Neville Kirk, *Change Continuity and Class: Labour in British Society 1850-1920* (Manchester, 1998), Ch. 8; Knox, *Industrial Nation*, Ch. 18; Mansfield, *English Farmworkers*.

79. McIvor, 'Clydeside Employers', in Kenefick and McIvor (eds.), *Roots of Red Clydeside*

80. McIvor, 'Clydeside Employers'; idem, *A History of Work in Britain 1880-1950* (Basingstoke, 2001), Ch. 4; Neville Kirk, *Labour and Society in Britain and the USA*

1780-1939, Vol. 2, *Challenge and Accommodation 1850-1939* (Aldershot, 1994), pp. 35-7.

81. Knox, *Industrial Nation,* pp. 129-31,Ch. 18; idem, 'Political and Workplace Culture', pp. 158-61; Biagini and Reid, *Currents.*

82. Owen R. Ashton and Paul A.Pickering, *Friends of the People: Uneasy Radicals in the Age of the Chartists* (London, 2002); Kirk, '"Traditional" Working-Class Culture'; Chris Waters, *British Socialists and the Politics of Popular Culture 1884-1914* (Manchester, 1990).

83. See above, pp. 10, 39.

84. *Highland News,* 13 June 1903.

85. *Highland News,* 13 June 1903; Grant, *Papers,* Introduction to the collection, Vol. 1, July 1902.

86. For the *Lancet's* comments see Grant, *Papers,* Vol. 3, December 1905.

87. For Grant's proposed medical reforms see Grant, *Papers,* Vol. 3, December 1905 (*Lancet, British Medical Journal, Medical Press and Circular*), January 1906 (for his pamphlet *Modern Highland Problems,* reprinted from the *Caledonian Medical Journal*), December 1906 (*Medical Press and Circular*).

88. See Grant, *Papers,* Vol. 1, August 1902 (*Edinburgh Medical Journal, British Medical Journal, Oban Telegraph and Express, Glasgow Weekly Mail*), Vol. 3, December 1905 (*Lancet*); *Oban Times,* 30 April 1904 (editorial).

89. Grant, *Papers,* Vol. 3, January 1906 (*Modern Highland Problems*).

90. Many of these measures foreshadowed Grant's proposed solutions for the depopulation and decline of the Highlands and Islands as expressed in his major work of 1935, *A New Deal for the Highlands.* This work set great store by re-population, 'if we are to avoid national and racial suicide'.

91. *Oban Times,* 2 January 1904; Grant, *Papers,* Vol. 3, December 1907 (for *Oban Weekly News,* 28 December), July 1908 (for *Oban Times,* 29 July).

92. Bernard Semmel, *Imperialism and Social Reform: English Social-Imperial Thought 1895-1914* (New York, 1968).

93. Grant, *Papers,* Vol. 4, February 1909, January, November, December 1910.

94. Harold Perkin, *The Rise of Professional Society: England since 1880* (London, 1989), Preface, Ch. 1.

95. Grant, *Papers,* Vol. 1, July 1902 (for *Highland News,* 26 July).

96. Grant, *Papers,* Vol. 1, July 1902 (for *Oban Telegraph and Express,* 25 July).

97. The term 'organic intellectuals' is taken from the writings of the early twentieth-century Italian Communist leader, Antonio Gramsci. Gramsci saw 'organic' intellectuals as 'the thinking and organising element of a particular fundamental social class'. See Quintin Hoare and Geoffrey Nowell Smith (eds. and translators), *Selections from the Prison Notebooks of Antonio Gramsci* (London, 1971), pp. 3-23.

98. Colin Barker, Alan Johnson and Michael Lavalette (eds.), *Leadership and Social Movements* (Manchester, 2001), pp. 17-20 and Ch. 6 by Alan Johnson, 'Self-Emancipation and Leadership: The Case of Martin Luther King'.

99. Barker, Johnson and Lavalette's *Leadership and Social Movements* makes a useful contribution towards redressing traditional neglect.

Chapter Four

1. See Carol McClurg Mueller, 'Building Social Movement Theory', Ch. 1, Mayer N. Zald, 'Looking Backward to Look Forward: Reflections on the Past and Future of The Resource Mobilization Research Program', Ch. 14 in Morris and McClurg (eds.), *Frontiers in Social Movement Theory*; Ron Eyerman and Andrew Jamison, *Social Movements: A Cognitive Approach* (Cambridge, 1991), Ch. 1; Nick Crossley, *Making Sense of Social Movements*, (Buckingham, 2002), pp. 10-13.

2. See, for example, Neil J. Smelser, *Theory of Collective Behaviour* (London, 1962),11-21, Chs. VI, VII, VIII; Eyerman and Jamison, *Social Movements*, p. 12; However, see Crossley, *Social Movements* (Chs. 2,3, p. 56), for the important qualification that 'not all collective behaviour approaches conform to the "irrationalist" stereotype'.

3. For excellent defences of the predominantly rational behaviour of a variety of protesters see, for example, Rudé, *Crowd in History*, pp. 7-10, Ch. 15; Lawrence Goodwyn, *The Populist Movement* (Oxford, 1978); Bryan D. Palmer, *Cultures of Darkness: Night Travels in the Histories of Transgression* (New York, 2000).

4. Sen, *Rationality and Freedom*, pp. 46-52.

5. Rudé, *Crowd in History*, p. 8.

6. Eyerman and Jamison, *Social Movements*, pp. 12-14; Smelser, *Theory*, pp. 17, 261-9.

7. William A. Gamson, 'The Social Psychology of Collective Action', in Morris and McClurg (eds.), *Frontiers*, Ch. 3.

8. McClurg,'Building Social Movement Theory', pp. 3, 22; Ferree,'The Political Context of Rationality', p. 29; Zald, 'Looking Backward', p. 332; Barker, Johnson, Lavalette, *Leadership*, p. 2; Crossley, *Social Movements*, Ch. 5.

9. Thompson, *The Making*, pp. 9-10.

10. Thompson, *The Making*, pp. 11- 12, Ch. 16.

11. See Harvey J. Kaye, *The British Marxist Historians* (Cambridge, 1984); Melvyn Dubofsky, *Hard Work:The Making of Labor History* (Chicago, 2000), Introduction, Ch.1.

12. Rudé, *Crowd in History*, pp. 3, 8-9, 252-3.

13. Eric J. Hobsbawm and George Rudé, *Captain Swing* (London, 1970), pp. 15-19.

14. Thompson, *Chartists*, p. 7.

15. Eugene Genovese, *Roll Jordan Roll: The World the Slaves Made* (New York, 1976); Herbert G. Gutman, *The Black Family in Slavery and Freedom 1750-1925* (New York, 1977); idem, *Work Culture and Society in Industrializing America: Essays in American Working Class and Social History* (New York, 1976); David Montgomery, *The Fall of the House of Labor: The Workplace, the State and American Labor Activism 1865-1925* (Cambridge,1987).

16. Ferree, 'Political Context', p. 29.

17. Thompson, *Customs*, pp. 185-9, for a devastating critique of a reductionist and spasmodic view of the protests of the eighteenth-century English crowd.

18. Barker, Johnson, Lavalette, *Leadership*, p. 2.

19. Rudé, *Crowd in History*, Ch. 13.

20. See, for example, Thompson, *Chartists*, Ch.7; idem, 'Women and Nineteenth-Century Radical Politics: A Lost Dimension', Ch. 3 in her *Outsiders*; Bush, 'The Women at Peterloo', pp. 215-16.

21. See, for example, Asa Briggs, 'The Local Background of Chartism', Ch. 1 in Briggs's edited *Chartist Studies* (London, 1959); R.S. Neale, *Class and Ideology in the Nineteenth Century* (London, 1972), pp. 22-9, Ch. 2; Gray, *Labour Aristocracy*, pp. 18-27, 158-64, Ch. 5; Crossick, *Artisan Elite*, Ch. 10; Biagini and Reid, *Currents*; Ashton and Pickering, *Friends*; J.P.D. Dunbabin, *Rural Discontent in Nineteenth- Century Britain* (London, 1974), pp. 75-84, Ch. V (by Pamela Horn); Alun Howkins, *Poor Labouring Men:Rural Radicalism in Norfolk 1870-1923* (London,1985), pp. 63-66.

22. Howkins, *Poor Labouring Men*, p. 66; Thompson, *Chartists*, Ch.8; MacGill, *Children of the Dead End*, Chs. XXIV, XXX, XXIX.

23. For the heavy and very problematic reliance of resource mobilization practitioners upon rational choice theory see Crossley, *Social Movements*, Chs. 4,5.

24. Ferree, 'Political Context', p. 31; Crossley, *Social Movements*, pp. 67-8.

25. For the Kinlochleven strike see Grant, *Papers*, Vol. 3, September 1910; *Oban Times*, 3, 10 September 1910; *Report by the Chief Constable*, 12 October 1910, Argyll and Bute Council Archives, Lochgilphead. Courtesy of Murdo MacDonald.

26. *Oban Times*, 10 September 1910.

27. Dunbabin, *Rural Discontent*, p. 123; Howkins, *Poor Labouring Men*, pp. 63-6, 82, 105, 111; Mansfield, *English Farmworkers*, pp. 141-5; James G.M. Cranstoun, 'Farm Servants and Collective Bargaining in War and Peace; the Experience of the Scottish Farm Servants' Union in East Lothian, 1912-1932', *Scottish Labour History*, Vol. 35 (2000), pp. 8- 24; Richard Anthony, *Herds and Hinds:Farm Labour in Lowland Scotland 1900-1939* (East Linton, 1997).

28. Howkins, *Poor Labouring Men*, p.111; Mansfield, *English Farmworkers*, pp. 30- 6, 193-8; Cranstoun, 'Farm Servants', pp. 12, 21.

29. Cranstoun, 'Farm Servants', p. 8; Dunbabin, *Rural Discontent*, Introduction.

30. Mueller, 'Building social Movement Theory', pp. 3-5; Ferree, 'Political Context', p. 29; Crossley, *Social Movements*, pp. 84, 170.

31. Louis Maheu, 'Introduction' to Louis Maheu (ed.), *Social Movements and Social Classes: The Future of Collective Action* (London, 1995), p. 4; Bert Klandermans and Sidney Tarrow, 'Mobilization into Social Movements: Synthesizing European and American Approaches', in Bert Klandermans, Hanspeter Kriesi and Sidney Tarrow (eds.), *International Social Movement Research*, Vol. 1, *From Structure to Action: Comparing Social Movement Research Across Cultures* (London,1988), p. 9.

32. Maheu, 'Introduction', p. 4. See Crossley, *Social Movements*, Ch.9, for a stimulating and very helpful discussion of the connections between agency and structure

and the importance of Bourdieu's notions of *habitus* and *field* to the understanding of social movements.

33. Eyerman and Jamison, *Social Movements*, p. 4. See also J. Craig Jenkins and Kevin Leicht, ' Class Analysis and Social Movements: A Critique and Reformulation', in Hall, *Reworking Class*, p. 392.
34. Klandermans and Tarrow, 'Mobilization into Social Movements', p. 10.
35. Ferree,' Political Context', pp. 29-30.
36. Ferree,' Political Context', pp. 30-1.
37. Sen, *Rationalty and Freedom*, p. 46.
38. Sen, *Rationalty and Freedom*, p. 66.
39. Sen, *Rationality and Freedom*, p. 46.

Afterword

1. *Oban Times*, 4, 11, 18 January 1908.
2. *Oban Times*, 18 January 1908.
3. *Oban Times*, 4 January, 21 March 1908.
4. *Oban Times*, 28 August 1909.
5. *Oban Times*, 4 September 1909.
6. *Oban Times*, 23, 30 October 1909.
7. *Oban Times*, 5 January, 5 March 1910.
8. *Oban Times*, 3 September 1910.
9. For such coexistence in the areas of consumer culture and credit relations see, for example, the stimulating study by Margot C. Finn, *The Character of Credit: Personal Debt in English Culture 1740-1914* (Cambridge, 2003).
10. Kris Misselbrook, 'The 1903 Ballachulish Lockout', *Lochaber Free Press*, 18 February 1977; idem, 'Lockout: Solidarity Brings Victory', *Lochaber Free Press*, 25 February 1977; Lachlan Grant, MD., D.P.H., J.P., *Ballachulish and its Quarries: An Address Delivered to the Quarriers' Committee 5th May, 1919* (Glasgow, 1919). Both the Misselbrook articles and Grants' 'Address' were kindly supplied to the author by Duncan Clark.

Appendix 1
Valuation Rolls, County of Argyll, 1901-1906

Courtesy of National Library of Scotland and the National Archives of Scotland

418 VALUATION ROLL FOR THE COUNTY OF ARGYLL, FOR THE YEAR 1901-1902. LISMORE AND APPIN PARISH. LORN DISTRICT.

No.	Description and Situation of Subject	Proprietor	Tenant	Occupier	Inhabitant Occupier and rental (40 Vic. cap. 8, &S 2 and 7)	Accrued Value	Yearly rent or Value	No.
						Forward	£15,849 15 1	
		BALLACHULISH WATER AND DRAINAGE DISTRICT—CONTINUED.						
14278	House and Store, East Laroch	F. C. Beresford Drummond and another	Barr, & Co., storekeepers	Tenants	Robert Paton Grant, manager	£4 0 0	90 0 0	14278
14279	„ and Mill	„			Tenant			25 0 0	14279
14280	Cottage, Shop, and Land	„	Archibald McAlpine, joiner	Tenant			50 0 0	14280
14281	Sheep, Farm, & House, Gortenorn, East Laroch	„	Hugh Maclennan, butcher				13 0 0	14281
14282	Land	„	Donald Campbell, farmer				1 0 0	14282 A
14283	Drill Hall, Armoury, Mechanics Institute, and House, No. 4	„	The Village Committee, per Secretary Argyll Highland Rifle Volunteers	Tenants	Peter Campbell, drill instructor	5 0 0	30 10 0	14283
14284	Part of Slate Quarries—Rent and Lordship	„	The Ballachulish Slate Quarries Co., Limited, per E. Bruce Low, S.S.C., 23 York Place, Edinburgh				300 0 0	14284
14285	House, South Ballachulish	„	„	Vacant		4 0 0	1 0 0	14285
14286	Quarry Cottage, No. 47, East Laroch	„	„	Mrs. McKenzie, pauper			Rent free.	14286
14287	„ 19, West Laroch	„	„	Paul McInnes, quarrier			3 0 0	14287
14288	„ 1, West Laroch	„	„	Widow Cameron, pauper			0 10 0	14288
14289	„ 20	„	„	Vacant			1 0 0	14289
14290	„ 21	„	„	Dugald McLaren, quarrier			1 7 0	14290
14291	„ 41	„	„	Mrs. Christina Lawson			1 0 0	14291
14292	„ 47	„	„	Donald Rankin, pauper			1 10 0	14292
14293	„ 76	„	„	Sarah McInnes			1 5 0	14293
14294	„ 77	„	„	Mrs. Donald Macdonald			1 2 6	14294
14295	„ 81	„	„	Bella McInnes			0 15 0	14295
14296	„ 46	„	„	Margaret Mackenzie			0 15 0	14296
14297	Quarries' Pier, Ballachulish	„	„	Tenants	David MacBraynes, Glasgow	5 0 0	20 0 0	14297
14298					The West Highland Carrying Co., Limited	5 0 0		14298
14299	Quarry Cottages, No. 15, East House	„	„		Dugald Henderson, quarrier	2 2 6	550 11 0	14299
14300	„ 16, Laroch	„	„					14300
14301	„ 16,	„	„		Angus McInnes	2 0 0		14301
14302	„ 17,	„	„		Donald McColl, „	4 10 0		14302
14303	„ 18, & Grazing	„	„		John Stewart, „	4 0 0		14303
14304	„ 19A,	„	„		Ronald McInnes, labourer	1 7 0		14304
14305	„ 19B,	„	„		Archd. McKenzie, quarrier	1 13 0		14305
14306	„ 19C,	„	„		Archd. Rankin, „	1 12 0		14306
14307	„ 30,	„	„		Duncan Clark, „	4 1 6		14307
14308	„ 22,	„	„		Catherine McKenzie	2 16 0		14308
14309	„ 23,	„	„		Allan Robertson, „	4 1 0		14309
14310	„ 24,	„	„		John Kennedy, „	1 10 0		14310
14311	„ 25,	„	„		Alexander McDonald	1 5 0		14311
14312	„ 25A,	„	„		Mrs. William Cameron	1 15 0		14312
14313	„ 26,	„	„		Alexander Cameron, quarrier	1 10 0		14313
14314	„ 97,	„	„		Alexander Macdonald, quarrier	1 16 3		14314
14315	„ „	„	„		Thomas McDonald, „	1 16 3		14315
14316	„ 28,	„	„		Archibald Carmichael, „	2 14 0		14316
14317	„ 29,	„	„		Mrs. Duncan Clark, widow	3 2 0		14317
						Forward	£16,943 0 7	

53 a

VALUATION ROLL FOR THE COUNTY OF ARGYLL, FOR THE YEAR 1901–1902.   LISMORE AND APPIN PARISH.   LORN DISTRICT.   419

No.	DESCRIPTION AND SITUATION OF SUBJECT.	PROPRIETOR.	TENANT.	OCCUPIER.	INHABITANT OCCUPIER. not rated (48 Vic. cap. 3, s.s. 3 and 9).	Annual Value of Dwelling	Yearly Rent or Value.	No.
						Forward	£16,943 0 7	
	BALLACHULISH WATER AND DRAINAGE DISTRICT—*Continued.*					£3 9 6		
4818	House, No. 30, East Laroch	E. C. Beresford Drummond and another.	The Ballachulish Slate Quarries Co., Limited		Donald Turner, quarrier			14318
4819	" " 31, "		"		John McDonald, labourer	2 0 0		14319
4820	Grazing, " 32, "		"		Robert M'Innes, quarrier	3 15 0		14320
4821	" " 33, "		"		Archibald Fallow, "	3 12 6		14321
4822	" " 34, "		"		Alexander Livingston, "	3 16 0		14322
4823	" " 35, "		"		Mrs. James Clark	2 14 0		14323
4824	" " 36, "		"		Archibald McQuarrie	2 4 6		14324
4825	" " 37, "		"		John M'Innes, labourer	1 16 0		14325
4826	" " 38, "		"		James Robertson, quarrier	4 2 6		14326
4827	" " 39, "		"		Donald Robertson, labourer	1 16 0		14327
4828	" " 40, "		"		Alexander Macleggatt, labourer	3 0 0		14328
4829	" " 41, "		"		John Macintosh, quarrier	8 14 0		14329
4830	" " 42, "		"		Alexander M'Taggart, quarrier	3 0 0		14330
4831	" " 43, "		"		John McLean,	2 0 0		14331
4832	" " 44, "		"		Allan McDougall	2 0 0		14332
4833	" " 45, "		"		Archibald M'Millan, labourer	2 0 0		14333
4834	" " 46, "		"		Duncan Livingston, engineman	1 10 0		14334
4835	" " 47, "		"		Hugh Cameron, quarrier	1 4 6		14335
4836	" " 48, "		"		Donald Maclennan, quarrier	1 4 0		14336
4837	" " 49, "		"		James Brown, engineman	3 0 0		14337
4838	" " 49a, "		"		John M'Gillivray, quarrier	1 15 0		14338
4839	" " 50, "		"		Alexander M'Kenzie, "	1 13 0		14339
4840	" " 51, "		"		Duncan Livingston, "	1 7 0		14340
4841	" " 52, "		"		Duncan Cameron, "	4 2 6		14341
4842	" " 53, "		"		Neil McNeill	4 2 6		14342
4843	" " 54, "		"		Mrs. Margaret Morrison, nurse	4 0 0		14343
4844	" " 55, "		"		John Macdonald, quarrier	4 2 6		14344
4845	" " 56, "		"		Archibald McCallum, smith	4 2 6		14345
4846	" " 57, "		"		John Carmichael, quarrier	4 2 6		14346
4847	" " 58, "		"		Dugald Livingston, "	4 2 6		14347
4848	" " 59, "		"		Donald Rankin,	4 2 0		14348
4849	" " 60, "		"		Hugh Lowrie,	4 2 6		14349
4850	" " 61, "		"		Duncan McKenzie,	4 0 0		14350
4851	" " 62, "		"		Donald Macgregor,	4 2 6		14351
4852	" " 63, "		"		John M'Innes, foreman	4 0 0		14352
4853	" " 64, "		"		John M'Innes, quarrier	4 0 0		14353
4854	" " 65, "		"		John Clark,	4 12 0		14354
4855	" " 66, "		"		Duncan M'Intyre, ——— (a minor)	4 0 0		14355
4856	" " 67, "		"		Duncan M'Intyre, quarrier	4 11 0		14356
4857	" " 68, "		"		Mrs. J. Campbell	4 0 0		14357
4858	" " 69, "		"		John Robertson, quarrier	4 5 0		14358
4859	" " 70, "		"		Mrs. John Campbell	4 0 0		14359
4860	" " 71, "		"		William McKenzie, quarrier	4 12 0		14360
4861	" " 72, "		"		Duncan Rankine, quarrier	4 0 0		14361
4862	Laroch Cottage and Garden, No. 73,		"		Alexander Maccoll, foreman	18 0 0		14362
4863	House, " 73a,		"		John Graham, piermaster	2 0 0		14363
4864	" " 73b,		"	Vacant		6 0 0		14364
4865	" " 74,		"		Alexander Wilson, quarrier	1 10 0		14365
						Forward	£16,948 0 7	

420　VALUATION ROLL FOR THE COUNTY OF ARGYLL, FOR THE YEAR 1901-1902.　LISMORE AND APPIN PARISH.　LORN DISTRICT.

No.	DESCRIPTION AND SITUATION OF SUBJECT.	PROPRIETOR.	TENANT.	OCCUPIER.	INHABITANT OCCUPIER not rated (48 Vic. cap. 3, S.S. 2 and 9).	Annual Value of Lands and Heritages if Inhabited (Standard Act, 1867) per Pro-Rata or otherwise	Yearly Rent or Value.	No.
						Forward	£16,943　0　7	
14366	House,	BALLACHULISH WATER AND DRAINAGE DISTRICT.—Continued		Alexander Anderson		£2　0　0		14366
14367	No. 7¼, East Lorach & Grazing, 76,	F. C. Beresford Drummond and another	The Ballachulish Slate Quarries Co., Limited		Alexander M'Laren, joiner	3　0　0		14367
14368	77,				Donald M'Intyre, quarrier	2　11　0		14368
14369	78,				Archibald Rankin,	2　0　0		14369
14370	79,				Donald Kennedy,	2　0　0		14370
14371	80,				Catherine M'Kenzie	0　10　0		14371
14372	81,				Mrs. Duncan M'Coll	1　5　0		14372
14373	82,				Allan Brown, smith	2　6　0		14373
14374	83,				John Livingston, quarrier	2　8　0		14374
14375	84,				Donald Lawrie, - (a minor)	2　16　0		14375
14376	85,				Agnes M'Fadzen, pauper	0　1　0		14376
14377	86,				Archibald Black, quarrier	2　0　0		14377
14378	87,				Mrs. Christina Colquhoun	1　0　0		14378
14379	88,				Donald M'Donald, labourer	2　0　0		14379
14380	89,				Paul M'Coll, quarrier	1　10　0		14380
14381	90,				Donald M'Millan, quarrier	2　0　0		14381
14382	1, West Lorach				Catherine Cameron, pauper	0　1　0		14382
14383	2,				Dugald Ferguson, quarrier	4　4　6		14383
14384	3,				James Stewart,	3　6　0		14384
14385	4,				John M'Dougall,	2　19　6		14385
14386	5,				Alexander M'Coll,	4　7　6		14386
14387	6,				John Cameron,	3　10　0		14387
14388	7,				Donald Campbell, blacksmith	4　4　0		14388
14389	7a,				David Gemmell	4　9　0		14389
14390	7b,				Hugh M'Innes, quarrier	4　11　0		14390
14391	8,				Archibald M'Taggart,	4　7　0		14391
14392	9,				Angus M'Kenzie,	4　11　0		14392
14393	10,				John M'Lachlan,	4　11　0		14393
14394	11,				John M'Lachlan,	0　15　0		14394
14395	12,				James M'Innes, labourer	2　15　0		14395
14396	13,					4　9　6		14396
14397	14,				John M'Coll, quarrier	3　3　6		14397
14398	15,				Hugh M'Coll, foreman	3　6　6		14398
14399	16,				Mrs. Christina M'Callum, widow	1　10　0		14399
14400	17,				John Cameron, quarrier	4　0　0		14400
14401	18,				Hugh Graves	4　4　0		14401
14402	19,				Alexander M'Innes,	0　1　0		14402
14403	20,				Miss Catherine M'Kenzie, pauper	1　7　0		14403
14404	21,				John M'Kenzie, quarrier	2　13　0		14404
14405	22,				Alexander M'Pherson, -	4　1　0		14405
14406	23,				Duncan M'Kenzie, postman	2　19　0		14406
14407	24,				Donald Ferguson	3　5　6		14407
14408	25,				John M'Coll, quarrier	4　6　6		14408
14409	26,				Jane Clark,	2　18　6		14409
14410	27,				Donald Stewart,	3　3　0		14410
14411	28,				Hugh Campbell,	4　4　0		14411
14412	29,				John Thomson,			14412
14413	30,				Hugh Robertson,			14413
14414	31,				Allan M'Kenzie,			14414
						Forward	£16,943　0　7	

VALUATION ROLL FOR THE COUNTY OF ARGYLL, FOR THE YEAR 1901–1902.   LISMORE AND APPIN PARISH.   LORN DISTRICT.   421

Ss.	Description and Situation of Subject	Tenant	Proprietor	Occupier	Inhabitant Occupier, not being (36 Vic. cap. 3, §§ 3, 4 and 6).	Yearly Rent or Value	Annual Value of Dwelling House...	No.
						Forward £16,943 0 7		
1415	House, No. 311, West Larach.	The Ballachulish Slate Quarries Co., Limited	F. C. Bereford Drummond and another		Jens McEachern, pauper	£0 1 0		14415
1416	„ „ 311a, „	„	„		James Watson, labourer	2 5 0		14416
1417	„ „ 32, „	„	„		James McInnes, quarrier	1 15 0		14417
1418	„ „ 32, „	„	„		Mrs. John McIntyre	0 1 0		14418
1419	„ „ 33, „	„	„		John McGregor	2 18 6		14419
1420	„ „ 34, „	„	„		Donald McKenzie	2 15 0		14420
1421	„ „ 35, „	„	„		Dugald Lowrie	4 0 0		14421
1422	„ „ 35a, „	„	„		Robert McColl	4 0 0		14422
1423	„ and Grazing, „ 35b, „	„	„		Donald Cameron	3 6 0		14423
1424	„ „ 35c, „	„	„		Ewen McDonald	3 0 0		14424
1425	„ „ 36, „	„	„		William Fleming	3 1 0		14425
1426	„ „ 37, „	„	„		John McEachern	3 0 0		14426
1427	„ „ 38, „	„	„		Donald McLaren	3 0 0		14427
1428	„ „ 39, „	„	„		Duncan McDonald	2 19 0		14428
1429	„ „ 40, „	„	„		Hugh McKenzie	2 19 0		14429
1430	„ „ 41, „	„	„		Hugh Cameron	3 1 6		14430
1431	„ „ 42, „	„	„		Mrs. Mary McDonald, pauper	3 11 6		14431
1432	„ „ 43, „	„	„		Peter Cameron, quarrier	3 11 6		14432
1433	„ „ 44, „	„	„		Angus Benton	2 0 0		14433
1434	„ „ 45, „	„	„		Alexander Cameron	2 0 0		14434
1435	„ „ 46, „	„	„		Mary McColl	1 5 0		14435
1436	„ „ 47, „	„	„		John Clark	3 11 0		14436
1437	„ „ 48, „	„	„		Margaret McKenzie, pauper	0 1 0		14437
1438	„ „ 49, „	„	„		Alexander McTaggart, quarrier	1 10 0		14438
1439	„ „ 50, „	„	„		Lachlan McTaggart	3 16 0		14439
1440	„ „ 51, „	„	„		Donald Cameron	2 8 0		14440
1441	„ „ 52, „	„	„		Archibald McPhee	2 16 0		14441
1442	„ „ 53, „	„	„		James Cameron, roadman	2 14 0		14442
1443	„ „ 54, „	„	„		Finlay Rankin, quarrier	2 9 0		14443
1444	„ „ 55, „	„	„		Donald Clark	4 0 0		14444
1445	„ „ 55, „	„	„		James McGillivray	2 0 0		14445
1446	„ „ 56, „	„	„		Ann Lowrie, pauper	0 1 0		14446
1447	„ „ 57, „	„	„		John McColl, quarrier	2 5 0		14447
1448	„ „ 58, „	„	„		Hugh McDonald, labourer	3 8 0		14448
1449	„ „ 59, „	„	„		Dugald McColl, quarrier	2 19 6		14449
1450	„ „ 60, „	„	„		Ronald Robertson	3 3 6		14450
1451	„ „ 63, „	„	„		Donald McGillivray	2 18 6		14451
1452	„ „ 64, „	„	„		Duncan McColl, engineman	2 17 6		14452
1453	„ „ 65, „	„	„		William Grieve, quarrier	4 0 0		14453
1454	„ „ 66, „	„	„		Angus Cameron, engineman	3 6 0		14454
1455	„ „ 67, „	„	„		Mrs. Mary Kesson	3 6 0		14455
1456	„ „ 68, „	„	„		Neil McDonald, quarrier	2 14 0		14456
1457	„ „ 69, „	„	„		John McKenzie	3 0 0		14457
1458	„ „ 70, „	„	„		Mrs. John Cameron, widow	3 0 0		14458
1459	„ „ 71, „	„	„		John Rankin, quarrier	2 5 0		14459
1460	„ „ 72, „	„	„		Hugh McIntyre	2 9 0		14460
1461	„ „ 73, „	„	„		Hugh McEachmor, labourer	4 5 6		14461
1462	„ „ 73, „	„	„		Allan McDougall, quarrier	4 5 6		14462
1463	„ „ 74, „	„	„		Duncan Fraser	4 5 6		14463
1464	„ „ 74, „	„	„		Alexander McGregor, -	4 0 0		14464
						Forward £16,943 0 7		

432   VALUATION ROLL FOR THE COUNTY OF ARGYLL, FOR THE YEAR 1901-1902.   LISMORE AND APPIN PARISH.   LORN DISTRICT.

No.	Description and Situation of Subject	Proprietor	Tenant	Occupier	Inhabitant Occupier and rated (58 Vic. cap A. SS. 2 and 3).	Annual Value of Dwelling-House or Portion thereof, &c., used as a Dwelling-House (58 Vic. cap A, SS. 2), Annual Value in such case.	Yearly Rent or Value.	No.
		BALLACHULISH WATER AND DRAINAGE DISTRICT—Continued					Forward £16,943 0 7	
14465	House and Grazing, No. 75, West Laroch	P. C. Beresford Drummond and another	The Ballachulish Slate Quarries Co., Limited		Donald M'Innes, quarrier	£4 11 0		14465
14466	,, ,, 76, ,,	,,	,,		Sarah M'Innes	1 5 0		14466
14467	,, ,, 77, ,,	,,	,,		Mrs. Donald M'Donald, pauper	1 6 0		14467
14468	,, ,, 78, ,,	,,	,,		Angus Cameron, grieve	2 14 6		14468
14469	,, ,, 79, ,,	,,	,,		Charles Livingston, quarrier	0 18 0		14469
14470	,, ,, 80, ,,	,,	,,		Mrs. Peter Rankin, pauper	0 7 0		14470
14471		,,	,,		Allan Cumming, labourer	1 0 0		14471
14472	,, ,, 81, ,,	,,	,,		Bella M'Innes, pauper	0 14 6		14472
14473	,, ,, 82, ,,	,,	,,		Duncan M'Intyre, quarr	2 14 6		14473
14474	,, ,, 83, ,,	,,	,,		Miss Ann M'Coll	2 14 0		14474
14475		,,	,,		Allan M'Lachlan,	3 0 0		14475
14476	(Old Store), East Laroch	,,	,,		Mrs. Alexander Rankin	3 0 0		14476
14477	,, ,, 84, ,,	,,	,,		Archibald M'Innes, quarrier	3 0 0		14477
14478	{ No. 1 Inskinno Buildings, East Laroch	,,	,,		Allan M'Coll,	3 10 0		14478
14479		,,	,,		Malcolm M'Kenzie, ,,			14479
14480	,, 2 ,,	,,	,,		John M'Millan,	3 0 0		14480
14481	,, 2A ,,	,,	,,		Paul M'Innes,	3 0 0		14481
14482	,, 3 ,,	,,	,,		Neil Carmichael, labourer	2 0 0		14482
14483	,, Bank, ,,	,,	,,		Alexander M'Coll, baker	3 0 0		14483
14484		,,	,,		Angus M'Intyre, quarrier	2 12 0		14484
14485	Workshop, ,,	,,	,,		Angus M'Donald, ,,	0 15 0		14485
14486	,, ,,	,,	,,		Duncan Clark	0 5 0		14486
14487	Laroch House	,,	£1,128 5 6		Archibald M'Coll	25 0 0		14487
		FEUS AND BUILDING LEASES.						
14488	Benbhan Cottage, West Laroch, Ballachulish	Misses Marion and Margaret Weir		Proprietors		0 2 6	25 0 0	14488
14489	House, ,, ,,	Robert M'Innes, grocer		Vacant		2 0 0	18 0 0	14489
14490	,, shop, & bakehouse, ,,	Archd. M'Coll, quarry manager	Andrew Cowlem,	Proprietor			30 0 0	14490
14491	,, West Laroch	Dugald Cameron, tailor	Lachlan Grant, M.D.	Tenant			30 0 0	14491
14492	,, and shop, ,,			Proprietor			6 0 0	14492
14493	Water Works, Ballachulish	Lorn District Committee, per John D. Sutherland		Proprietors			25 0 0	14493
		PUBLIC BUILDINGS.						
14495	South, Ballachulish U.P. Church	Rev. Duncan M'Murchy, minister		The Board		3 14 3	10 0 0	14495
14496	Public School, Ballachulish	The School Board of the Parish, per D. Macintyre, Port-Appin					15 0 0	14496
14497	,, Dwelling-house, ,,	,,		The Teacher, Arch. M'Callum, M.A.			10 0 0	14497
							Forward £17,112 0 7	

VALUATION ROLL FOR THE COUNTY OF ARGYLL, FOR THE YEAR 1902–1903. LISMORE AND APPIN PARISH. LORN DISTRICT. 425

BALLACHULISH WATER AND DRAINAGE DISTRICT.

No.	Description and Situation of Subject	Proprietor	Tenant	Occupier	Inhabitant Occupier (as rated)	Annual Value of Dwelling	Yearly Rent or Value	No.
							Forward £15,763 17 0	
	Cottage and Shop, East Laroch	F. C. Beresford Drummond and another, trustees of the late Sir George de la Poer Beresford, of Ballachulish, per Millar, Robson & M'Lean, W.S., Edinburgh	Hugh M'Coll, baker	Tenant			35 0 0	14574
	House and Store, and Mill	"	Barr & Co., storekeepers	Tenants	Robert Paton Grant, manager	£4 0 0	20 0 0	14575
	Cottage, Shop, and Land	"	Archibald McAlpine, joiner	Tenant			25 0 0	14576
	Shop, Farm, & House, Gortenorm, East Laroch	"	Hugh MacInnes, butcher				50 0 0	14377
	Land, East Laroch	"	Donald Campbell, farmer				15 0 0	14378
	Drill Hall, Armoury, Mechanics' Institute, and House, No. 4	"	The Village Committee, per Secy.	Tenants			1 0 0	14379
	Institute Buildings	"	Argyll Highland Rifle Volunteers				30 10 0	14380
	Part of Slate Quarries—Rent and Lordship	"	The Ballachulish Slate Quarries Co., Limited, per E. Bruce Low, S.S.C., 23 York Place, Edinburgh		Peter Campbell, drill instructor	5 0 0	300 0 0	14381
	House, South Ballachulish	"	"	Vacant				14382
	Quarry Cottage, No. 47, East Laroch	"	"	Mrs. M'Kenzie, pauper		Rent free	1 0 0	14383
	19, West Laroch	"	"	Paul M'Innes, quarrier			3 0 0	14384
	1, West Laroch	"	"	Widow Cameron, pauper			0 10 0	14385
	20	"	"	Samuel M'Taggart			1 0 0	14386
	21	"	"	Dugald McLaren, quarrier			7 0 0	14387
	41	"	"	Mrs. Christian Lawson			1 0 0	14388
	47	"	"	Donald Rankin, pauper			1 10 0	14389
	76	"	"	Sarah M'Innes			1 5 0	14390
	77	"	"	Mrs. Donald Macdonald			1 2 0	14391
	81	"	"	Bella M'Innes			0 15 0	14392
	46	"	"	Margaret Mackenzie			0 15 0	14393
	Quarries' Pier, Ballachulish	"	"	Tenants	David MacBrayne, Glasgow	5 0 0	20 0 0	14394
		"	"		The West Highland Carrying Co., Limited	5 0 0		14395
	Quarry Cottages, No. 15, East Laroch, House	"	"		Dugald Henderson, quarrier	2 2 6	495 14 0	14396
	16	"	"		Angus M'Innes	2 0 0		14397
	17	"	"		Donald McColl	2 10 0		14398
	18	"	"		John Stewart	2 14 0		14399
	19a & Grazing	"	"		Ronald M'Innes, labourer	1 7 0		14400
	19c	"	"		Archd. M'Kenzie, quarrier	1 15 0		14401
	90	"	"		Archd. Rankin	1 12 0		14402
	22	"	"		Duncan Clark	4 9 6		14403
	23	"	"		Catherine M'Kenzie	2 16 0		14404
	24	"	"		Allan Robertson	2 13 0		14405
	25	"	"		John Kennedy	1 10 0		14406
	25a	"	"		Alexander M'Donald	1 5 0		14407
	26	"	"		Mrs. Margaret Cameron, widow	1 15 0		14408
		"	"		Alexander Cameron, quarrier	1 10 0		14409
							Forward £16,857 5 6	14410

426   VALUATION ROLL FOR THE COUNTY OF ARGYLL, FOR THE YEAR 1902-1903, LISMORE AND APPIN PARISH. LORN DISTRICT.

BALLACHULISH WATER AND DRAINAGE DISTRICT—Continued.

No.	Description and Situation of Subject	Proprietor	Tenant	Occupier	Inhabitant Occupier	Amount Value of Dwelling	Yearly Rent or Value	No.
					Forward	£1 16 3	Forward £16,837 5 6	
14411	House, No. 27, East Laroch	F. C. Beresford Drummond and another	The Ballachulish Slate Quarries Co., Limited		Alexander Macdonald, quarrier			14411
14412	,, 28, ,,	,,	,,		Thomas M'Donald	1 16 3		14412
14413	,, 29, ,,	,,	,,		Archibald Carmichael	2 14 6		14413
14414	,, 30, ,,	,,	,,		Mrs. Duncan Clark, widow	2 8 6		14414
14415	,, 31, ,,	,,	,,		Donald Turner, quarrier	2 6 0		14415
14416		,,	,,		John M'Donald, labourer	2 9 0		14416
14417		,,	,,		Robert M'Innes, quarrier	2 9 6		14417
14418	,, 32, ,,	,,	,,		Archibald Fallow	2 12 6		14418
14419	,, 33, ,,	,,	,,		Alexander Livingston	2 16 0		14419
14420	,, 34, ,,	,,	,,		Mrs. Christina May, widow	2 14 0		14420
14421	,, 35, ,,	,,	,,		Mrs. Margaret Clark	2 14 0		14421
14422	,, 36, ,,	,,	,,		Archibald M'Quarrie, quarrier	4 — 6		14422
14423	,, 37, ,,	,,	,,		John M'Innes, labourer	2 15 0		14423
14424	,, 38, ,,	,,	,,		James Robertson, quarrier	4 0 0		14424
14425	,, 39, ,,	,,	,,		Donald Cameron, labourer	4 0 0		14425
14426	,, 40, ,,	,,	,,		Alexander MacTaggart, quarrier	2 14 0		14426
14427	,, 41, ,,	,,	,,		Alexander M'Taggart, quarrier	2 9 0		14427
14428	,, 42, ,,	,,	,,		John Macinnes	2 8 0		14428
14429	,, 43, ,,	,,	,,		John M'Lean	2 8 0		14429
14430	,, 44, ,,	,,	,,		Allan M'Dougall	2 8 0		14430
14431	,, 45, ,,	,,	,,		Archibald M'Millan, labourer	1 10 0		14431
14432	,, 46, ,,	,,	,,		Duncan Livingstone, engineman	1 4 0		14432
14433		,,	,,		Angus Macintyre, quarrier	3 0 0		14433
14434	,, 47, ,,	,,	,,		John Mackenzie	1 15 0		14434
14435	,, 48, ,,	,,	,,		James Brown, engineman	1 15 0		14435
14436	,, 49, ,,	,,	,,		John M'Gillivray, quarrier	1 7 0		14436
14437	,, 49a, ,,	,,	,,		Alexander M'Kenzie	4 2 0		14437
14438	,, 50, ,,	,,	,,		Duncan Livingstone	4 2 6		14438
14439	,, 51, ,,	,,	,,		John Cameron	4 8 0		14439
14440	,, 52, ,,	,,	,,		Neil M'Neill	4 2 6		14440
14441	,, 53, ,,	,,	,,		Mrs. Margaret Morrison, nurse	4 2 6		14441
14442	,, 54, ,,	,,	,,		John Macdonald, quarrier	4 2 6		14442
14443	,, 55, ,,	,,	,,		Archibald M'Callum, smith	4 2 0		14443
14444	,, 56, ,,	,,	,,		John Carmichael, quarrier	4 0 0		14444
14445	,, 57, ,,	,,	,,		Dugald Livingston	4 0 0		14445
14446	,, 58, ,,	,,	,,		Duncan Rankin	4 0 0		14446
14447	,, 59, ,,	,,	,,		Hugh Leslie	4 0 0		14447
14448	,, 60, ,,	,,	,,		Duncan M'Kenzie	4 0 0		14448
14449	,, 61, ,,	,,	,,		Donald Macgregor	4 0 0		14449
14450	,, 62, ,,	,,	,,		John M'Innes, foreman	4 0 0		14450
14451	,, 63, ,,	,,	,,		John M'Innes, quarrier	4 0 0		14451
14452	,, 64, ,,	,,	,,		John Clark	4 0 0		14452
14453	,, 65, ,,	,,	,,		Duncan M'Intyre	4 11 0		14453
14454	,, 66, ,,	,,	,,		Mrs. J. Campbell	4 5 0		14454
14455	,, 67, ,,	,,	,,		John Robertson	4 0 0		14455
14456	,, 68, ,,	,,	,,		Miss Bella Campbell	4 0 0		14456
14457	,, 69, ,,	,,	,,		William M'Kenzie	4 12 6		14457
14458	,, 70, ,,	,,	,,		Duncan Rankin	4 0 0		14458
14459	Laroch Cottage and Garden, No. 73	,,	,,		Alexander Maccoll, foreman	13 0 0		14459
14460	House, No. 73	,,	,,		John Graham, piermaster	2 0 0		14460
							Forward £16,837 5 6	

M a

VALUATION ROLL FOR THE COUNTY OF ARGYLL, FOR THE YEAR 1902–1903.   LISMORE AND APPIN PARISH.   LORN DISTRICT.

427

No.	Description and Situation of Subject.	House.	Proprietor.	Tenant.	Occupier.	Inhabitant Occupier, not rated (48 Vic. cap. 1, 2, & 3 and 4).	Annual Value and Rental of Subject Occupier (Gross Rent deducted) or Valued Rent.	Yearly Rent or Value.	No.
							Forward	£16,837 5 6	14461
			BALLACHULISH WATER AND DRAINAGE DISTRICT—CONTINUED.				Forward	£1 10 0	
14461	House,	No. 73A, East Laroch	F. C. Beresford Drummond and another	The Ballachulish Slate Quarries Co., Limited		Alexander Macoll, quarrier			14461
14462	„ 74, „		„	„		Alexander Wilson,	1 10 0		14462
14463	„ 75, „		„	„		Alexander Anderson	2 0 0		14463
14464	„ 76, „		„	„		Alexander M'Laren, joiner	2 0 0		14464
14465	„ 77, „		„	„		Donald M'Intyre, quarrier	2 11 0		14465
14466	„ 78, „		„	„		Archibald Rankin,	2 0 0		14466
14467	„ 79, „		„	„		Donald Kennedy,	2 0 0		14467
14468	„ 80, „		„	„		Catherine M'Kenzie	0 10 0		14468
14469	„ 81, „		„	„		Mrs. Duncan M'Coll	1 5 0		14469
14470	„ 82, „		„	„		Allan Brown, smith	2 6 0		14470
14471	„ 83, „		„	„		John Livingston, quarrier	2 8 0		14471
14472	„ 84, „		„	„		Donald Lowrie,	2 16 0		14472
14473	„ 85, „		„	„		Agnes M'Farlane, pauper	0 1 0		14473
14474	„ 86, „		„	„		Archibald Black, quarrier	1 0 0		14474
14475	„ 87, „		„	„		Mrs. Christina Colquhoun	2 0 0		14475
14476	„ 88, „		„	„		Donald M'Donald, labourer	2 0 0		14476
14477	„ 89, „		„	„		Paul M'Coll, quarrier	1 10 0		14477
14478	„ 90, „		„	„		Donald M'Millan,	2 0 0		14478
14479	„ 1, West Laroch		„	„		Catherine Cameron, pauper	0 1 0		14479
14480	„ 2, „		„	„		Dugald Ferguson, quarrier	4 4 6		14480
14481	„ 3, „		„	„		James Stewart,	3 6 0		14481
14482	„ 4, „		„	„		John M'Dougall,	2 15 0		14482
14483	„ 5, „		„	„		Alexander M'Coll,	4 10 6		14483
14484	„ 6, „		„	„		John Cameron,	4 7 0		14484
14485	„ 7, „		„	„		Donald Campbell, blacksmith	3 10 0		14485
14486	„ 7A, „		„	„		David Drummond	4 0 0		14486
14487	„ 7B, „		„	„		Hugh M'Innes, quarrier	4 11 0		14487
14488	„ 8, „		„	„		Archibald M'Taggart,	4 0 0		14488
14489	„ 9, „		„	„		Angus M'Kenzie,	4 7 0		14489
14490	„ 10, „		„	„		John Clark,	4 11 0		14490
14491	„ 11, „		„	„		John M'Lachlan,	4 11 0		14491
14492	„ 12, „		„	„		Dugald M'Innes,	0 15 0		14492
14493	„ 13, „		„	„			2 15 0		14493
14494	„ 14, „		„	„		John M'Coll,	4 9 6		14494
14495	„ 15, „		„	„		Hugh M'Coll, foreman	3 6 0		14495
14496	„ 16, „		„	„		Mrs. Christina M'Callum, widow	3 6 0		14496
14497	„ 17, „		„	„		John Cameron, quarrier	1 10 0		14497
14498	„ 18, „		„	„		Hugh Grieve	4 0 0		14498
14499	„ 19, „		„	„		Alexander M'Innes,	4 4 0		14499
14500	„ 20, „		„	„		Miss Catherine M'Kenzie, pauper	0 1 0		14500
14501	„ 21, „		„	„		John M'Kenzie, quarrier	1 7 0		14501
14502	„ 22, „		„	„		Alexander M'Pherson,	2 0 0		14502
14503	„ 23, „		„	„		Duncan M'Kenzie, postman	2 13 0		14503
14504	„ 24, „		„	„		Donald Ferguson	4 1 0		14504
14505	„ 25, „		„	„		John M'Coll, quarrier	2 0 0		14505
14506	„ 26, „		„	„		James Clark,	2 19 0		14506
14507	„ 27, „		„	„		Donald Stewart,	3 5 6		14507
14508	„ 28, „		„	„		Hugh Campbell,	4 4 6		14508
14509	„ 29, „		„	„		John Thomson,	2 18 6		14509
							Forward	£16,837 5 6	

VALUATION ROLL FOR THE COUNTY OF ARGYLL, FOR THE YEAR 1902-1903.   LISMORE AND APPIN PARISH.   LORN DISTRICT.

No.	DESCRIPTION AND SITUATION OF SUBJECT.	PROPRIETOR.	TENANT.	OCCUPIER.	INHABITANT OCCUPIER, not rated (65 Vic. cap. 3, S.S. 3 and 9).	Annual Value of Dwelling-houses of Inhabitant Occupiers (included) not rated.	Yearly Rent or Value.	No.
		BALLACHULISH WATER AND DRAINAGE DISTRICT—Continued.					Forward £16,837 3 6	
14510	House, No. 30, West Larach,	F. C. Beresford Drummond and another	The Ballachulish Slate Quarries Co. Limited		Hugh Robertson, quarrier	£3 3 0		14510
14511	„ 31, „	„	„		Alan M'Kenzie, „	4 4 0		14511
14512	„ 31a, „	„	„		Jean M'Eachern, pauper	4 0 0		14512
14513	„ 31a, „	„	„		James Watson, labourer	2 0 0		14513
14514	„ 31a, „	„	„		James M'Innes, quarrier	1 16 0		14514
14515	„	„	„		Mrs. John M'Intyre	0 1 0		14515
14516	„ 32, „	„	„		John M'Gregor	2 18 0		14516
14517	„ 33, „	„	„		Miss Catharine M'Kenzie	2 18 6		14517
14518	„ 34, „	„	„		Dugald Lowrie, quarrier	2 0 0		14518
14519	„ 35, „	„	„		Robert M'Coll	4 0 0		14519
14520	„ 35a, „	„	„		Donald Cameron	4 0 0		14520
14521	„ 35a, „	„	„		Ewen M'Donald	5 0 0		14521
14522	„ 35a, and Grazing,	„	„		William Fleming	2 1 0		14522
14523	„ 36, „	„	„		John M'Eachern	3 1 0		14523
14524	„ 37, „	„	„		Donald M'Intyre	3 1 0		14524
14525	„ 38, „	„	„		Duncan M'Donald	2 19 0		14525
14526	„ 39, „	„	„		Mrs. Margaret M'Kenzie, widow	2 19 0		14526
14527	„ 40, „	„	„		Hugh Cameron, quarrier	0 1 0		14527
14528	„ 41, „	„	„		Mrs. Mary M'Donald, pauper	3 0 0		14528
14529	„ 42, „	„	„		Peter Cameron, quarrier	3 11 6		14529
14530	„ 43, „	„	„		Angus Benton, quarrier	3 0 0		14530
14531	„ 44, „	„	„		Alexander Cameron, „	2 9 0		14531
14532	„ 45, „	„	„		Mary M'Coll	1 5 0		14532
14533	„	„	„		John Clark	3 11 0		14533
14534	„ 46, „	„	„		Margaret M'Kenzie, pauper	0 1 0		14534
14535	„ 47, „	„	„		Alexander M'Taggart, quarrier	1 10 0		14535
14536	„ 48, „	„	„		Lachlan M'Taggart	3 16 0		14536
14537	„ 49, „	„	„		Donald Cameron	2 16 0		14537
14538	„ 50, „	„	„		Archibald M'Phee	2 16 6		14538
14539	„ 51, „	„	„		James Cameron, roadman	2 14 0		14539
14540	„ 52, „	„	„		Alex. Macintyre, quarrier	2 0 0		14540
14541	„ 53, „	„	„		Donald Clark	4 0 0		14541
14542	„ 54, „	„	„		James M'Gillivray, „	2 0 0		14542
14543	„ 55, „	„	„		Ann Lowrie, pauper	0 1 0		14543
14544	„ 56, „	„	„		John M'Coll, quarrier	2 5 0		14544
14545	„ 57, „	„	„		Hugh M'Donald, labourer	3 0 0		14545
14546	„ 58, „	„	„		Dugald M'Coll, quarrier	2 12 0		14546
14547	„ 59, „	„	„		Ronald Robertson	2 0 0		14547
14548	„ 60, „	„	„		Donald M'Gillivray, „	2 18 0		14548
14549	„ 62, „	„	„		Duncan M'Coll, engineman	2 17 6		14549
14550	„ 63, „	„	„		William Grieve, quarrier	4 0 0		14550
14551	„ 64, „	„	„		Angus Cameron, engineman	3 6 0		14551
14552	„ 65, „	„	„		Mrs. Mary Keston	2 14 0		14552
14553	„ 66, „	„	„		Neil M'Donald, quarrier	3 6 0		14553
14554	„ 67, „	„	„		John M'Kenzie	3 6 0		14554
14555	„ 68, „	„	„		Miss Jessie Cameron	2 6 0		14555
14556	„ 69, „	„	„		John Rankin, quarrier	2 6 0		14556
14557	„ 70, „	„	„		Hugh M'Intyre, „	4 0 0		14557
14558	„ 71, „	„	„		Hugh M'Eachran, labourer	4 5 0		14558
14559	„ 72, „	„	„		Allan M'Dougall, quarrier	4 0 0		14559
							Forward £16,857 5 6	

VALUATION ROLL FOR THE COUNTY OF ARGYLL, FOR THE YEAR 1902–1903. LISMORE AND APPIN PARISH. LORN DISTRICT.

429

No.	Description and Situation of Subject	Proprietor	Tenant	Occupier	Inhabitant Occupier not rated (55 Vic. cap. 4, §§ 3 and 9)	Yearly Rent or Value	No.
					Forward	£16,837 5 6	
	BALLACHULISH WATER AND DRAINAGE DISTRICT.—Continued.						
14460	House, No. 73, West Laroch	F. C. Beresford Drummond and another	The Ballachulish Slate Quarries Co., Limited	Duncan Fraser, quarrier	£4 5 6		14460
14461	do. 74, do.	do.	do.	Alexander M'Gregor	4 0 0		14461
14462	do. 75, do.	do.	do.	Donald M'Innes	4 11 0		14462
14463	do. 76, do.	do.	do.	Sarah M'Innes	1 5 0		14463
14464	do. and Grazing 77, do.	do.	do.	Mrs. Donald M'Donald, pauper	0 1 0		14464
14465	do. 78, do.	do.	do.	Angus Cameron, grieve	2 14 6		14465
14466	do. 79, do.	do.	do.	Charles Livingston, quarrier	0 18 0		14466
14467	do. 80, do.	do.	do.	Mrs. Peter Rankin, pauper	0 1 0		14467
14468	do. 81, do.	do.	do.	Allan Cumming, labourer	0 1 0		14468
14469	do. 82, do.	do.	do.	Bella M'Innes, pauper	0 1 0		14469
14470	do. 83, do.	do.	do.	Duncan M'Intyre, quarrier	2 14 0		14470
14471	do. 84, do.	do.	do.	Miss Ann M'Coll	2 2 6		14471
14472	do. (Old Store), East Laroch	do.	do.	Mrs. Alexander Rankin	2 14 0		14472
14473	do. No. 1 Institute Buildings, East Laroch	do.	do.	Allan M'Lachlan	3 0 0		14473
14474	do. do.	do.	do.	Archibald M'Innes, quarrier	3 0 0		14474
14475	do. do.	do.	do.	Allan M'Coll	3 0 0		14475
14476	do. do.	do.	do.	Malcolm M'Kenzie	4 10 0		14476
14477	do. 2, do.	do.	do.	John M'Millan	3 0 0		14477
14478	do. 2A, do.	do.	do.	Paul M'Innes	2 0 0		14478
14479	do. 3, do.	do.	do.	Neil Carmichael, labourer	3 0 0		14479
14480	do. 3, do.	do.	do.	Alexander M'Coll, baker	2 0 0		14480
14481	Bank, do.	do.	do.	Angus M'Intyre, quarrier	0 12 0		14481
14482	do. do.	do.	do.	Dugald Johnson	0 12 0		14482
14483	Laroch House	do.	do.	Archibald M'Coll	25 0 0		14483
				£1,073 8 6			
	FEUS AND BUILDING LEASES.						
14484	Benban Cottage, West Laroch, Ballachulish	Misses Marion and Margaret Weir		Proprietrices	0 2 6	25 0 0	14484
14485	House, do.	Robert M'Innes, grocer		Vacant			14585
14486	House, do.	Robert M'Innes, grocer		Proprietor	2 0 0	18 0 0	14586
14487	House, shop, & bakehouse, do.	Archd. M'Coll, quarry manager	Andrew Cochran, baker	Tenant		30 0 0	14587
14488	do. and shop, West Laroch	Dugald Cameron, tailor	Lachlan Grant, M.D.		£40 0 0	30 0 0	14588
14489	Water Works, Ballachulish	Lorn District Committee, per John D. Sutherland		Proprietor		10 0 0	14589
14490				Proprietors		25 0 0	14590
	PUBLIC BUILDINGS.						
14491	South Ballachulish U.F. Church, Ballachulish	Rev. Duncan M'Murchy, minister		The Board		10 0 0	14591
14492	Public School, Ballachulish	The School Board of the Parish, per D. Macintyre, Port-Appin		The Board	3 14 3	15 0 0	14592
14493	do. Dwelling-house, do.			The Teacher, Arch. M'Callum, M.A.		10 0 0	14593
					Forward	£17,010 5 6	

444   VALUATION ROLL FOR THE COUNTY OF ARGYLL, FOR THE YEAR 1905-1906.   LISMORE AND APPIN PARISH.   LORN DISTRICT.

No.	Description and Situation of Subject.	Proprietor.	Tenant.	Occupier.	Inhabitant Occupier. Not rated (48 Vic. cap. 3, S.S. 7 and 9).	Annual Value of Lands and Heritages included in the Valuation Roll, whether Subject, Owner or Occupier; deducting Public Burdens, Feu-duty or Ground Annual if either applicable.	Yearly Rent or Value.	No.
						Forward	£16,062 0 7	Forward	
		BALLACHULISH WATER, DRAINAGE, AND SCAVENGING DISTRICT.						
14777	House and Shop, East Laroch	F. C. Beresford Drummond and another, trustee of the late Sir George de la Poer Beresford, of Ballachulish, per Millar, Robson & M'Lean, W.S., Edinburgh.	Miss Nancy M'Coll, baker	Tenant			36 0 0	14772
14778	House and Store,	„	Barr & Co., storekeepers	Tenants	Robert Paton Grant, manager	£4 0 0	90 0 0	14778
14779	and Mill,	„	Archibald M'Alpine, joiner	Tenant			35 0 0	14779
14780	Land,	„	Hugh MacInnes, butcher				14 0 0	14780 A
14781	Sheep Farm & House, Gorteneorn East Laroch	„	Donald Campbell, farmer	Tenants			1 0 0	14781
14782	Land,	„	The Village Committee, per Secy, 5th V. B. Argyll and Sutherland Highland Rifle Volunteers				20 10 0	14782 A
14783	Drill Hall, Armoury, Mechanics Institute, and House, No. 4	„			Peter Campbell, drill instructor	5 0 0		14783
14784	Institute Buildings Part of Slate Quarries—Rent and Lordship	„	The Ballachulish Slate Quarries Co., Limited, per E. Bruce Low, S.S.C., 23 York Place, Edinburgh	„			360 0 0	14784
14785	House, South Ballachulish	„	„	Vacant			1 0 0	14785
14786	Quarry Cottage, No. 47, East Laroch	„	„	Mrs. M'Kenzie, pauper			1 0 0	14786 Rent free.
14787	„ 19, „	„	„	Paul M'Innes, quarrier			3 0 0	14787
14788	„ 1, West Laroch	„	„	Widow Cameron, pauper			0 10 0	14788
14789	„ 20, „	„	„	Vacant			1 0 0	14789
14790	„ 21, „	„	„	Mrs. Christina Lawson			1 7 0	14790
14791	„ 41, „	„	„	Donald Rankin, pauper			1 0 0	14791
14792	„ 47, „	„	„	Sarah M'Innes			1 10 0	14792
14793	„ 76, „	„	„	Mrs. Donald Macdonald			1 5 0	14793
14794	„ 77, „	„	„	Bella M'Innes			1 0 0	14794
14795	„ 81, „	„	„	Margaret Mackenzie			0 15 0	14795
14796	„ 46, „	„	„	Tenant			0 15 0	14796
14797	Ground,	„	Hugh M'Coll, tailor	Tenants			0 2 6	14797
14798	Quarries' Pier, Ballachulish	„	The Ballachulish Slate Quarries Co., Limited, per E. Bruce Low, S.S.C., 23 York Place, Edinburgh				20 0 0	14798
14799		„			David MacBrayne, Glasgow	5 0 0		14799
14800	Quarry Cottages, No. 15, East	„			The West Highland Carrying Co., Limited	5 0 0	495 14 0	14800
14801	House,	„			Dugald Henderson, quarrier	1 10 0		14801
14802	„ 16, Laroch	„			Angus M'Innes,	2 0 0		14802
14803	„ 17, „	„			Alexander M'Coll,	3 17 0		14803
14804	& Grazing, „ 18, „	„			John Stewart,	2 1 0		14804
14805	„ 19a, „	„			Ronald M'Innes, labourer	2 7 0		14805
14806	„ 19a, „	„			Archd. M'Kenzie, quarrier	1 15 0		14806
14807	„ 19b, „	„			Jessie Rankin, pauper	1 0 0		14807
14808	„ 20, „	„			Duncan Clark, „	3 17 0		14808
14809	„ 22, „	„			Catherine M'Kenzie	2 0 0		14809
14810	„ 23, „	„			Allan Robertson, „	2 0 6		14810
						Forward	£17,120 11 7	

VALUATION ROLL FOR THE COUNTY OF ARGYLL, FOR THE YEAR 1905–1906.   LISMORE AND APPIN PARISH.   LORN DISTRICT.   445

No.	Description and Situation of Subject	Proprietor	Tenant	Occupier	Inhabitant Occupier not rated (59 Vic. cap. 4, §§ 7 and 8)	Yearly Rent or Value	No.
		BALLACHULISH WATER, DRAINAGE, AND SCAVENGING DISTRICT—*continued.*					
						Forward £17,130 11 7	
1811	House, No. 34, East Laroch	F. C. Bensford Drummond, and another	The Ballachulish Slate Quarries Co., Limited		John Kennedy, quarrier	£1 10 0	14811
1812	„ 25a „	„	„		Alexander M'Donald	1 5 0	14812
1813	„ 25a „	„	„		Mrs. Margaret Cameron, widow	1 15 0	14813
1814	„ 26a „	„	„		Alexander Cameron, quarrier	1 10 0	14814
1815	„ 27 „	„	„		Alexander Macdonald, „	1 16 3	14815
1816	„ 98 „	„	„		Thomas M'Donald, „	1 16 3	14816
1817	„ 99 „	„	„		Archibald Carmichael, „	2 1 6	14817
1818	„ 29 „	„	„		John Clark, „	2 10 0	14818
1819	„ 30 „	„	„		Donald Turner, „	2 1 6	14819
1820	„ 31 „	„	„		John M'Donald, labourer	2 10 0	14820
1821	Grazing, 32 „	„	„		Robert M'Innes, quarrier	1 16 6	14821
1822	„ 33 „	„	„		Archibald Fallow, „	3 3 6	14822
1823	„ 34 „	„	„		Alexander Livingston, „	3 6	14823
1824	„ 35 „	„	„		Mrs. Christina May, widow	3 1 6	14824
1825	„ 36 „	„	„		John Clark, „	1 6	14825
1826	„ 37 „	„	„		Archibald M'Quarrie, quarrier	3 10 0	14826
1827	„ 38 „	„	„		John M'Innes, labourer	1 15 0	14827
1828	„ 39 „	„	„		James Robertson, quarrier	4 0 0	14828
1829	„ 40 „	„	„		Donald Robertson, labourer	3 0 0	14829
1830	„ 41 „	„	„		Alexander Mavor, quarrier	3 1 6	14830
1831	„ 42 „	„	„		John Maciness, „	2 1 6	14831
1832	„ 43 „	„	„		Alexander M'Taggart, „	2 7 6	14832
1833	„ 44 „	„	„		John M'Lean, „	2 9 0	14833
1834	„ 45 „	„	„		Allan M'Dougall, „	2 0 0	14834
1835	„ 46 „	„	„		Archibald M'Millan, labourer	1 0 0	14835
1836	„ 47 „	„	„		Duncan Livingston, engineman	1 0 0	14836
1837	„ 48 „	„	„		Ann Macintyre, pauper	0 1 0	14837
1838	„ 49 „	„	„		John Mackenzie, quarrier	2 0 0	14838
1839	„ 49a „	„	„		James Brown, engineman	2 7 6	14839
1840	„ 49a „	„	„		John M'Gillivray, quarrier	1 15 0	14840
1841	„ 50 „	„	„		Alexander M'Kenzie, „	18 0	14841
1842	„ 51 „	„	„		Duncan Livingston, „	0 14 6	14842
1843	„ 54 „	„	„		John Cameron, „	4 3 0	14843
1844	„ 55 „	„	„		Neil M'Neill, „	4 2 6	14844
1845	„ 56 „	„	„		Mrs. Margaret Morrison, nurse	4 0 0	14845
1846	„ 57 „	„	„		John Macdonald, quarrier	4 2 6	14846
1847	„ 58 „	„	„		Archibald M'Callum, smith	4 2 6	14847
1848	„ 59 „	„	„		John Carmichael, quarrier	4 2 6	14848
1849	„ 60 „	„	„		Dugald Livingston, „	4 2 6	14849
1850	„ 61 „	„	„		Donald Rankin, „	4 2 6	14850
1851	„ 62 „	„	„		Hugh Lowrie, „	4 2 6	14851
1852	„ 63 „	„	„		Mrs. Isabella M'Kenzie, widow	4 2 6	14852
1853	„ 53 „	„	„		Donald Macgregor, quarrier	4 0 0	14853
1854	„ 64 „	„	„		John M'Innes, foreman	4 0 0	14854
1855	„ 65 „	„	„		John M'Innes, quarrier	4 0 0	14855
1856	„ 66 „	„	„		John Clark, „	4 0 0	14856
1857	„ 67 „	„	„		Duncan M'Intyre, „	4 11 0	14857
1858	„ 68 „	„	„		Mrs. J. Campbell	4 0 0	14858
1859	„ 69 „	„	„		John Robertson, „	4 5 0	14859
1860	„ 70 „	„	„		Miss Bella Campbell	4 0 0	14860
						Forward £17,130 11 7	

446   VALUATION ROLL FOR THE COUNTY OF ARGYLL, FOR THE YEAR 1905-1906.   LISMORE AND APPIN PARISH.   LORN DISTRICT.

No.	Description and Situation of Subject	Proprietor	Tenant	Occupier	Inhabitant Occupier, and rated (68 Vic. cap. 4, S.S. 3 and 9).	Annual Value	Yearly Rent or Value.	No.
					Forward	£4 0 0	£17,120 11 7	
14861	House, No. 71, East Larach	F. C. Beresford Drummond and another			William M'Kenzie, quarrier			14861
			The Ballachulish Slate Quarries Co., Limited					
14862	,, 72, ,,				Duncan Rankin,	4 0 0		14862
14863	Larach Cottage and Gardens,				Alexander Maccoll, foreman	15 0 0		14863
14864	,, No. 73, ,,				John Graham, pier master	2 2 0		14864
14865	House, ,, 73a, ,,				Alexander Maccoll, quarrier	1 10 0		14865
14866	,, 74, ,,				Alexander Wilson,	2 0 0		14866
14867	,, 75, ,,				Alexander Anderson	1 10 0		14867
14868	& Grazing, 76, ,,				Alexander M'Laren, joiner	2 0 0		14868
14869	,, 77, ,,				Donald M'Intyre, quarrier	3 0 0		14869
14870	,, 78, ,,				Archibald Rankin,	2 11 0		14870
14871	,, 79, ,,				Donald Kennedy,	2 0 0		14871
14872	,, 80, ,,				Catherine M'Kenzie	0 10 0		14872
14873	,, 81, ,,				Duncan M'Innes	1 5 0		14873
14874	,, 82, ,,				Mrs. Mary Brown	2 8 0		14874
14875	,, 83, ,,				John Livingston, quarrier	2 8 0		14875
14876	,, 84, ,,				Donald Lowrie,	2 16 0		14876
14877	,, 85, ,,				Agnes M'Farlane, pauper	0 1 0		14877
14878	,, 86, ,,				Nicol Black, quarrier	2 0 0		14878
14879	,, 87, ,,				John M'Coll,	1 0 0		14879
14880	,, 88, ,,				Archibald Black,	1 0 0		14880
14881	,, 89, ,,				Mrs. Paul M'Coll	1 10 0		14881
14882	,, 90, West				Donald M'Millan,	2 0 0		14882
14883	,, 1, Larach				Catherine Cameron, pauper	0 1 0		14883
14884	,, 2, ,,				Dugald Ferguson, quarrier	4 6 0		14884
14885	,, 3, ,,				Angus Macdonald,	3 6 0		14885
14886	,, 4, ,,				John M'Dougall,	2 5 0		14886
14887	,, 5, ,,				Alexander M'Coll,	4 19 0		14887
14888	,, 6, ,,				John Cameron,	4 7 0		14888
14889	,, 7, ,,				Donald Campbell, blacksmith	3 10 0		14889
14890	,, 7a, ,,				John Gemmell	4 0 0		14890
14891	,, 7b, ,,				Hugh M'Innes, quarrier	1 11 0		14891
14892	,, 8, ,,				Archibald M'Taggart, ,,	4 11 0		14892
14893	,, 9, ,,				Angus M'Kenzie,	4 7 0		14893
14894	,, 10, ,,				John Clark,	4 11 0		14894
14895	,, 11, ,,				John M'Lachlan,	0 15 0		14895
14896	,, 12, ,,				Dugald M'Innes,	3 15 0		14896
14897	,, 13, ,,					4 6 0		14897
14898	,, 14, ,,				John M'Coll,	4 9 0		14898
14899	,, 15, ,,				Hugh M'Coll, foreman	3 6 0		14899
14900	,, 16, ,,				Mrs. Christina M'Callum, widow	3 6 0		14900
14901	,, 17, ,,				John Cameron, quarrier	1 10 0		14901
14902	,, 18, ,,				Hugh Grieve	4 4 0		14902
14903	,, 19, ,,				Alexander M'Eachern, joiner	4 4 0		14903
14904	,, 20, ,,				Miss Catherine M'Kenzie, pauper	0 1 0		14904
14905	,, 21, ,,				John M'Kenzie, quarrier	1 7 0		14905
14906	,, 22, ,,				Alexander M'Phorson,	2 0 0		14906
14907	,, 23, ,,				Duncan M'Kenzie, postman	2 13 0		14907
14908	,, 24, ,,				Donald Ferguson	4 1 0		14908
14909	,, 25, ,,				Mrs. Mary M'Coll, widow	2 0 0		14909
					Forward		£17,120 11 7	

BALLACHULISH WATER, DRAINAGE, AND SCAVENGING DISTRICT—Continued.

VALUATION ROLL FOR THE COUNTY OF ARGYLL, FOR THE YEAR 1905–1906.   LISMORE AND APPIN PARISH.   LORN DISTRICT.   447

BALLACHULISH WATER, DRAINAGE, AND SCAVENGING DISTRICT—Continued.

No.	Description and Situation of Subject	Proprietor	Tenant	Occupier	Inhabitant Occupier not rated (48 Vic. cap. 2, ss. 2 and 9).	Annual Value	Yearly Rent or Value	No.
							Forward £17,120 11 7	
4910	House, No. 26, West Laroch	F. C. Beresford Drummond and another	The Ballachulish Slate Quarries Co., Limited		James Clark, quarrier	£2 19 0		14910
	" 27, " and Grazing	"	"		Donald Stewart	1 5 6		14911
	" 28, "	"	"		Hugh Campbell	4 6		14912
	" 29, "	"	"		John Thompson	2 18 6		14913
	" 30, "	"	"		Hugh Robertson	3 5 0		14914
	" 31, "	"	"		Allan McKenzie	4 0		14915
	" 31a, "	"	"		John McEachern, pauper	0 1 0		14916
	" 31b, "	"	"		James Watson, labourer	2 4 0		14917
		"	"		James McInnes, pauper	5 0		14918
		"	"		Kenneth Maguire	0 5 0		14919
	" 32, "	"	"		John McGregor, quarrier	2 18 6		14920
	" 33, "	"	"		Miss Catherine McKenzie	2 15 6		14921
	" 34, "	"	"		Dugald Lowrie, quarrier	2 15 0		14922
	" 35, "	"	"		Robert McColl	4 0 0		14923
	" 35a, "	"	"		Donald Cameron	4 0		14924
	" 35b, "	"	"		Ewen McDonald	3 0		14925
	" 35c, "	"	"		William Fleming	3 0 0		14926
	" 36, "	"	"		John McEachern	3 6 0		14927
	" 37, "	"	"		Donald McIntyre	3 0		14928
	" 38, "	"	"		Duncan McDonald	3 6 0		14929
	" 39, "	"	"		Mrs. Margaret McKenzie, widow	2 19 0		14930
	" 40, "	"	"		Hugh Cameron, quarrier	2 19 0		14931
	" 41, "	"	"		Mrs. Mary McDonald, pauper	0 1 0		14932
	" 42, "	"	"		Peter Cameron, quarrier	3 1 0		14933
	" 43, "	"	"		Angus Beaton	3 0 0		14934
	" 44, "	"	"		Alexander Cameron	2 0		14935
	" 45, "	"	"		Mary McColl	1 5 0		14936
		"	"		John Clark	3 11 0		14937
	" 46, "	"	"		Margaret McKenzie, pauper	0 1 0		14938
	" 48, "	"	"		Lachlan McTaggart, quarrier	3 16 0		14939
	" 49, "	"	"		Donald Cameron	2 8 0		14940
	" 50, "	"	"		Archibald McPhee	2 16 0		14941
	" 51, "	"	"		James Cameron, roadman	2 14 0		14942
	" 52, "	"	"		Alex. Macintyre, quarrier	2 9 0		14943
	" 53, "	"	"		Donald Clark	4 0 0		14944
	" 54, "	"	"		James McGillivray	2 9 0		14945
	" 54a, "	"	"		Hugh McDonald, labourer	2 12 0		14946
	" 55, "	"	"		Ann Lowrie, pauper	0 1 0		14947
	" 59, "	"	"		Ronald Robertson, quarrier	8 3 6		14948
	" 60, "	"	"		Donald McGillivray, "	2 18 0		14949
	" 62, "	"	"		Duncan McColl, engineman	2 17 0		14950
	" 63, "	"	"		Angus Grieve, quarrier	2 14 0		14951
	" 64, "	"	"		Angus Cameron, engineman	3 8 6		14952
	" 65, "	"	"		Mrs. Mary Kenon	0 6 0		14953
	" 66, "	"	"		Neil McDonald, quarrier	2 14 0		14954
	" 67, "	"	"		John McKenzie	3 6 0		14955
	" 68, "	"	"		Miss Jessie Cameron	3 6 0		14956
	" 69, "	"	"		John Rankin, quarrier	2 5 0		14957
	" 70, "	"	"		Hugh McIntyre	2 6 0		14958
	" 71, "	"	"		Hugh McEachran, labourer	4 5 6		14959
							Forward £17,190 11 7	

448   VALUATION ROLL FOR THE COUNTY OF ARGYLL, FOR THE YEAR 1905-1906.   LISMORE AND APPIN PARISH.   LORN DISTRICT.

No.	Description and Situation of Subject	Proprietor	Tenant	Occupier	Inhabitant Occupier not rated (48 Vic. cap. 3, S.S. 1 and 3).	Annual Value of Dwellinghouses of less than £4, occupied by householders, etc. (1882) or Annual Value of Lands and other subjects.	Yearly Rent or Value	No.
					Forward	£17,120 11 7		
		BALLACHULISH WATER, DRAINAGE, AND SCAVENGING DISTRICT—Continued.						
14960	House, No. 73, West Laroch	R. C. Beresford Drummond and another	The Ballachulish Slate Quarries Co., Limited		Allan M'Dougall, quarrier	£4 0 0		14960
14961	73,	,,	,,		Duncan Fraser, ,,	4 5 6		14961
14962	74,	,,	,,		Alexander M'Gregor, ,,	4 6 0		14962
14963	& Grazing 75,	,,	,,		Alexander MacInnes, ,,	8 5 0		14963
14964	76,	,,	,,		Sarah M'Innes, pauper	1 0 0		14964
14965	77,	,,	,,		John M'Donald, a minor	1 0 0		14965
14966	78,	,,	,,		Angus Cameron, grieve	2 14 6		14966
14967	79,	,,	,,		Charles Livingston, quarrier	2 14 0		14967
14968	80,	,,	,,		John Rankin, a minor	1 0 0		14968
14969	81,	,,	,,		Allan Cumming, labourer	1 0 0		14969
14970	82,	,,	,,		Bella M'Innes, pauper	1 0 0		14970
14971	83,	,,	,,		Duncan M'Intyre, quarrier	2 14 0		14971
14972	84,	,,	,,		Dugald M'Coll, ,,	2 13 6		14972
14973	(Old Store), East Laroch	,,	,,		Allan M'Lachlan, ,,	2 14 0		14973
14974	,,	,,	,,		Mrs. Alexander Rankin	3 0 0		14974
14975	,,	,,	,,		Archibald M'Innes, quarrier	3 0 0		14975
14976	No. 1 Institute Buildings, East Laroch	,,	,,		Allan M'Coll, ,,	3 0 6		14976
14977	,,	,,	,,		Malcolm M'Kenzie, ,,	4 10 0		14977
14978	2	,,	,,		John McMillan, ,,	3 0 0		14978
14979	2A	,,	,,		Paul M'Innes, ,,	3 0 0		14979
14980	3	,,	,,		Neil Carmichael, labourer	2 0 0		14980
14981	Bank,	,,	,,		Alexander M'Coll, baker	0 12 0		14981
14982	,,	,,	,,		Dugald M'Intyre, quarrier	0 12 0		14982
14983	,,	,,	,,		Dugald Johnson, ,,	0 12 0		14983
14984	Laroch House	,,	£1,058 11 0		Archibald M'Coll	25 0 0		14984
		FEUS AND BUILDING LEASES.						
14985	Benliah Cottage, West Laroch, Ballachulish	Misses Marion and Margaret Weir		Proprietrices		0 2 6	25 0 0	14985
14986	House, ,,	Dugald Cameron, tailor		Vernut		2 0 0	30 0 0	14986
14987	,, & Shop, ,,	,,	£40 0 0	Tenant		1 10 0	10 0 0	14987
14988	Feu, ,,	Miss Annie M'Coll		Proprietor			0 0 0	14988
14989	Quarrier's	,,		Building	Building.	1 0 0	0 0 0	14989
14990	Cottage, ,,	Alex. MacTaggart, quarrier, lessee		Proprietor	Part of a year.		0 0 0	14990
14991	House, Lonsfern, East Laroch	Robert M'Innes, grocer		,,		1 0 0	2 0 0	14991
14992	,, Shop, & Bakehouse, ,,	Archd. M'Coll, quarry manager	Andrew Cochran, tacker	Tenant		1 12 0	18 0 0	14992
14993	Workmen's House, Ballachulish	Callander and Oban Railway Company, per R. Watson, 15 Hope Street, Glasgow		Proprietors		3 0 0	32 10 0	14993
14994	House, ,,	,,			James Skinner, station master	6 10 0		14994
14995	,, ,,	,,			Donald McColl, porter	4 11 0		14995
14996	,, ,,	,,			Murdoch M'Taggart, guard	4 11 0		14996
					Forward	£17,268 1 7		

Appendix 2
Census Returns, 1901: West Laroch

Courtesy of General Register Office for Scotland

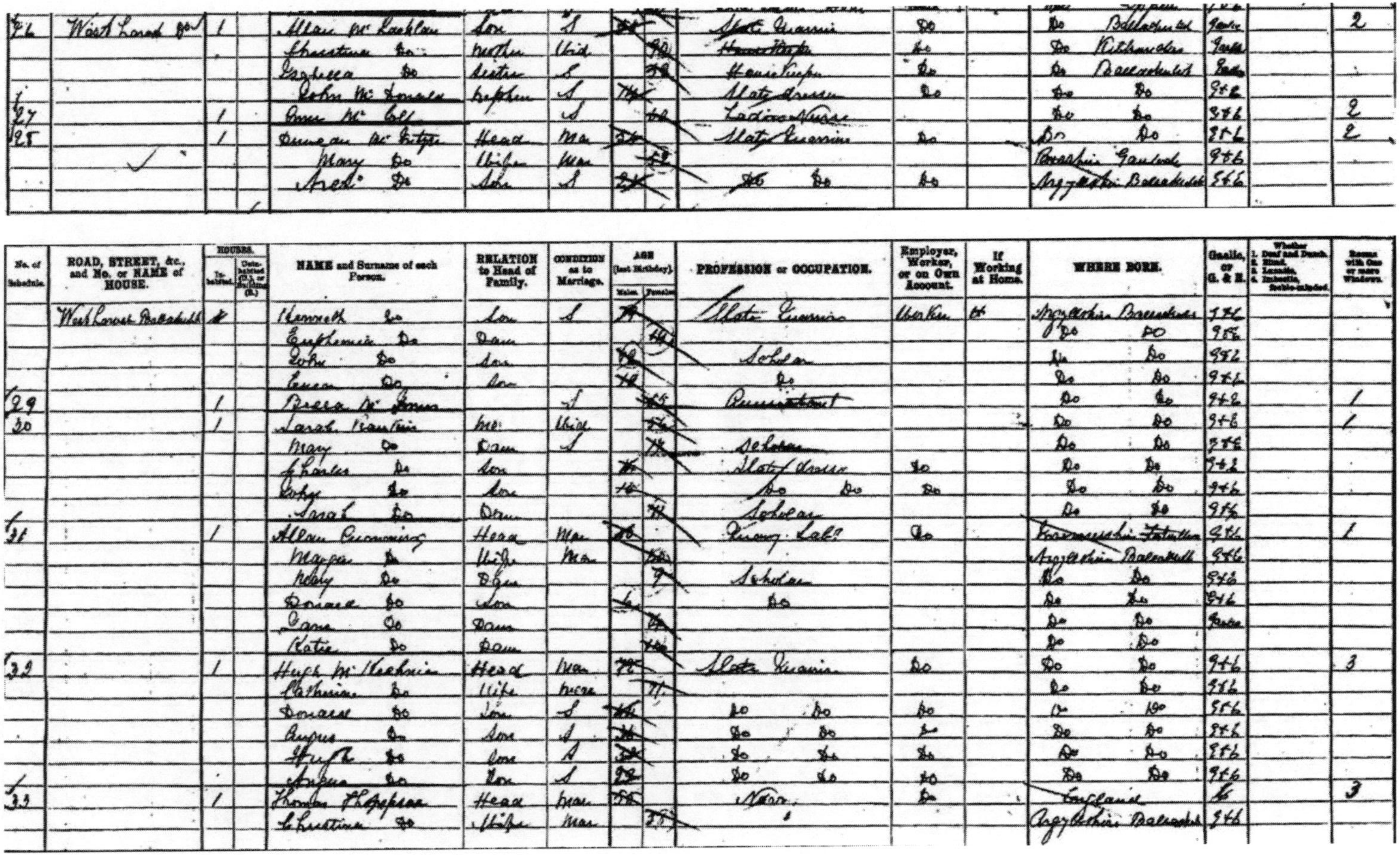

No. of Schedule	ROAD, STREET, &c., and No. or NAME of HOUSE.	HOUSES: Inhabited	Uninhabited (U.), or Building (B.)	NAME and Surname of each Person.	RELATION to Head of Family.	CONDITION as to Marriage.	AGE [last Birthday]. Males	Females	PROFESSION or OCCUPATION.	Employer, Worker, or on Own Account.	If Working at Home.	WHERE BORN.	Gaelic, or G. & E.	Whether 1. Deaf and Dumb. 2. Blind. 3. Lunatic. 4. Imbecile, Feeble-minded.	Rooms with One or more Windows.
26	West Land Rd	1		Allan McLachlan	Son	S	[illegible]		Slate Quarrier	Do		Do Ballachulish	Gaelic		2
				Christina Do	Mother	Wid		[illegible]	Housewife	Do		Do Kilmonivaig	Gaelic		
				Isabella Do	Sister	S		[illegible]	Housekeeper	Do		Do Ballachulish	Gaelic		
				John McDonald	Nephew	S	[illegible]		Slate Dresser	Do		Do Do	G&E		
27		1		Ann McColl		S		[illegible]	Ladies Nurse			Do Do	G&E		2
28		1		Duncan McIntyre	Head	Ma	[illegible]		Slate Quarrier	Do		Do Do	G&E		2
				Mary Do	Wife	Mar		[illegible]				Perthshire Garland	G&E		
				Archd Do	Son	S	[illegible]		Do Do	Do		Argyllshire Ballachulish	G&E		
	West Laroch Ballachulish			Kenneth Do	Son	S	[illegible]		Slate Quarrier	Worker		Argyllshire Ballachulish	G&E		
				Euphemia Do	Dau			[illegible]				Do Do	G&E		
				John Do	Son		[illegible]		Scholar			Do Do	G&E		
				Ewen Do	Son		[illegible]		Do			Do Do	G&E		
29		1		Grace McInnes		S		[illegible]	Pensioner			Do Do	G&E		1
30		1		Sarah Rankin	Mo	Wid		[illegible]				Do Do	G&E		1
				Mary Do	Dau	S		[illegible]	Scholar			Do Do	G&E		
				Charles Do	Son		[illegible]		Slate Dresser	Do		Do Do	G&E		
				John Do	Son		[illegible]		Do Do	Do		Do Do	G&E		
				Sarah Do	Dau			[illegible]	Scholar			Do Do	G&E		
31		1		Allan Cumming	Head	Ma	[illegible]		Quarry Labr	Do		Inverness-shire Fort William	G&E		1
				Maggie Do	Wife	Ma		[illegible]				Argyllshire Ballachulish	G&E		
				Mary Do	Dau			9	Scholar			Do Do	G&E		
				Donald Do	Son		[illegible]		Do			Do Do	G&E		
				Jane Do	Dau			[illegible]				Do Do	Gaelic		
				Katie Do	Dau			[illegible]				Do Do			
32		1		Hugh McKechnie	Head	Mar	[illegible]		Slate Quarrier	Do		Do Do	G&E		3
				Catherine Do	Wife	Mar		71				Do Do	G&E		
				Donald Do	Son	S	[illegible]		Do Do	Do		Do Do	G&E		
				Angus Do	Son	S	[illegible]		Do Do	Do		Do Do	G&E		
				Hugh Do	Son	S	[illegible]		Do Do	Do		Do Do	G&E		
				Archd Do	Son	S	[illegible]		Do Do	Do		Do Do	G&E		
33		1		Thomas Thompson	Head	Mar	[illegible]		Navvy	Do		England	E		3
				Christina Do	Wife	Mar		[illegible]				Argyllshire Ballachulish	G&E		

No. of Schedule.	ROAD, STREET, &c., and No. or NAME of HOUSE.	HOUSES. In-habited.	HOUSES. Uninhabited (U.), or Building (B.)	NAME and Surname of each Person.	RELATION to Head of Family.	CONDITION as to Marriage.	AGE (last Birthday). Males.	AGE (last Birthday). Females.	PROFESSION or OCCUPATION.	Employer, Worker, or on Own Account.	If Working at Home.	WHERE BORN.	Gaelic, or G. & E.	Whether 1. Deaf and Dumb. 2. Blind. 3. Lunatic. 4. Imbecile, feeble-minded.	Rooms with One or more Windows.
				Flora Do	Daur			[illegible]				Argyllshire Ballachulish	G & E		
				Mary Do	Sister	S		46	Gen Ser Domestic			Do Do	G & E		
				Duncan Do	Brother	S	38		Slate Quarrier	Worker		Do Do	G & E		
				Alex M' [illegible]	Boarder	Mar	[illegible]		Navvy	Do		[illegible]	G & E		
				Gregor M' Donald	Do	S	[illegible]		Do	Do		Do [illegible]	G & E		
41		1		Duncan Fraser	Head	S	[illegible]		Slate Quarrier	Do		Argyllshire Ballachulish	G & E		3
				Janet Fraser	Sister	S		[illegible]	Housekeeper			Do Do	G & E		
				Jane Do	Do	S		[illegible]	Dressmaker	Own Acct	At home	Do Do	G & E		
				Angus Do	Brother	S	[illegible]		Tailor	Do	Do	Do Do	G & E		
42		1		Alex M' Gregor	Head	S	[illegible]		Slate Quarrier	Worker		Lanarkshire Glasgow	G & E		3
				Malcolm Do	Brother	S	[illegible]		Do Do	Do		Argyllshire Ballachulish	G & E		
				Donald Do	Do	S	[illegible]		Do Do	Do		Do Do	G & E		
				Margaret Do	Sister	S		47	Laundrymaid			Do Easdale	G & E		
				Isabella Do	Do	S		31	Housekeeper			Do Ballachulish	G & E		3
43		1		Donald M' Innes	Head	S	[illegible]		Slate Quarrier	Do		Do Do	G & E		
				Dorothy Do	Mother	Wid		[illegible]	Housekeeper			Do Do	G & E		
				Duncan Do	Brother	S	[illegible]		Slate Quarrier	Do		Do Do	G & E		
				Alex Do	Do	S	[illegible]		Do Do	Do		Do Do	G & E		
				John Do	Do	S	[illegible]		Do Do	Do		Do Do	G & E		
				Robert Do	Do	S	[illegible]		Slate dresser	Do		Do Do	G & E		
				Bella M' Donald	Niece			11	Scholar			Lanarkshire Glasgow	G & E		
44		1		John Naughton	Head	S	[illegible]		Slate Quarrier	Do		Argyllshire Ballachulish	G & E		1
45		1		Catherine Cameron	Head	Wid		73	Housekeeper			Do Do	G & E		1
				John Do	Son	Wid	[illegible]		Slate Quarrier	Do		Do Do	G & E		

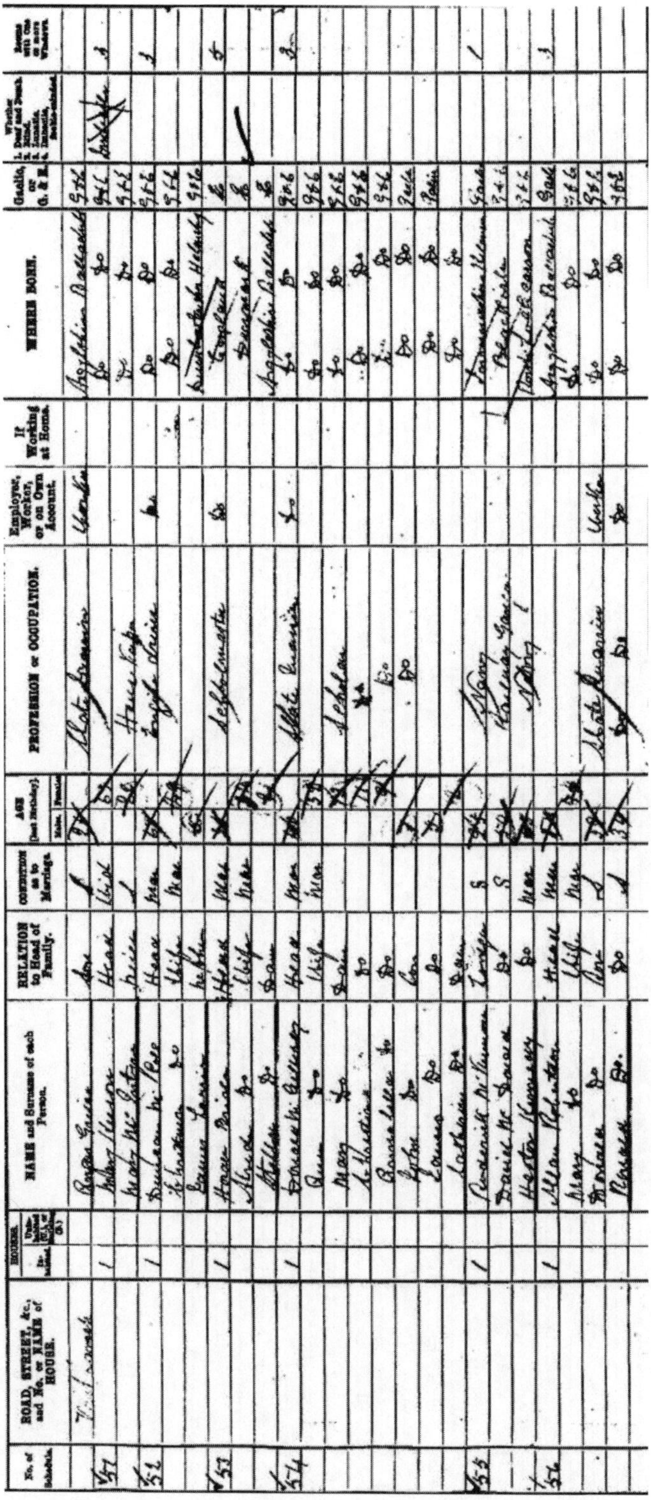

No. of Schedule	ROAD, STREET, &c., and No. or NAME of HOUSE	Houses: Inhabited	Houses: Uninhabited (U.), or Building (B.)	NAME and Surname of each Person	RELATION to Head of Family	CONDITION as to Marriage	AGE [last Birthday] Males	AGE [last Birthday] Females	PROFESSION or OCCUPATION	Employer, Worker, or on Own Account	If Working at Home	WHERE BORN	Gaelic, or G. & E.	Whether 1. Deaf and Dumb 2. Blind 3. Lunatic 4. Imbecile, Feeble-minded	Rooms with One or more Windows
	[illegible]			Angus Grieve	Son	S	[illegible]		Slate Quarrier	Worker		Argyllshire Ballachulish	G&E		
51		1		Mary [illegible]	Head	Widow		[illegible]				Do Do	G&E	[illegible]	3
				Mary McIntyre	Niece	S		[illegible]	Housekeeper			Do Do	G&E		
52		1		Duncan McRae	Head	Mar	[illegible]		Engine Driver	Do		Do Do	G&E		3
				Christina Do	Wife	Mar		[illegible]				Do Do	G&E		
				James [illegible]	Nephew		[illegible]					[illegible]	G&E		
53		1		Horace [illegible]	Head	Mar	[illegible]		Schoolmaster	Do		England	E		5
				[illegible] Do	Wife	Mar		[illegible]				Denmark	E	✓	
				Stella Do	Dau			[illegible]				Argyllshire Ballachulish	E		
54		1		Donald McGillivray	Head	Mar	[illegible]		Slate Quarrier	Do		Do Do	G&E		3
				Ann Do	Wife	Mar		[illegible]				Do Do	G&E		
				Mary Do	Dau			[illegible]	Scholar			Do Do	G&E		
				Christina	Do			[illegible]	Do			Do Do	G&E		
				Rosabella Do	Do			[illegible]	Do			Do Do	G&E		
				John Do	Son		[illegible]		Do			Do Do	Gaelic		
				James Do	Do		[illegible]					Do Do	Gaelic		
				Catherine Do	Dau			[illegible]				Do Do			
55		1		Roderick McKinnon	Lodger	S	[illegible]		Navvy			[illegible]	Gaelic		1
				David McDonald	Do	S	[illegible]		Railway Ganger			Black Isle	G&E		
				Hector Kennedy	Do	Mar	[illegible]		Navvy			[illegible] Lochcarron	G&E		
56		1		Allan Robertson	Head	Mar	[illegible]					Argyllshire Ballachulish	Gaelic		3
				Mary Do	Wife	Mar		[illegible]				Do Do	G&E		
				Donald Do	Son	S	[illegible]		Slate Quarrier	Worker		Do Do	G&E		
				Ronald Do	Do	S	[illegible]		Do Do	Do		Do Do	G&E		

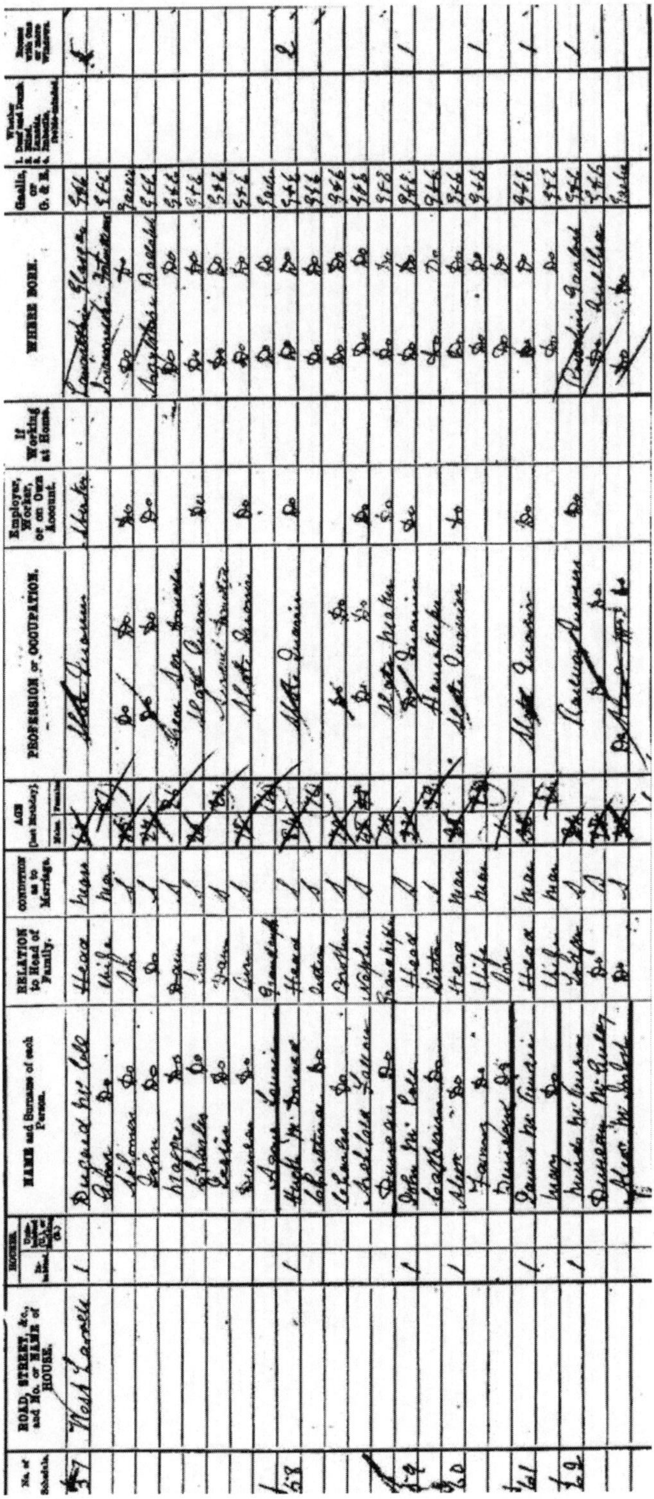

No. of Schedule	ROAD, STREET, &c., and No. or NAME of HOUSE	HOUSES: In-habited	HOUSES: Uninhabited (U.), or Building (B.)	NAME and Surname of each Person	RELATION to Head of Family	CONDITION as to Marriage	AGE (last Birthday): Males	AGE (last Birthday): Females	PROFESSION or OCCUPATION	Employer, Worker, or on Own Account	If Working at Home	WHERE BORN	Gaelic, or G. & E.	Whether 1. Deaf and Dumb, 2. Blind, 3. Lunatic, 4. Imbecile, feeble-minded	Rooms with One or more Windows
57	West Laroch	1		Dugald McColl	Head	Mar	[illegible]		Slate Quarrier	Worker		Lanarkshire Glasgow	G&E		2
				Anne Do	Wife	Mar		[illegible]				Invernesshire [illegible]	G&E		
				Solomon Do	Son	S	[illegible]		Do Do	Do		Do Do	Gaelic		
				John Do	Do	S	[illegible]		Do Do	Do		Argyllshire Ballachulish	G&E		
				Maggie Do	Daur	S		[illegible]	Gen Ser Domestic			Do Do	G&E		
				Charles Do	Son	S	[illegible]		Slate Quarrier	Do		Do Do	G&E		
				Jessie Do	Daur	S		[illegible]	Assistant [illegible]			Do Do	G&E		
				Duncan Do	Son	S	[illegible]		Slate Quarrier	Do		Do Do	G&E		
				Agnes Lewis	Granddaughter			[illegible]				Do Do	Gaelic		
58		1		Hugh McInnes	Head	S	[illegible]		Slate Quarrier	Do		Do Do	G&E		2
				Christina Do	Sister	S		[illegible]				Do Do	G&E		
				Charles Do	Brother	S	[illegible]		Do Do			Do Do	G&E		
				Archibald Lamont	Nephew	S	[illegible]		Do Do	Do		Do Do	G&E		
				Duncan Do	Grandnephew		[illegible]		Slate Maker	Do		Do Do	G&E		
59		1		John McColl	Head	S	[illegible]		Do Quarrier	Do		Do Do	G&E		1
				Catherine Do	Sister	S		[illegible]	Housekeeper			Do Do	G&E		
60		1		Alex Do	Head	Mar	[illegible]		Slate Quarrier	Do		Do Do	G&E		
				Fanny Do	Wife	Mar		[illegible]				Do Do	G&E		1
				Duncan Do	Son		[illegible]					Do Do			
61		1		James McKenzie	Head	Mar	[illegible]		Slate Quarrier	Do		Do Do	G&E		1
				Mary Do	Wife	Mar		[illegible]				Do Do	G&E		
62		1		[illegible] McInnes	Lodger	S	[illegible]		Railway Surfaceman	Do		Perthshire [illegible]	G&E		1
				Duncan McAulay	Do	S	[illegible]		Do Do			Do [illegible]	G&E		
				Alex McIntosh	Do	S	[illegible]		Do [illegible]			Do Do	Gaelic		

[Page 13]

The undermentioned Houses are situate within the Boundaries of the

Civil Parish of	Ecclesiastical Parish of	Quoad Sacra Parish of	Parliamentary Division of	Parliamentary Burgh of
Leven & Dysart		Glasser		Rossland City

No. of Schedule	ROAD, STREET, &c., and No. or NAME of HOUSE	HOUSES		NAME and Surname of each Person	RELATION to Head of Family	CONDITION as to Marriage	AGE		PROFESSION or OCCUPATION	Employer, Worker, or on Own Account	If Working at Home	WHERE BORN	Whether Deaf and Dumb, Blind, Lunatic, &c.	Rooms with one or more Windows
		Inhabited	Uninhabited				Males	Females						

Appendix 3
Census Returns, 1891: Ballachulish Road, West Laroch

Courtesy of the General Register Office for Scotland

[Page 8]

The undermentioned Houses are situate within the Boundaries of the

Civil Parish of	Quoad Sacra Parish of	School Board District of	Parliamentary Burgh of	Royal Burgh of
Municipal Burgh of	Police Burgh of	Burgh Ward of	Town of	Village or Hamlet of	Island of

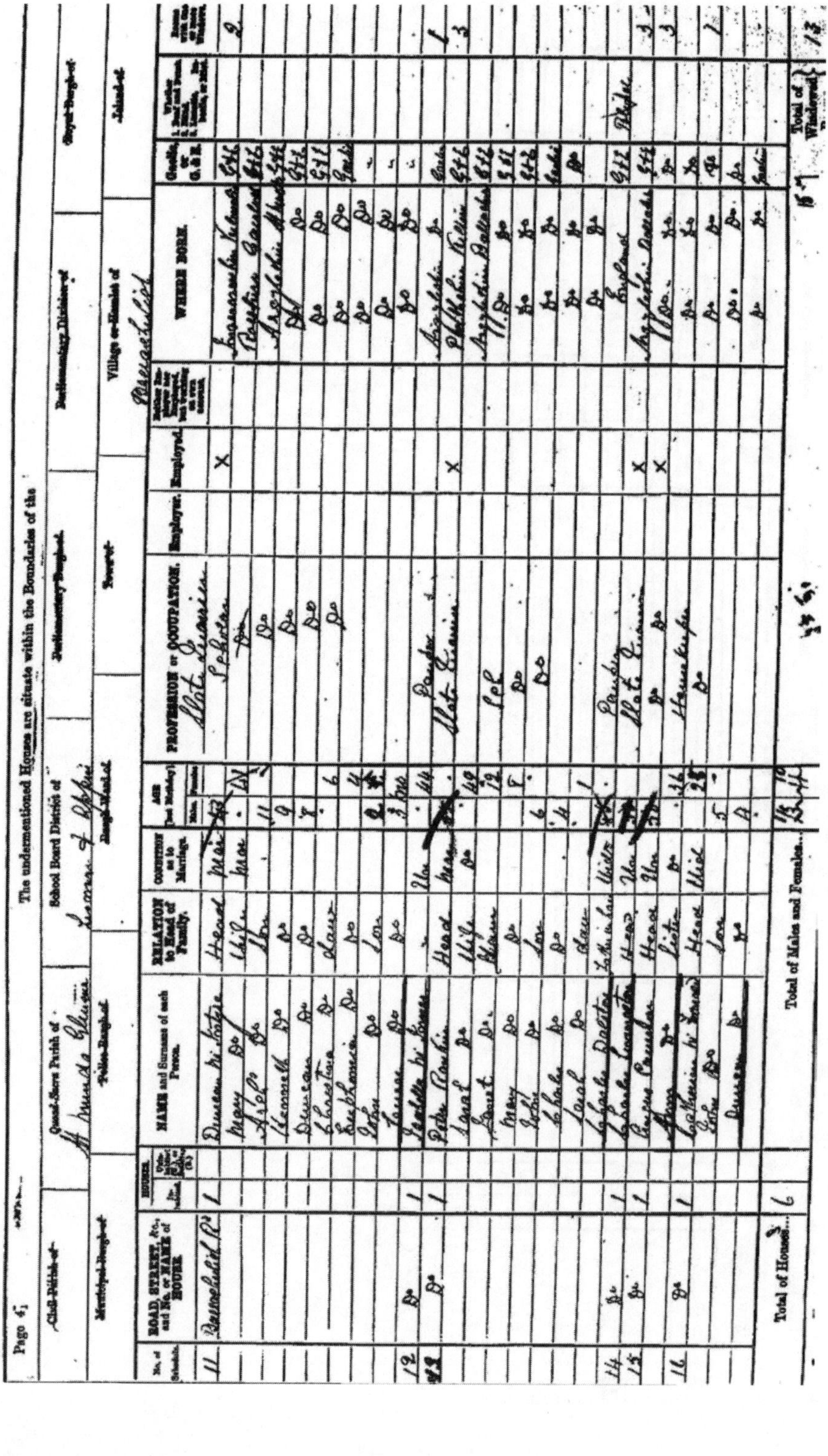

[Page 5]

The undermentioned Houses are situate within the Boundaries of the

Civil Parish of — | County Shire Parish of H. Munde's Clu. | School Board District of ... | Parliamentary Division of ... | Municipal Borough of — | Parliamentary Division of — | Village or Hamlet of Breac... | ... | ...

No. of Schedule	ROAD, STREET, &c., and No. or NAME of HOUSE	HOUSES (Inhabited / Uninhabited / Building)	NAME and Surname of each Person	RELATION to Head of Family	CONDITION as to Marriage	AGE (Males / Females)	PROFESSION or OCCUPATION	Employer	Employed	Neither employer nor employed but working on own account	WHERE BORN	(Deaf / Dumb / Blind / Lunatic)
17	Braeshabul	1	Jno? M. Innes	Head	Un	24	Farmer			X	Argyllsh. Balantrie		1
18	Do	1	Mary Scott	dau			do				Do		
			Alex McColgan	Head	mar	43	Mot Servic		X		Do Godour		3
			Margaret Do	Wife	mar	44	Wife				Do Dacinshik		
			Hugh Do	son		14	Scholar				Do		
			Baby Do	dau							Do		
			Duncan Do	son		11					Do		
			Lizzie Do	dau		9					Do		
			James Do	son		4					Do		
			Alex Do	son							Do		
19	Do	1	Euan McFachan	Head	mar	54	Mot Servic		X		Do		3
			Cath McFachanDo	Wife	mar		do				Do		
			John Do	son			do		X		Do		
			Hugh Do	do					X		Do		
			Mart Do	do			Servant		X		Do Gira		
			Lizzie Do	do			Mot Servic				Do		
20	Do	1	Catherine McDugald	Head	Wid	53	Housekeeper		X		Do Balnahuid		3
			Jno Do	son			Mot Servic				Do		
			Nessie Do	do		12	do				Do Do		
			Lizzie Do	dau			Sen Scholar				Do Do		

Total of Houses.... 4 | Total of Males and Females.... 10 / 24 | Total of Windowed Rooms 19 — 10

[Page 7]

The undermentioned Houses are situate within the Boundaries of the

Civil Parish of	Quoad Sacra Parish of	School Board District of	Parliamentary Burgh of	Royal Burgh of	Village or Hamlet of	Parliamentary Division	Royal Burgh of

No. of Schedule	ROAD, STREET, &c., and No. or NAME of HOUSE	HOUSES Inhabited	NAME and Surname of each Person	RELATION to Head of Family	CONDITION as to Marriage	AGE (last Birthday) Males / Females	PROFESSION or OCCUPATION	Employer / Employed / Working on own account	WHERE BORN	(Whether) Deaf-and-Dumb / Blind / Lunatic / etc.
25	Borrowdale Rd	1		Head			Met Lamer	X		
26	Do	1		Head			Do	X		
27	Do	1		Wife			Do			
							Retired			
							Do	X		
							Housekeeper			
							Retired Queen			
28	Do	1		Head			Housekpr			
							Son			
29	Do	1		Head			Met Queen	X		
							Housekpr			
							Petticoat	X		
30	Do	1		Head			Met Queen	X		
							Housekpr	X		
							Met Queen			
							Do			
							Housemaid			
							Housemaid	X		
31	Do	1		Head			Tapmbin	X		
							Met Queen	X		
Total of Houses		7				Total of Males and Females ... 13 7				

[Page 9]

The undermentioned Houses are situate within the Boundaries of the

Page 10]

The undermentioned Houses are situate within the Boundaries of the

School Board District of

The undermentioned Houses are situate within the Boundaries of the [Page 11

Civil Parish of	Quoad Sacra Parish of	School Board District of	Parliamentary Burgh of	Parliamentary Division of	Royal Burgh of
	St Munda Glencoe	Lismore & Appin			

Municipal Burgh of	Police Burgh of	Burgh Ward of	Town of	Village or Hamlet of	Island of
				Ballachulish	

No. of Schedule	ROAD, STREET, &c., and No. or NAME of HOUSE	Houses: Inhabited	Houses: Uninhabited	NAME and Surname of each Person	RELATION to Head of Family	CONDITION as to Marriage	AGE Males	AGE Females	PROFESSION or OCCUPATION	Employer	Employed	Neither Employer nor Employed	WHERE BORN	Gaelic, or G. & E.	Whether Deaf and Dumb, Blind, Lunatic, Imbecile, or Idiot	Rooms with One or more Windows
	Ballachulish Rd			Duncan Clark	Son		9						Argyllshire Ballachulish			
53	Do Do	1		John Cameron	Head	Mar	[illegible]		Slate Quarrier				Do Do	G&E		2
				Sarah Do	Wife	Mar		55	Do Wife				Do Do	Do		
				Duncan Do	Son	Un	[illegible]		Do Quarrier				Do Do	Do		
				Hugh Do	Do	Do	[illegible]		Do Do				Do Do	Do		
				Alexr Do	Do	Do	19?		Do Do				Do Do	Do		
				Bella Do	dau			18?	Ser. dom.				Do Do	Do		
				Lizzie Do	Do			13	Sch				Do Do	Do		
54	Do Do	1		Alexr Barton	Head	Mar	[illegible]		Crofter		X		Inverness-shire Glencoe	Gaelic		3
				Ann Do	Wife	Mar		61	Do Wife				Argyllshire Ballachulish	G&E		
				Angus Do	Son	Un	[illegible]		Slate Quarrier		X		Do Do	G&E		
				[illegible] McColl	Grandau			11	Sch				Do Do	G&E		
55	Do Do	1		Peter Cameron	Head	Mar	[illegible]		Slate Quarrier		X		Do Do	G&E		2
				Catherine Do	Wife	Mar		36	Do Wife				Do Do	G&E		
				Angus Do	Son		9		Sch				Do Do	Do		
				Lachlan Do	Do		7		Do				Do Do	Do		
				Catherine Do	dau			5	Do				Do Do	Gaelic		
				Jessie Do	Do			3	Do				Do Do	Do		
56	Do Do	1		Margaret McKenzie	Head	Un		5?	Retired Ser.				Do Do	G&E		1
57	Do Do	1		Hugh Cameron	Head	Mar	38?		Slate Quarrier		X		Do Do	Do		3
				Clementina Do	Wife	Mar		33	Do Wife				Do Do	Do		
				Angus Do	Son		13		Do Ser				Do Do	Do		
				Donald Do	Do		11		Sch				Do Do	Do		
				Mary Do	dau			10	Do				Do Do	Do		
				Lilly Do	Do			8	Do				Do Do	Do		
	Total of Houses	5		Total of Males and Females			[illegible]	[illegible]					21-5		Total of Windowed Rooms	11

Index